# THE
# ULTIMATE ASCENT

*The Divine Comedy* stands as one of the towering creations of world literature, and its climactic section, *The Paradiso,* is perhaps the most ambitious poetic attempt ever made to represent the ultimate goal of human striving, the merging of individual destiny with universal order.

*Having passed through Hell and Purgatory, the poet-narrator is led by his beloved Beatrice through the upper sphere wherein lie the sublime truths of Divine will and purpose. The symbols of medieval Christianity mingle with those of classical antiquity, the boundaries separating science, religion, and art are dissolved by a passionate unity of vision. Presented here in a great and definitive new translation is a work of almost mystical intensity and indescribable power—an immortal hymn to God, Nature, Eternity, and, above all, "the Love that moves the Sun and other stars."*

"Dante and Shakespeare divide the modern world between them, there is no third." —T. S. Eliot

Poetry Editor of *The Saturday Review,* John Ciardi has taught at Harvard and Rutgers universities and is a Fellow of the American Academy of Arts and Sciences and of the National Institute of Arts and Letters. In 1955 he won the Harriet Monroe Memorial Award, and in 1956, the Prix de Rome. He has published twelve volumes of poetry. His translations of *The Inferno,* Part One of *The Divine Comedy,* and *The Purgatorio,* Part Two, are also available in Mentor editions.

## Other Literary Classics
## in MENTOR Editions

*Dante Alighieri*

# THE PARADISO

a verse rendering for the modern
reader by JOHN CIARDI

Introduction by John Freccero

A MENTOR BOOK from
**NEW AMERICAN LIBRARY**
TIMES MIRROR
New York and Scarborough, Ontario
The New English Library Limited, London

Library of Congress Catalog Card Number: 72-130872

Canto I was first published in *Italian Quarterly*, 1965.
Canto VIII was first published in *Arbor*, 1961.
Canto XXI was first published in *Hartwick Review*, 1967.
Canto XXXIII was first published in *The Rarer Action: Essays in Honor of Francis Fergusson*, ed. Alan Cheuse and Richard Koffler, 1970.

SECOND PRINTING

MENTOR TRADEMARK REG. U.S. PAT. OFF. AND FOREIGN COUNTRIES
REGISTERED TRADEMARK—MARCA REGISTRADA
HECHO EN CHICAGO, U.S.A.

SIGNET, SIGNET CLASSICS, SIGNETTE, MENTOR AND PLUME BOOKS
are published *in the United States* by
The New American Library, Inc.,
1301 Avenue of the Americas, New York, New York 10019,
*in Canada* by The New American Library of Canada Limited,
81 Mack Avenue, Scarborough, 704, Ontario,
*in the United Kingdom* by The New English Library Limited,
Barnard's Inn, Holborn, London, E.C. 1, England

PRINTED IN THE UNITED STATES OF AMERICA

## ACKNOWLEDGMENTS

I must thank Professor Mark Musa and especially Professor John Freccero for reading and commenting on this version of *The Paradiso*. I am not a Dante scholar; I have undertaken what I hope is poet's work. The learning of these good men has saved me from some of the gaps in my own. At times I have not followed their suggestions, feeling that the points raised, though important to scholars, might interfere with the pleasure of a beginning student reading in translation. If I have been wrong in so deciding, the responsibility is mine. Their suggestions have been invaluable, and I owe them a most grateful thanks, gladly offered.

For Connie—
as all things draw to what they most are.

# Contents

### ILLUSTRATIONS

# Introduction

Dante's claim for the *Paradiso*, the last *cantica* of his poem, is as daring as it is clear: "My course is set for an uncharted sea." History has in fact granted him the unique place that he claimed with that navigational metaphor, both as pilgrim and as poet. Just as, within the fiction of the poem, the pilgrim's course is privileged beyond the aspiration of ordinary men, so in its final course the poem accomplishes what no other poet had ever dared. Throughout the *Divine Comedy*, the metaphor of the ship serves to describe both the pilgrim's journey and the progress of the poem: on both counts, Dante can refer to himself as a new Jason, who returns with the Golden Fleece that is at once the vision of God and the poem that we read.

For the twentieth-century reader, the fiction of the story requires a great effort of the imagination—few of us still believe in a paradise in any form, much less in the possibility of reaching it in this life. The claim of the pilgrim to have reached the absolute seems to us even more fantastic than the fiction of the *Inferno*, where at least the characters, if not the landscape, are quite familiar. For this reason, the *Paradiso* is often thought of as the most "medieval" part of the poem. This reputation should not, however, obscure for us the sense in which, as poetry, it remains daring and even contemporary. By attempting to represent poetically that which is by definition beyond representation, this *cantica* achieves what had scarcely seemed possible before (even for the poet of the *Inferno* and the *Purgatorio*) and has remained the ultimate aspiration of poets ever since. The quest of Romantic poets and their successors for "pure poetry" has for its prototype the *Paradiso*.

The poetry of the *Paradiso* represents a radical departure from that of the *Purgatorio*, as the latter represented a departure from the poetry of the *Inferno*. The changes may be thought of as a gradual attenuation of the bond between poetry and representation, from the immediacy of the *Inferno* to the dreamlike mediation of the *Purgatorio* to the attempt to create a non-representational poetic world in the last *cantica*. This refinement of poetic representation perfectly matches the evolution of the pilgrim's understanding within the story: he learns first of all from his senses, from the sights and sounds of a hell that seems actually to exist, now and forever, thanks to the celebrated mimetic power of Dante's verses in the *Inferno*. As the pilgrim depends upon his senses in his travels, so the reader seems to be with him in a world which exists autonomously, almost as if it had not been created by an act of the imagination.

In the *Purgatorio*, on the other hand, the major revelations come to the pilgrim subjectively, as interior events in what Francis Fergusson has called a "drama of the mind." The dream-vision is the primary vehicle for this illumination; Dante refers to the power which receives it as the *imaginativa* (*Purgatorio* XV). According to medieval physchology, this is the same power that enables poets to create a totally new world from the fragments of sense experience and memory, so that in Dante's view, the poetic power that created the poem is the same power that is illuminated within the pilgrim during his ascent of the mountain. The poet's imagination, hidden by its own concreteness in the first part of his poem, becomes the focus of his attention and of ours in the *Purgatorio*. Thus, the landscape is suffused with mist, the tone is nostalgic, and the reader is called upon to respond with his imagination to both the sensory and the emotional suggestiveness, to imagine "visible speech" in the bas-reliefs, to hear the music of familiar hymns, to recall the lessons from the Sermon of the Mount. The substantiality of this part of the poem resides in the subjectivity of the pilgrim and in our reaction to it more than in an explicit architectonic creation of the poet.

In the last part of the poem, the pilgrim's vision is transformed until it no longer has need of any representational media whatever in its communication with the absolute. The technical problem involved in finding a stylistic correspondence to this transformation reaches insoluble proportions by the poem's ending, for it demands straining the representational value of poetry to the ultimate, approaching silence as its limit. Insofar as the *Paradiso* exists at all, therefore, it is an accommodation, a compromise short of silence, as Dante suggests in the first canto:

> How speak trans-human change to human sense?
> Let the example speak until God's grace
> grants the pure spirit the experience.

This sense of compromise, of poetic inadequacy for the ultimate experience, is what accounts for the poignancy of much of the *cantica*, but particularly of the last cantos, where both memory and *fantasia* fail the poet, who can describe only the sweetness distilled within his heart.

The prodigious achievement of the poet is that he manages, within the limits of this compromise, to represent nonrepresentation without falling either into unintelligibility or into silence. Within the story, this accommodation takes the form of a "command performance" of all of the souls of the blessed for the exclusive benefit of the pilgrim. In the fourth canto, Beatrice tells him that all of what he sees in the heavenly spheres of the Moon, the Sun, and the planets is there only temporarily, until he is able to behold all of Paradise without any such "condescension":

> So must one speak to mortal imperfection,
> which only from the *sensible* apprehends
> whatever it then makes fit for intellection.

One might incidentally extend the principle to include a justification of the effort to translate into English what at first appears to be this least translatable of all poems. As the pilgrim's experience is out of the reach of his powers of expression, so is the original poetry out of the reach of the average reader of English, who requires the "accommodation" of a translation; in the case of a superb translation, such as this, the "accommodation" is also a work of art, dependent upon an original experience for its inspiration, but autonomous in terms of literary value for those to whom the original is out of reach.

To return to the fiction of the descent of the souls to the various spheres for the sake of the pilgrim, the extraordinary implication of Beatrice's remark is that the whole of the *Paradiso*, at least until the crossing of the river of light toward the poem's ending, has no existence, even fictional, beyond the metaphoric. When the souls return to their home in the Empyrean, the last heaven beyond time and space, they leave the spheres, presumably forever, and no subsequent voyager will ever see them again as the pilgrim saw them. If the *Inferno* may be said to have a fictionally autonomous existence and the *Purgatorio* a subjective substantiality, paradise and the poem are co-extensive, like the terms of a metaphor and, even within the fiction of the story, neither can exist without the other.

The metaphoric quality of the story has a stylistic counterpart in some of the distinctive features of the poetry, the most startling of which may be referred to as anti-images. One of the most memorable occurs in the first heaven (III, 15), where spirits appear within the Moon and are described as "a pearl upon a milk white brow." The comparison is obviously self-defeating as far as its function to convey information is concerned: we are told simply that the poet saw white upon white. The point is of course the *difference*, which we are unable to see, yet within which all of the reality of the *Paradiso* is contained. The juxtaposition of the pearl and the brow, in their concreteness, serve in a negative way to block the attempt to leave the confines of the text, defying us, as it were, to find more than a shadow of reference to the real world.

It cannot be coincidence that the comparison is found in a section of the poem where the moon spots are discussed at great length in what at first seems to be a superfluous digression. Its point becomes apparent when we realize that for Dante the spots on the Moon were visible only from the earth, while the heavenly body shone with a uniform radiance on the side closest to the Sun. The spots are therefore also shadows, in a sense an accommodation of God's light to the eyes of mortal men below, gradations within a unity which might not otherwise be perceived. Finally, the literary significance of the complicated interplay becomes clear when one recalls the terms with which Dante had set forth his ambition in the prologue of Canto I:

> O power divine, but lend to my high strain
> so much as will make clear even the shadow
> of that High Kingdom stamped upon my brain . . .

The experience of the pilgrim, like the experience of pure whiteness or, for that matter, the experience of the divine light, remain out of reach to mortal minds, which can proceed to unity only analogically. It is in difference that meaning is born, like the difference between two phonetic sounds, unintelligible in themselves, yet constituting meaning when linked together. So with the poem, which manages to approach its conclusion and silence by the gradual dissipation of all difference between light and light, and yet remains as the shadow of all that the experience is not, as irreducibly literary as "a pearl upon a milk white brow."

There was a whole corpus of writings in the Middle Ages which dealt with the subject of "light metaphysics," an adaptation of light imagery, considered literally as the connecting link between God and the cosmos. These writings are obviously of doctrinal relevance to the study of the *Divine Comedy*; the point I wish to make here, however, is the poetic function of the interplay of light and shadow as a figure for the poem itself.

Dante's ascent through all of the heavenly spheres provides him with excellent occasions for modulating his poetic effects to suit the cosmic context. We have already seen the correspondence between poetic imagery and the specific nature of the Moon. Mercury's proximity to the Sun is an occasion for fugitive effects, Venus' shift in the sky suggests the dramatization of a didactic passage in terms of a solar "illumination," from behind and before the pilgrim, the heaven of the Sun calls forth zodiacal imagery and a dance of the hours, Mars colors even Beatrice with its ruddy glow, and so on; in each of the successive spheres, astronomical imagery contributes its color and its geometry to lend to the poem such concreteness as it possesses.

Perhaps the most daring of all sequences in the poem, again at the stylistic level, occurs in the heaven of Jupiter. I have already described what I have called an anti-image in the sphere of the Moon; Jupiter provides us with an anti-image which might almost be referred to as an anti-character: the figure of the eagle. In Canto XVIII, Dante sees the souls of the just and temperate rulers as so many lights that gradually arrange themselves in order to form the first sentence from the Book of Wisdom: *DILIGITE IUSTITIAM, QUI IUDICATIS TERRAM*— "Love righteousness, ye that are judges of the earth." The last letter of the Latin sentence, as it is spelled out, is gradually transformed into the shape of an eagle, the symbol of Justice, which then speaks to Dante of its universal history. Mr. Ciardi remarks quite rightly in his notes that, as image, it must have seemed unprecedented in Dante's time, while we, who are used to "spectaculars" and flashing billboards have no trouble imagining such a display. In terms that were set forth at the beginning of this essay, those of poetic representation, the figure is as astounding now as it ever was, for it seems to make a series of references beyond itself, yet the series is perfectly closed and self-contained, in effect leading nowhere beyond itself. In this dramatic sequence, there is no reality that is not a sign, pointing to another level of meaning: the words of the poem point to men of history, the men are lights that are the words of a text from the Bible, which in turn unfolds to its meaning, the eagle. But the eagle also points beyond itself to the words of the text we read, where the series began. Just as there is no concrete reality which may be distinguished in its own right as irreducible, not even the lives of men who serve as the signifiers of God's Providence, so there is no ultimate reality signified beyond the text itself. The eagle, as unlike an eagle as can be imagined, stands as a figure for the poem itself, a nonrepresentation that is its own reality.

If the logical series of references in the episode turns back upon itself, giving the eagle a purely literary meaning, independent of the natural world or extant eagles, it is also true that at the farthest remove from the text in that logical series there is another text: *Diligite Iustitiam* . . . , a Biblical verse. The Bible was considered by the Middle Ages to be the exemplar of all books, possessed of a totality to which mortals could only aspire with their books, for God was taken to be its Author. Moreover, it is this sense of the universe as a symbolic book, of which the Bible was the concrete manifestation, that gives to everything its quality of sign, pointing beyond itself to its Maker. So it is in Dante's poem, where the ultimate reality is seen precisely as a book:

> I saw within Its depth how It conceives
>      all things in a single volume bound by Love,
>      of which the universe is the scattered leaves . . .

The aspiration of the pilgrim throughout the poem is to pick up the scattered leaves of God's book, but as he achieves that in the last canto of the *Paradiso* with his vision, the vision escapes him: "On the wild wind that bore the tumbling leaves/ the Sybil's oracles were scattered so." His own book, the poem we read, is an attempt to reconstruct the archetypal book and it is in this sense that it may be said, in Charles Singleton's words, that Dante "imitates God's way of writing." For the twentieth-century reader, whatever his beliefs, the inference to be made is that the ultimate reality and coherence is that represented by the written word.

The observation about the ways in which Dante's poem is an imitation of God's book brings us to the substance of his revelation in the final *cantica*. Heretofore we have been concerned with the poet's stylistic daring, but the daring of Dante the theorist is no less. The entire poem, from the dark wood to the Empyrean, traces the gradually transcendent view of Dante on his own culture, his own country, and even his own family, from the isolated and alienated bewilderment of the pilgrim in the first scene to the soaring view of the eagle in the upper reaches of the universe. It is characteristic of Dante and of his faith that any such transcendence must begin with the self; Dante's own history occupies the central cantos of the *Paradiso* in the form of his meeting with his ancestor, Cacciaguida. The encounter is based on Aeneas' meeting with Anchises, his father, in the sixth book of the *Aeneid* and has for its principal function the clarification of all of the dark prophecies the pilgrim has received throughout his journey concerning the future course of his life. As early as the sixth canto of the *Inferno,* he had been warned about future exile and misery in ambiguous terms; in the canto of Cacciaguida it is spelled out for him "not in dark oracles . . . but in clear words":

You will come to learn how bitter as salt and stone
  is the bread of others, how hard the way that goes
  up and down stairs that are never your own.

In spite of the formal resemblance to an ancient model, the mode of the revelation is distinctively biblical, as the phrase "dark oracles" and the context suggests. As the coming of Christ gave meaning retrospectively to all of history, so the revelation of Cacciaguida, a surrogate for the divine perspective in the poem, gives meaning to all of the prophecies in the poem.

The essential thing about an oracular utterance is that it contains the truth without revealing it; only in retrospect, after the fact, can its truth be appreciated. At the same time, when those ancient oracles deal with death, their truth can be tested only from beyond the grave, that is, when their truth is too late to be of value to humans. The coming of Christ changed all of this, for Christians, by providing a point of closure, an ending in time within time, an Archimedean place to stand from which the truth in life and in world history might be judged. It was therefore a death-and-resurrection perspective on the oracular utterance, at once an understanding and a survival. This mode of structuring history according to the Christ event forms the basis of Dantesque revelation in the poem: to tell the story of one's life in retrospect with confidence in the truth and the completeness of the story is somehow to be outside of, or beyond, one's own life. It is to undergo a kind of death and resurrection, the process of conversion, a recapitulation of the Christ event in the history of the individual soul. The retrospective illumination of Dante's own life by Cacciaguida is the dramatization of the poet's self-transcendence, the achievement of a place to stand from which the course of time, its trajectory, may be viewed as though it were completed.

It was St. Augustine in his *Confessions* who first drew the analogy between the unfolding of syntax and the flow of human time. As words move toward their conclusion in a sentence in order to arrive at meaning and as the sentences flow toward the poem's ending in order to give it meaning, so the days of a man's life flow toward his death, the moment of closure that gives meaning to his life. Meaning in history is revealed in the same way, from the standpoint of the ending of history or Apocalypse, to use the biblical term. The same analogy is operative in Dante's poem, which is why the *Paradiso* is inseparable from the earlier *cantiche*. As we approach the poem's ending (and, incidentally, the literal ending of the poet's life), the closure that gives meaning to the verses and to the life that they represent, so all of history is reviewed under the aspect of eternity, beginning with Adam and ending with an indeterminate triumph of Justice on earth.

As the dark prophecies concerning the poet's life are given meaning by the revelation of Cacciaguida, so the dark political struggles which are a counterpoint to the pilgrim's story throughout his voyage are finally revealed, in a way that no historian today would consider historical. Indeed, the ultimate structure of history, from the perspective of paradise, would seem to be the very opposite of the history we learn from the chronicles. St. Peter's invective against the corruption of the Church, for example, insists three times on the sacredness of his chair in Rome, which from his perspective appears to be empty, when we know it to have been filled, during the fictional time of the poem, by Boniface VIII, perhaps the most secularly powerful Pope of the Middle Ages. Again, we know that Henry VII of Luxemburg, upon whose entry into Italy Dante had placed so much of his hope for the restoration of the Empire, died rather miserably in 1313, eight years before the poet's death and the conclusion of the poem. Yet, Dante awards him the very highest place among contemporaries in the heavenly spheres. This is the implication of Beatrice's remark in Canto XXX as she points out an empty throne:

> That great throne with the crown already set
>     above it draws your eyes. To it shall come—
>     before your own call to this nuptial banquet—
> the soul, already anointed, of Henry the Great,
>     who will come to Italy to bring law and order
>     before the time is ripe to set things straight.

In the last phrase, "before the time is ripe," Dante almost casually points up the difference between fallen time and the fullness of time that is the Christian eternity. Henry's death seems the merest accident of history, in no way affecting its meaning, as the presence and continued existence of a powerful Pope, Dante's bitter enemy on earth, is inconsequential under the aspect of eternity.

One of the last figures used by Dante in order to describe his transcendent view of universal history and of his own life seems particularly contemporary in an age when the view from the stars is no longer a poetic dream but a reality. In the heaven of the fixed stars, as the poet looks down from his constellation, Gemini, he describes the entire terrestrial surface:

> And turning there with the eternal Twins,
>   I saw the dusty little threshing ground
>   that makes us ravenous for our mad sins,
> saw it from mountain crest to lowest shore.
> Then I turned my eyes to Beauty's eyes once more.

The convulsions of war and cataclysm are contained and almost domesticated by the figure of the threshing floor on which the winnowing is a contained violence with a purpose: the separation of the wheat from the chaff, the traditional biblical figure for judgment. At the same time, the pronoun "us" strains to have it both ways: the pilgrim is elevated far enough beyond human concerns to give him a perspective that seems supernatural, but the pronoun involves him in the fate of the whole human community so that even in the starry heaven he is not alone. This integration of the pilgrim into the human family, after the isolation of the dark wood, points to an essential feature of this poem and to the central paradox of the faith to which it bears witness: the Incarnation.

The last stages of the poem prepare the way for the final resolution of all paradoxes in terms of the paradox of the Incarnation. First of all, it should be observed that the final revelation that comes to the pilgrim is not simply Beatific Vision, but a vision of the principle that renders intelligible the union of humanity and divinity in the person of Christ. This mystery forms the basis, in Dante's view, for all of the "concrete universals" involved in the story as well as in the poem itself. It explains (to the pilgrim, if not to us) *how* an individual man, Dante Alighieri, can at the same time be all men, without any compromise of his identity. It also helps to explain, retrospectively, how an apparently chance encounter of a boy and a girl in medieval Florence on an exactly specified day could at the same time contain within it the pattern of universal salvation, without any surrender of historicity to a vague realm of ideas. Finally, perhaps most importantly for the modern reader, the vision of the Incarnation coincides with the coming together in the poem of the pilgrim and the author and narrator who has been with us from the beginning of the poem. It is as if the abstracted, confident voice of Dante-poet were an all-knowing principle of intelligibility and the figure of Dante-pilgrim were a flesh-and-blood reality, for that very reason struggling to understand his own meaning. When pilgrim and poet meet at the last stage of the journey, the circle is squared, to use Dante's figure, the poet's word joins the flesh of his experience and, in a sense that is at once paradoxical and exact, the poem is born.

At the beginning of this essay, I suggested that Dante could think of himself as a new Jason, returning with the Golden Fleece of his vision and of the poem that we read. In the last canto of the poem, this is in fact the figure that he uses:

> Twenty-five centuries since Neptune saw
> the Argo's keel have not moved all mankind,
> recalling that adventure, to such awe
> As I felt in an instant . . .

The perspective of Neptune, from the bottom of the ocean looking up to witness man's first navigation, is our perspective on the poet's journey, a celestial navigation, of which the "mad flight" of Ulysses' journey is the Promethean anti-type. The figure completes the navigational imagery with which the *Paradiso* began. At the same time, the perspective from the depths is the poet's as well, who, like all prophets worthy of the name, has returned to tell us all. This didactic intent is finally what separates Dante's vision from its more romantic successors or from its heroic predecessors. The final scene is not an apotheosis of the self in splendid isolation, but a return to the darkness of this world for its own good and a reintegration of poetry into society. There is a precise syntactic moment that marks his return in the final verses:

> Here my powers rest from their high fantasy,
>     but already I could feel my being turned—
>     instinct and intellect balanced equally
> as in a wheel whose motions nothing jars—
> by the Love that moves the Sun and the other stars.

The restless drive of Dante's verse reaches its climax and its repose with the word "Love" in the last verse, just as the desire that is in human terms insatiable finds its satisfaction in the Love of God. What follows after the word represents a fall to earth, which is to say to us, after the ecstatic moment. Dante's personal fulfillment of his own most intimate desires is perfectly harmonized with the Love that is the motive force of the entire universe, of the Sun and the other stars. Spatially, to speak of the Sun and stars is to return to our perspective, looking up at the heavenly bodies which had long been surpassed by the pilgrim's journey to the Empyrean. The word "Love" is therefore the link that binds heaven to earth and the poet to his audience, containing within it the substance of the poem.

—John Freccero

# CANTO I

---

*DANTE STATES his supreme theme as Paradise itself and invokes the aid not only of the Muses but of Apollo.*

*Dante and Beatrice are in THE EARTHLY PARADISE, the Sun is at the Vernal Equinox, it is noon at Purgatory and midnight at Jerusalem when Dante sees Beatrice turn her eyes to stare straight into the sun and reflexively imitates her gesture. At once it is as if a second sun had been created, its light dazzling his senses, and Dante feels the ineffable change of his mortal soul into Godliness.*

*These phenomena are more than his senses can grasp, and Beatrice must explain to him what he himself has not realized: that he and Beatrice are soaring toward the height of Heaven at an incalculable speed.*

*Thus Dante climaxes the master metaphor in which purification is equated to weightlessness. Having purged all dross from his soul he mounts effortlessly, without even being aware of it at first, to his natural goal in the Godhead. So they pass through THE SPHERE OF FIRE, and so Dante first hears THE MUSIC OF THE SPHERES.*

The glory of Him who moves all things rays forth
　　through all the universe, and is reflected
　　from each thing in proportion to its worth.　　　3

I have been in that Heaven of His most light,
　　and what I saw, those who descend from there
　　lack both the knowledge and the power to write.　6

For as our intellect draws near its goal
　　it opens to such depths of understanding
　　as memory cannot plumb within the soul.　　　9

Nevertheless, whatever portion time
　　still leaves me of the treasure of that kingdom
　　shall now become the subject of my rhyme.　　12

O good Apollo, for this last task, I pray
　　you make me such a vessel of your powers
　　as you deem worthy to be crowned with bay.　　15

One peak of cleft Parnassus heretofore
　　has served my need, now must I summon both
　　on entering the arena one time more.　　　18

Enter my breast, I pray you, and there breathe
　　as high a strain as conquered Marsyas
　　that time you drew his body from its sheath.　　21

O power divine, but lend to my high strain
　　so much as will make clear even the shadow
　　of that High Kingdom stamped upon my brain,　　24

and you shall see me come to your dear grove
　　to crown myself with those green leaves which you
　　and my high theme shall make me worthy of.　　27

So seldom are they gathered, Holy Sire,
　　to crown an emperor's or a poet's triumph
　　(oh fault and shame of mortal man's desire!)　　30

that the glad Delphic god must surely find
  increase of joy in the Peneian frond
  when any man thirsts for it in his mind. 33

Great flames are kindled where the small sparks fly.
  So after me, perhaps, a better voice
  shall raise such prayers that Cyrrha will reply. 36

The lamp of the world rises to mortal view
  from various stations, but that point which joins
  four circles with three crosses, it soars through 39

to a happier course in happier conjunction
  wherein it warms and seals the wax of the world
  closer to its own nature and high function. 42

That glad conjunction had made it evening here
  and morning there; the south was all alight,
  while darkness rode the northern hemisphere; 45

when I saw Beatrice had turned left to raise
  her eyes up to the sun; no eagle ever
  stared at its shining with so fixed a gaze. 48

And as a ray descending from the sky
  gives rise to another, which climbs back again,
  as a pilgrim yearns for home; so through my eye 51

her action, like a ray into my mind,
  gave rise to mine: I stared into the sun
  so hard that here it would have left me blind; 54

but much is granted to our senses there,
  in that garden made to be man's proper place,
  that is not granted us when we are here. 57

I had to look away soon, and yet not
  so soon but what I saw him spark and blaze
  like new-tapped iron when it pours white-hot. 60

And suddenly, as it appeared to me,
   day was added to day, as if He who can
   had added a new sun to Heaven's glory.      63

Beatrice stared at the eternal spheres
   entranced, unmoving; and I looked away
   from the sun's height to fix my eyes on hers.      66

And as I looked, I felt begin within me
   what Glaucus felt eating the herb that made him
   a god among the others in the sea.      69

How speak trans-human change to human sense?
   Let the example speak until God's grace
   grants the pure spirit the experience.      72

Whether I rose in only the last created
   part of my being, O Love that rulest Heaven
   Thou knowest, by whose lamp I was translated.      75

When the Great Wheel that spins eternally
   in longing for Thee, captured my attention
   by that harmony attuned and heard by Thee,      78

I saw ablaze with sun from side to side
   a reach of Heaven: not all the rains and rivers
   of all of time could make a sea so wide.      81

That radiance and that new-heard melody
   fired me with such a yearning for their Cause
   as I had never felt before. And she      84

who saw my every thought as well as I,
   saw my perplexity: before I asked
   my question she had started her reply.      87

Thus she began: "You dull your own perceptions
   with false imaginings and do not grasp
   what would be clear but for your preconceptions.      90

You think you are still on earth: the lightning's spear
   never fled downward from its natural place
   as rapidly as you are rising there."         93

I grasped her brief and smiling words and shed
   my first perplexity, but found myself
   entangled in another, and I said:         96

"My mind, already recovered from the surprise
   of the great marvel you have just explained,
   is now amazed anew: how can I rise         99

in my gross body through such aery substance?"
   She sighed in pity and turned as might a mother
   to a delirious child. "The elements         102

of all things," she began, "whatever their mode,
   observe an inner order. It is this form
   that makes the universe resemble God.         105

In this the higher creatures see the hand
   of the Eternal Worth, which is the goal
   to which these norms conduce, being so planned.    108

All Being within this order, by the laws
   of its own nature is impelled to find
   its proper station round its Primal Cause.     111

Thus every nature moves across the tide
   of the great sea of being to its own port,
   each with its given instinct as its guide.     114

This instinct draws the fire about the moon.
   It is the mover in the mortal heart.
   It draws the earth together and makes it one.    117

Not only the brute creatures, but all those
   possessed of intellect and love, this instinct
   drives to their mark as a bow shoots forth its
                          arrows.     120

The Providence that makes all things hunger here
    satisfies forever with its light
the heaven within which whirls the fastest sphere.   123

And to it now, as to a place foretold,
    are we two soaring, driven by that bow
    whose every arrow finds a mark of gold.               126

It is true that oftentimes the form of a thing
    does not respond to the intent of the art,
    the matter being deaf to summoning—                   129

just so, the creature sometimes travels wide
    of this true course, for even when so driven
    it still retains the power to turn aside               132

(exactly as we may see the heavens' fire
    plunge from a cloud) and its first impulse may
    be twisted earthward by a false desire.                135

You should not, as I see it, marvel more
    at your ascent than at a river's fall
    from a high mountain to the valley floor.              138

If you, free as you are of every dross,
    had settled and had come to rest below,
    that would indeed have been as marvelous               141

as a still flame there in the mortal plain."
So saying, she turned her eyes to Heaven again.

## Notes

1. *of Him who moves all things*: God as the unmoved mover.
Since any change from perfection would have to be toward a
lessening, God is changeless in Dante's conception. Himself
changeless (unmoved), therefore, he imparts the creating motion
to all things.

2-3. *reflected . . . in proportion to its worth*: The more perfect the thing, the more perfectly it will reflect God's perfect shining. The more clouded the glass, so to speak, the less its ability to reflect the light.

4. *that Heaven of His most light*: Literally: "that heaven that takes (i.e., "receives" and, by implication, "reflects again") the most of His light." The Empyrean.

5-12. *those who descend . . . lack*: Dante was not a mystic in the pure sense of the word, but all mystics have stressed the ineffability of the mystical experience. How does one convey any rapturous experience once the rapture is over? William James in his *Varieties of Religious Experience* offers a fine introductory discussion of this question. *as our intellect draws near its goal*: The goal of intellect is God.

13-36. THE INVOCATION. Heretofore, Dante has invoked the Muses. Now he invokes Apollo himself as the God of Poetry, and as the father of the Muses. Note, too, that Apollo is identified with the Sun and that Dante has consistently used the Sun as a symbol for God.

15. *crowned with bay*: The laurel wreath awarded to poets and conquerors. See also line 29 and XXV, 1-12.

16. *one peak of cleft Parnassus*: Parnassus has two peaks: Nisa, which was sacred to the Muses; and Cyrrha, which was sacred to Apollo. Heretofore Nisa has been enough for Dante's need, but for this last canticle he must summon aid from both peaks (i.e., from all the Muses and from Apollo as well).

20-21. *Marsyas*: The satyr Marsyas challenged Apollo to a singing contest and was defeated. Ovid (*Metamorphoses*, VI, 382-400) recounts in gory detail how Apollo thereupon punished him by pulling him out of his skin leaving all the uncovered organs still functioning.

Note that in this godly sport the skin was not pulled off Marsyas but that Marsyas was pulled out of his skin. In citing this incident Dante may be praying that he himself, in a sense, be pulled out of himself (i.e., be made to outdo himself), however painfully. *its sheath*: its skin.

23-27. *make clear even the shadow*: Sense: "Lend me enough power to make clear so much as the shadow of the ineffable light, and your power and my lofty theme will win me a laurel crown." *your dear grove*: The grove in which grows the sacred laurel, or bay.

31. *the glad Delphic god*: Apollo.

32. *Peneian frond*: The laurel or bay, so called for Daphne, daughter of the river god Peneus. Cupid, to avenge a taunt, fired an arrow of love into Apollo and and an arrow of aversion into Daphne. Fleeing from the inflamed Apollo, Daphne prayed to her father and was changed into a laurel tree.

36. *Cyrrha will reply*: Cyrrha, Apollo's sacred peak, is here taken for Apollo himself. If Apollo does not heed his prayer, Dante will at least show the way, and perhaps a better poet will come after him and have his prayer answered by Apollo, whereby Paradise will at last be well portrayed.

37-42. THE POSITION OF THE SUN AT THE VERNAL EQUINOX. Short of pages of diagrams, there is no way of explaining Dante's astronomical figure in detail. A quick gloss must do: *the lamp*: The Sun. *various stations*: various points on the celestial horizon from which the sun rises at various times of the year. *four circles with three crosses*: The four circles here intended are: (1) the celestial horizon, (2) the celestial equator, (3) the ecliptic, and (4) equinoxial colure. The equinoxial colure is the great circle drawn through both poles and the two equinoxial points (the solsticial colure, similarly, passes through both poles and the two solsticial points). Since the equinox occurs when the sun crosses the celestial equator, both equinoxial points must lie on the equator and the equinoxial colure must be at right angles to the celestial equator. The celestial equator is the infinite extension of the plane of the earth's equator into the celestial sphere.

When the sun is in the position shown in the diagram the time is sunrise of the vernal equinox and all four circles meet, each of the other three forming a cross with the celestial horizon. Astrologers took this to be a particularly auspicious conjunction. Its *happier course* (line 40) brings the brighter and longer days of summer. Its *happier conjunction* (line 40) with the stars of Aries bring it back to the sign of the first creation (see *Inferno*, I, 38-39, note). And certainly the fact that the diagram forms three crosses would weigh it with the good omens of both the cross and trinity. All would once more be in God's shaping hand. So the *wax of the world* (line 41) is warmed and sealed, in a first sense by the warmth of approaching summer, and in a clearly implicit spiritual sense by the favor of God's will upon His creation.

This complicated figure could hardly have failed to suggest, further, some reference to the Four Cardinal Virtues, the Three Theological Virtues, and to the approaching Sun as Divine Illumination, now drawing to the full summer of mankind—for bear in mind that the southern hemisphere, in Dante's geography, was all water: there would be no mankind for the Sun to shine upon in its southern summer.

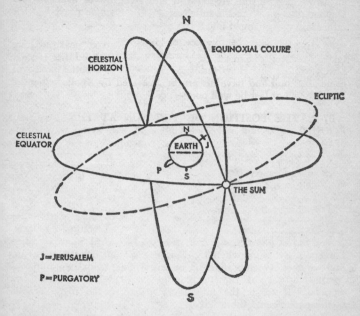

43-44. *evening here and morning there*: At the time Dante returned from drinking the waters of Eunöe. It is now noon, for only at noon could the entire southern hemisphere be alight and the north dark—or so Dante must clearly intend, though I do not understand how that could be.

46. *had turned left*: Beatrice had been facing east with Eunöe before her. She now turns her eyes north to the sun.

47. *no eagle ever*: In the Middle Ages men believed that the eagle was able to stare directly into the sun.

49-54. *and as a ray*: Just as a descending ray of light strikes a reflecting surface and sends a reflected ray back upward, and at the same angle at which it struck the surface, so Beatrice's action in looking at the sun descends upon Dante like a ray from on high that enters through his eyes and strikes upward to his mind giving rise to a "reflected" action.

62. *day was added to day*: Dante perceives the increased brilliance of the light as if God had added a second sun to the sky, and he wonders at it. He does not yet know that the light has grown so much more brilliant because he is soaring through space toward the sun. He believes himself to be still in the Terrestrial Paradise.

Dante's device here, in showing himself as soaring toward God at enormous speed without, at first, realizing that he is soaring, is a superbly conceived climax to the whole theme of Purification as Gradual Weightlessness. In Hell all is gross and heavy. At the start of the Ascent of Purgatory, Dante almost drops from exhaustion. As he mounts and sin is stricken from him, he climbs ever more lightly. Now purified and perfected, he need not even think about mounting on high. His new nature draws effortlessly to God.

68. *Glaucus*: The fisherman Glaucus, noting how his catch revived and leaped into the sea after being laid upon a certain herb, ate some of it and was transformed into a god (Ovid, *Metamorphoses*, XIII, 898-968). Staring at Beatrice, Dante feels the beginning inside himself of that change that will make him, too, immortal.

73-75. *the last created part of my being*: The soul, which is created after the body. (See *Purgatorio*, XXV, 37-75.) *O Love that rulest Heaven*: God. *whose lamp*: Beatrice as the reflector of God's love.

76-78. *The Great Wheel etc.*: Dante says, literally: "The wheel that Thou, in being desired [i.e., loved] by it, makest eternal." The Great Wheel is the Primum Mobile, its motion deriving from the love of God. *captured my attention*: Indicates that Dante turned his eyes from Beatrice to look up again. *that harmony*: The Music of the Spheres.

80. *ablaze with sun*: Dante believed that the earth's atmosphere extended as high as the Sphere of the Moon. Beyond the Moon is another atmosphere of fire. This sphere of fire was believed to cause lightning. (See also line 115, "the fire about the moon".)

92. *natural place*: The Sphere of Fire. It summons all fire to itself. Conflicting forces of nature force the lightning downward, but the fiery elements dislocated under stress find their way back to their natural place. Dante still has not realized that he and Beatrice are soaring toward Heaven at an incalculable speed.

93. *there*: To the Sphere of Fire.

104. *an inner order*: In relation to one another, and each in its relation to the total and to its final end, as fire to fire (see line 115). The end of man is God; therefore, the purified soul ascends naturally and inevitably to Him.

106. *the higher creatures*: The rational beings of creation: angels, heavenly spirits, and men.

108. *these norms*: The mode and form of lines 103-104.

123-124. *that heaven*: The Empyrean. *the fastest sphere*: The Primum Mobile. The Empyrean does not move and it is beyond space. It is eternal and perfect Love (therefore unchangeable) and holds within its constancy all of space, including the outermost and greatest sphere, the Primum Mobile.

125. *that bow*: The innate impulse of all creatures to seek their place in God.

127-135. The free will of creatures allows them, despite the innate order of all things, to yield to false pleasures and so to resist God's plan as the matter in which the artist works, being base and imperfect, may resist his intent to give it ideal form. One might argue against this figure that the artist in this case, being God, is omnipotent and could, at will, work in perfect matter. But to enter into such an argument would only be to bump heads on the question of fallible free will within an omnipotent creation—a question that has vexed Christian theology for millennia.

141. *that would indeed have been . . . marvelous*: Because then it would be going against the order of the universe. What is purified must ascend to God as inevitably as earthly waters must flow downhill.

# CANTO II

---

ASCENT TO THE MOON                    *Warning to the Reader*

THE FIRST SPHERE: THE MOON           *Beatrice Explains the*
                                     *Markings on the Moon*

DANTE AND BEATRICE are soaring to THE
SPHERE OF THE MOON at a speed approaching that
of light. Dante warns back the shallow reader: only
those who have eaten of the knowledge of God may
hope to follow him into the last reaches of his infinite
voyage, for it will reveal such wonders as only faith can
grasp.

His warning concluded, he and Beatrice enter the
Sphere of the Moon and pass into the substances of
the moon as light into water, as God incarnated himself
into man, or as the saved soul reenters God, without
disruption of the substance thus entered.

Still unenlightened by the ultimate revelation, Dante
does not understand how there can appear on the
diamond-smooth surface on the moon (as he conceived
it) those markings we know as THE MAN IN THE
MOON, and which the Italians knew as CAIN WITH
HIS BUSH OF THORNS.

Beatrice asks for his explanation, refutes it, and
proceeds to explain the truth of the moon's markings.

O you who in your wish to hear these things
    have followed thus far in your little skiffs
    the wake of my great ship that sails and sings,          3

turn back and make your way to your own coast.
  Do not commit yourself to the main deep,
  for, losing me, all may perhaps be lost.          6

My course is set for an uncharted sea.
  Minerva fills my sail. Apollo steers.
  And nine new Muses point the Pole for me.         9

You other few who have set yourselves to eat
  the bread of angels, by which we live on earth,
  but of which no man ever grew replete;            12

you may well trust your keel to the salt track
  and follow in the furrow of my wake
  ahead of the parted waters that close back.        15

Those heroes who sailed to Colchis, there to see
  their glorious Jason turned into a plowman,
  were not as filled with wonder as you will be.    18

The connate and perpetual thirst we feel
  for the God-like realm, bore us almost as swiftly
  as the sight soars to see the heavens wheel.       21

Beatrice was looking upward and I at her
  when—in the time it takes a bolt to strike,
  fly, and be resting in the bowstring's blur—       24

I found myself in a place where a wondrous thing
  drew my entire attention; whereat she
  from whom I could not hide my mind's
                            least yearning      27

turned and said, as much in joy as beauty:
  "To God, who has raised us now to the first star
  direct your thoughts in glad and grateful duty."   30

It seemed to me a cloud as luminous
  and dense and smoothly polished as a diamond
  struck by a ray of sun, enveloped us.              33

We were received into the elements
   of the eternal pearl as water takes
   light to itself, with no change in its substance.   36

If I was a body (nor need we in this case
   conceive how one dimension can bear another,
   which must be if two bodies fill one space)   39

the more should my desire burn like the sun
   to see that Essence in which one may see
   how human nature and God blend into one.   42

There we shall witness what we hold in faith,
   not told by reason but self-evident;
   as men perceive an axiom here on earth.   45

"My lady," I replied, "in every way
   my being can, I offer up my thanks
   to Him who raised me from the world of clay.   48

But tell me what dark traces in the grain
   of this bright body show themselves below
   and cause men to tell fables about Cain?"   51

She smiled a moment and then answered me:
   "If the reckoning of mortals fails to turn
   the lock to which your senses hold no key,   54

the arrows of wonder should not run you through:
   even when led by the evidence of the senses
   the wings of reason often do not fly true.   57

But what do *you* believe the cause to be?"
   And I: "That these variations we observe
   are caused by bodies of varying density."   60

And she: "You will certainly come to know your view
   is steeped in falsehood. If you listen well
   to the counter-arguments I shall offer you.   63

The eighth sphere shines with many lamps, and these
  may be observed to shine with various aspects,
  both in their qualities and quantities.              66

If rare or dense alone could have produced
  all this, one power would have to be in all,
  whether equally or variously diffused.               69

Diversity of powers can only spring
  from formal principles, and all but one
  would be excluded by your reasoning.                 72

Now if rarity produced the marks you mention,
  then the matter of this planet must be transparent
  at certain points, due to its rarefaction;           75

or it must be arranged like fat and lean
  within a body, as, so to speak, a book
  alternates pages. But it may be seen                 78

in an eclipse that the first cannot be true,
  for then the sun's light, as it does in striking
  rare matter of any sort, would pass right through.   81

Since it does not, we may then pass along
  to the second case, and if I prove it false,
  I shall have shown that your whole thought
                                        is wrong.      84

If this rare matter is not spread throughout
  the planet's mass, then there must be a limit
  at which the denser matter will turn about           87

the sun's rays, which, not being allowed to pass,
  will be reflected as light and color are
  from the leaded back of a clear looking glass.       90

Now you may argue, in Avicenna's track,
  that the ray seems darker in one place than in others
  since it is being reflected from further back.       93

From such an *instance* (if you will do your part)
  you may escape by experiment (that being
  the spring that feeds the rivers of man's art).    96

Take three clear mirrors. Let two be set out
  at an equal distance from you, and a third
  between them, but further back. Now turn about    99

to face them, and let someone set a light
  behind your back so that it strikes all three
  and is reflected from them to your sight.    102

Although the image from the greater distance
  is smaller than the others, you must note
  that all three shine back with an equal brilliance.    105

Now, as the power of the sun's rays will strip
  the wintry ground on which the snow has lain
  of the cold and color that held it in their grip,    108

so you, with mind stripped clean, shall I delight
  with such a radiance of the living truth
  that it will leap and tremble in your sight.    111

Within the heaven of peace beyond the sky
  there whirls a body from whose power arises
  the being of all things that within it lie.    114

The next sphere, that which is so richly lit,
  distributes this power to many essences
  distinct from itself, yet all contained within it.    117

The other spheres, in various degrees,
  dispose the special powers they have within
  to their own causes and effects. All these    120

great universal organs, as you now know,
  proceed from grade to grade. Each in its order
  takes power from above and does its work below.    123

Now then, note carefully how I move on
    through this pass to the truth you seek, for thus
    you shall learn how to hold the ford alone.    126

The motion and the power of the sacred gyres—
    as the hammer's art is from the smith—must flow
    from the Blessed Movers. It is their power inspires. 129

And thus that Heaven made loveliest in its wheel
    by many lamps, from the deep mind that turns it
    takes the image and makes itself the seal.    132

And as the soul within your mortal clay
    is spread through different organs, each of which
    is shaped to its own end; in the same way    135

the high angelic Intelligence spreads its goodness
    diversified through all the many stars
    while yet revolving ever in its Oneness.    138

This varying power is variously infused
    throughout the precious body that it quickens,
    in which, like life in you, it is diffused.    141

Because of the glad nature from which it flows,
    this many-faceted power shines through that body
    as through the living eye the glad soul glows.    144

From this source only, not from rare and dense,
    comes that by which one light and another differs—
    the formal principle whose excellence,    147

conforming to its own purposes, makes appear
those markings you observe as dark and clear.

## Notes

3. *of my great ship*: See *Purgatorio*, I, 1-2. There Dante
refers to "the little bark of my indwelling powers." For the present
voyage nothing less than a great (God-inspired) ship will do.

**7-9.** No poet has ever undertaken any such subject as Dante now sings. Poetically, therefore, he is embarking on waters no man has ever sailed. Apollo will guide his helm by the rules of poetry, but it is Minerva, goddess of wisdom, who must fill his sails, and the Muses who must be his navigators. *nine new Muses*: Dante says, simply, *"nove Muse"*. But *"nove"* may mean either "nine" or "new." *the Pole*: Dante says "the Bears" (Ursa Major and Ursa Minor. The North Star is in Ursa Minor but its position in the sky is usually located by first identifying Ursa Major, the stars of Ursa Minor being dim.)

**11.** *the bread of angels*: The knowledge of God. It is by that, Dante says, that we are able to live, but no mortal man can grasp enough of it to become satisfied, the Divine Mystery being veiled from man.

**13-15.** The few who have sought the knowledge of God are described as having keels. Hence they sail in something more seaworthy than the little skiffs of the others. Those few may dare the voyage, but note how closely they must follow Dante—they must stay in the very furrow of his wake, ahead of the waters that flow back to close it. Clearly, Dante means that he must be followed with the most scrupulous attention if the truth of his poem is to be grasped.

**16-17.** *Those heroes*: The Argonauts. Jason led them to Colchis to get the Golden Fleece. The Colchian King offered to give Jason the fleece if he would subdue two fire-breathing brass-hooved bulls, yoke them, plow the field of Ares with them, sow the field with dragon's teeth, and then defeat the army of warriors that would spring up from the teeth.

**19.** *connate*: Dante says *"concreata."* The thirst for God is born in the instant the soul is formed.

**20-21.** *almost as swiftly as the eye*: Dante and Beatrice soar upward at almost the speed of light.

**23-24.** The bolt of a crossbow would leave the bowstring so rapidly that human sense could not measure the rate of change. Hence, the figure means "instantly." But Dante has deliberately reversed the motion, a daring hysteron-proteron. Prof. John Freccero cites it, in the best interpretation known to me, as an example of Dante's "retrospective technique." Bear in mind that Dante is looking backward at the world and sees earthly actions in reverse. See XXII, 109, for another such usage.

**27.** *drew my entire attention*: As noted in line 22, Dante's attention had been fixed on Beatrice.

29. *to the first star*: The "first star" is the Moon. Dante has reached the first sphere of the Ptolemaic system.

32. *dense and smoothly polished as a diamond*: Dante finds the surface of the Moon to be diamond-smooth and highly polished (the telescope that was to reveal the jagged surface had not yet been invented).

35. *the eternal pearl*: The Moon.

37-42. THE UNITY OF GOD AND MAN. Dante is dealing here in the mysteries of faith. On Earth two bodies, being conceived as solids, cannot occupy the same space ("one dimension cannot bear another"). Yet, as light is received by water with no change in its self-unity, so Dante enters into the substance of the Moon, and this miraculous unity with which he enters the Moon-substance without disrupting it, sends his mind soaring to the mystery of the incarnation of God, and to the ultimate reception of the good man into the ineffable Logos. *that Essence*: Christ as the Man-God.

44. *not told by reason*: Reason is only the handmaiden of faith. With his final purification in the Earthly Paradise, Dante passed beyond reason to the greater way of knowing. Virgil's last words to Dante were: "Lord of yourself I crown and miter you." With his subsequent purification Dante achieves the state in which every effort of the will and of the intellect cease. Yet the understanding grows, for now the soul perceives as self-evident what had seemed incomprehensible to mere reason.

49-51. *dark traces . . . Cain?* In Dante's Italy what we call the Man in the Moon was fabled to be Cain with a Bush of Thorns. Recall that Dante has just described the lunar surface as being diamond-smooth and polished: such a surface would not show dark traces.

52-57. Sense: No wonder men fable falsely when they have no sensory evidence on which to base their reasoning. Even in matters about which firm sensory evidence is available to them they do not always reason correctly.

64-66. *The eighth sphere*: The Sphere of the Fixed Stars. *lamps*: Stars. *qualities and quantities*: Coloration and intensity. The phrasing of Beatrice's disquisition is characteristically Scholastic: one can only repeat the admonition of the first six lines of the present Canto and hope the willing reader will accept the invitation of lines 10-18.

68. *power*: The influence of the stars upon the earth and upon the lives of men.

71. *formal principle*: Scholastic teaching distinguishes two principles in all bodies: the *material*, which is to say, the first matter, which is the same in all; and the *formal*, which is to say the substantial form that produces the various species and innate abilities of living forms. The *formal principle* is active; the *material principle*, passive. Dante's reasoning is false in that it would reduce all to a single principle.

73 ff. BEATRICE'S EXPLANATION OF THE MARKINGS OF THE MOON. In *Il Convivio*, II, 14, Dante had attributed these traces to differences in the density of the lunar matter, whereby the body reflected the light unequally. In this he followed Avicenna. (The reference to Avicenna in line 91 is not explicitly in the original text, but it is clearly implied.) Now, with Beatrice as his revelation, he refutes his earlier belief, having her first show that such a belief leads to impossible conclusions, and then having her assign the true cause to the special power diffused by the Primum Mobile. That power, though itself indivisible, dispenses itself with varying intensity according to the different bodies it permeates—as the soul, for example, permeates some parts of the body more intensely than it does others.

Beatrice's argument is a curious one, Scholastic, pragmatic, and mystical by turn. She begins by demonstrating that Dante's belief involves a true dilemma (an either/or) and proceeds to reduce either term to an absurdity, offering in evidence practical observations of an eclipse and an experiment she suggests to Dante. As noted above, she then explains the phenomenon by the mystic nature of the Primum Mobile.

93. *reflected*: Dante says *"rifratto"* (refracted). The physics of his time did not distinguish between reflection and refraction.

94. *instance*: A technical term (*"instanza"*) of Aristotelian and Scholastic logic signifying "counter-proposition." Dante's figure treats the *instance* as a trap from which one must escape with the aid of experiment.

96. *art*: Learning. See *Inferno*, XI, 97-105. In Dante "art" signifies the skills, the crafts, and all the methods by which man understands and wins control over nature. It is always distinct from the higher knowledge of faith.

97-105. THE EXPERIMENT. Dante assumes in this experiment that the heavenly bodies are highly reflective surfaces. Thus by shining a light into three mirrors, two equidistant from him and one further back, and noting (though the size of the remoter image is smaller) that the brightness of all three is equal, he seems to argue that light of equal intensity is equally brilliant from whatever distance it is reflected. The argument is ingenious but any reader interested in the rudiments of science will be able to offer his own refutation of the experiment when its conclusions are applied to heavenly bodies at astronomic distances as seen at varying angles through a varying atmosphere.

108-109. *cold and color*: Both the cold and the whiteness are removed from the ground. *so you, stripped in your mind*: So Dante, the cold and color of error stripped from his mind, will be flooded with the living light (like the fructifying light and heat of returning Spring) of the truth.

112. *the heaven of peace beyond the sky*: The Empyrean. I have had to take liberties here. A literal rendering would be: "within the heaven of the divine peace."

113. *a body*: The Primum Mobile. Since the Empyrean (which lies beyond) is beyond space, the sphere of the Primum Mobile contains all of the universe. Taking its power from the all-encompassing Godhead (the Empyrean), it gives rise to all being.

115. *the next sphere*: Of the Fixed Stars.

120. *to their own causes and effects*: Each sphere to those causes and effects influenced by its particular powers.

123. *takes power from above*: From God. *and does its work below*: Ultimately upon man (the influence of the heavens upon mortal lives) but intermediately some of the work of each sphere must be to transmit certain powers (undiminished) to the spheres below.

124-126. Beatrice, as ever, is acting as Dante's teacher. Here, in a military figure, she instructs him to take careful note of how her argument proceeds through the next point, that by her example Dante may learn how to defend the ford (the crossing to the truth) by himself.

127. *gyres*: Circlings.

129. *the Blessed Movers*: The Angels, Powers, Principalities, and Intelligences who influence each sphere.

130. *the Heaven made loveliest by many lamps*: The Sphere of the Fixed Stars.

131-132. *from the deep mind*: Of God. The Sphere of the Fixed Stars receives its power from God (through the Primum Mobile) and taking His image from above, makes itself the seal that impresses that image on the spheres below (as a seal impresses its given image upon wax).

135. *shaped to its own end*: As the eye to sight, the ear to sound, *etc.*

140. *the precious body*: Of the Sphere of the Fixed Stars, here compared to the human body, because its unity comprises so many varied organs.

142. *the glad nature*: Of God.

147. *formal principle*: (See also note to line 71.) The power of the Divine and Angelic Intelligence is the intrinsic and substantial cause which produces the effect of dark and clear according to the various ways in which it enters into conjunction with the stars.

# CANTO III

45

THE FIRST SPHERE: THE MOON

*The Inconstant*
*Piccarda, Constance*

*AS DANTE IS ABOUT TO SPEAK to Beatrice he
sees the dim traceries of human faces and taking them
to be reflections, he turns to see what souls are being
so reflected. Beatrice, as ever, explains that these pallid
images are the souls themselves. They are THE INCON-
STANT, the souls of those who registered holy vows
in Heaven, but who broke or scanted them.*

*Among them PICCARDA DONATI identifies herself,
and then identifies THE EMPRESS CONSTANCE.
Both, according to Dante's beliefs, had taken vows as
nuns but were forced to break them in order to contract
a political marriage. Not all the souls about them need
have failed in the same vows, however. Any failure
to fulfill a holy vow (of holy orders, to go on a
pilgrimage, to offer special services to God) might place
the soul in this lowest class of the blessed.*

*Piccarda explains that every soul in Heaven rejoices
in the entire will of God and cannot wish for a higher
place, for to do so would be to come into conflict with
the will of God. In the perfect harmony of bliss, everywhere in Heaven is Paradise.*

That sun that breathed love's fire into my youth
  had thus resolved for me, feature by feature—
    proving, disproving—the sweet face of truth.    3

I, raising my eyes to her eyes to announce
  myself resolved of error, and well assured,
  was about to speak; but before I could pronounce  6

my first word, there appeared to me a vision.
  It seized and held me so that I forgot
  to offer her my thanks and my confession.  9

As in clear glass when it is polished bright,
  or in a still and limpid pool whose waters
  are not so deep that the bottom is lost from sight, 12

a footnote of our lineaments will show,
  so pallid that our pupils could as soon
  make out a pearl upon a milk-white brow—  15

so I saw many faces eager to speak,
  and fell to the error opposite the one
  that kindled love for a pool in the smitten Greek. 18

And thinking the pale traces I saw there
  were reflected images, I turned around
  to face the source—but my eyes met empty air.  21

I turned around again like one beguiled,
  and took my line of sight from my sweet guide
  whose sacred eyes grew radiant as she smiled.  24

"Are you surprised that I smile at this childish act
  of reasoning?" she said, "since even now
  you dare not trust your sense of the true fact,  27

but turn, as usual, back to vacancy?
  These are true substances you see before you.
  They are assigned here for inconstancy  30

to holy vows. Greet them. Heed what they say,
  and so believe; for the True Light that fills them
  permits no soul to wander from its ray."  33

So urged, I spoke to those pale spirits, turning
   to one who seemed most eager, and began
   like one whose mind goes almost blank with
                      yearning.    36

"O well created soul, who in the sun
   of the eternal life drinks in the sweetness
   which, until tasted, is beyond conception;    39

great would be my joy would you confide
   to my eager mind your earthly name and fate."
   That soul with smiling eyes, at once replied:    42

"The love that fills us will no more permit
   hindrance to a just wish than does that Love
   that wills all of Its court to be like It.    45

I was a virgin sister there below,
   and if you search your memory with care,
   despite my greater beauty, you will know    48

I am Piccarda, and I am placed here
   among these other souls of blessedness
   to find my blessedness in the slowest sphere.    51

Our wishes, which can have no wish to be
   but in the pleasure of the Holy Ghost,
   rejoice in being formed to His decree.    54

And this low-seeming post which we are given
   is ours because we broke, or, in some part,
   slighted the vows we offered up to Heaven."    57

And I then: "Something inexpressibly
   divine shines in your face, subliming you
   beyond your image in my memory:    60

therefore I found you difficult to place;
  but now, with the assistance of your words,
  I find the memory easier to retrace.                    63

But tell me, please: do you who are happy here
  have any wish to rise to higher station,
  to see more, or to make yourselves more dear?"          66

She smiled, as did the spirits at her side;
  then, turning to me with such joy she seemed
  to burn with the first fire of love, replied:           69

"Brother, the power of love, which is our bliss,
  calms all our will. What we desire, we have.
  There is in us no other thirst than this.               72

Were we to wish for any higher sphere,
  then our desires would not be in accord
  with the high will of Him who wills us here;            75

and if love is our whole being, and if you weigh
  love's nature well, then you will see that discord
  can have no place among these circles. Nay,             78

the essence of this blessed state of being
  is to hold all our will within His will,
  whereby our wills are one and all-agreeing.             81

And so the posts we stand from sill to sill
  throughout this realm, please all the realm as much
  as they please Him who wills us to His will.            84

In His will is our peace. It is that sea
  to which all moves, all that Itself creates
  and Nature bears through all Eternity."                 87

Then was it clear to me that everywhere
  in Heaven is Paradise, though the Perfect Grace
  does not rain down alike on all souls there.            90

But as at times when we have had our fill
   of one food and still hunger for another,
  we put this by with gratitude, while still     93

asking for that—just so I begged to know,
   by word and sign, through what warp she had not
   entirely passed the shuttle of her vow.     96

"The perfection of her life and her great worth
   enshrine a lady hereabove," she said,
   "in whose rule some go cloaked and veiled
                           on earth,     99

that till their death they may live day and night
   with that sweet Bridegroom who accepts of love
   all vows it makes that add to His delight.     102

As a girl, I fled the world to walk the way
   she walked, and closed myself into her habit,
   pledged to her sisterhood till my last day.     105

Then men came, men more used to hate than love.
   They tore me away by force from the sweet cloister.
   What my life then became is known above.     108

This other splendor who lets herself appear
   here to my right to please you, shining full
   of every blessedness that lights this sphere,     111

understands in herself all that I say.
   She, too, was a nun. From her head as from mine
   the shadow of the veil was ripped away.     114

Against her will and all propriety
   she was forced back to the world. Yet even there
   her heart was ever veiled in sanctity.     117

She is the radiance of the Empress Constance,
   who by the second blast of Swabia
   conceived and bore its third and final puissance."     120

She finished, and at once began to sing
   *Ave Maria,* and singing, sank from view
   like a weight into deep water, plummeting      123

out of my sight, which followed while it could,
   and then, having lost her, turned about once more
   to the target of its greater wish and good,      126

and wholly gave itself to the delight
   of the sweet vision of Beatrice. But she
   flashed so radiantly upon my sight      129

that I, at first, was blinded, and thus was slow
   to ask of her what I most wished to know.

## Notes

1. *That sun*: Beatrice. It was she who first breathed love's fire into Dante's youth. (See also *Purgatorio*, XXX, 40-42 and *Paradiso*, XXX, 75.)

3. *proving*: Her views, the truth. *and disproving*: My views, error.

9. *my confession*: Of the error Dante now recognizes (concerning the markings of the moon).

13. *a footnote of our lineaments*: The figure seems oddly out of context but its intent is clear: Dante is suggesting that the image is related to the face as a footnote is related to the text.

15. *a pearl upon a milk-white brow*: The brow would have to be death-pale as marble, but perhaps Dante intends these spirits to be chalky-white.

16. THE INCONSTANT. All these spirits registered vows in Heaven and then either broke or slighted them. Both of those cited took vows as nuns and were then forced to break them against their own wishes. One must assume, however, that the same category would include not only monks and priests who similarly gave up holy orders, but all who offered up a vow of any sort and then failed to observe it strictly.

They are "assigned here" (line 30), which is to say they appear on the moon (the inconstant planet), but each has his throne in the Empyrean (see IV, 23). All the souls of the blessed, whatever their rank in Heaven, experience as much bliss as they are capable of and cannot wish for more. Within the divine order each seeks and finds its proper place.

18. *the smitten Greek*: Narcissus. His error was in taking a reflection (his own) to be a real face. Dante's opposite error is in taking real faces to be reflections.

32. *the True Light*: God.

33. *permits no soul to wander*: So Dante's phrasing, but it should be understood that filled as these souls are by the True Light, their inability to stray from its ray (contrast Dante's situation in line 27) is not a prohibition but a choice of their own perfected volition. They are not capable of error.

44. *that Love*: God, as the essence of *Caritas*.

46. *virgin sister*: A nun.

49. *Piccarda*: Piccarda Donati was the daughter of Simone Donati (*Inferno*, XXV, 32) and sister of Forese (*Purgatorio*, XXIII, 48) and of the war-leader, Corso (*Purgatorio*, XXIV, 82ff.). Forese was Dante's friend. Dante was married to Gemma Donati, who also had a brother named Forese, but Piccarda's family was grander than Dante's in-laws.

Piccarda was already a nun and living in her convent when her brother Corso, needing to establish a political alliance, forced her to marry Rossellino della Tossa of Florence. Various commentators report that Piccarda sickened and soon died as a consequence of having been so forced against her will and vows.

52-54. THE BLISS OF THE BLESSED. Every soul in Heaven, whatever its station, is entirely happy because it is entirely identified with God's plan and has no joy but in being formed to His will. The essence of God is love, i.e., *caritas*, the love of others. With *caritas* as the essential mood of the *Paradiso*, no soul can help but rejoice in the joy of all about it. Contrast the state of things in the *Inferno*: the infernal souls have all refused to accept and to identify themselves with the Divine Love; each, therefore, is closed into itself, and no soul in Hell can derive any comfort from any other (see *Inferno*, V, note to line 102). Joy finds its increase exactly in being freely given to others. As Piccarda soon makes clear to Dante, that joy is expressed in Heaven in no way but in the complete identification with God's love.

63. *easier to retrace*: A desperate simplification of Dante's untranslatable *"m'è più latino"* (literally: "it is more Latin to

me"). Learned men of Dante's time used Latin naturally and gracefully. Thus to make a thing "more Latin" was to facilitate it. An opposite form of a similar idiom is our still current "It's Greek to me."

66. *to make yourselves more dear*: To God.

69. *the first fire of love*: Could variously be taken to mean God, the Moon (the first lit sphere of the Universe, which is Love), or the bliss mortals feel in the fire of newly awakened love. On the narrative level the last seems most likely, but the other meanings could function along with it.

95-96. *warp . . . shuttle*: The vertical strings of a loom are the warp. Across them the shuttle draws the woof. Not to draw the shuttle entirely through is to leave the weaving unfinished, hence her vow unfulfilled.

98. *a lady*: Saint Clara of Assisi (1194-1253). Born Chiara Sciffi, she became a disciple of St. Francis and, under his influence, founded in 1212 an order of nuns. *hereabove*: Higher in Heaven. Probably in the Empyrean, but Dante does not mention her again.

101. *that sweet Bridegroom*: Christ. He is so-called several times in the New Testament.

102. *all vows . . . that add to His delight*: Only those vows that conform to His love are acceptable. A vow to perform a trivial or an evil action would have no standing.

109. *This other splendor*: The Empress Constance (1154-1198). As the last of the line of Norman kings who took southern Italy in the eleventh century, she was Empress of the Two Sicilies (Sicily and Naples). She married the Emperor Henry VI in 1185 and became the mother of Frederick II. Dante follows a legend, for which there was no basis in fact, that she had become a nun and was forced to leave her convent to marry Henry.

109. *lets herself appear*: Dante says, "who shows herself to you." Clearly, the souls in Paradise can make themselves visible or invisible at will (i.e., Heaven reveals itself of its own love). At the end of the conversation the whole company withdraws from sight.

119. THE THREE BLASTS OF SWABIA. These are the three great princes whose origins were in Swabia (in Germany). Frederick Barbarossa was the first. His son, Henry VI, was the second. To Henry, Constance bore the third, Frederick II.

# CANTO IV

THE FIRST SPHERE: THE MOON　　　*Beatrice Discourses:*
*The True Seat of the Blessed*
*Plato's Error*
*Free Will*
*Recompense for Broken Vows*

*PICCARDA HAS TOLD DANTE that she inhabits the
sphere of the inconstant Moon because she broke her
vows against her will. Dante is torn by doubts that could
lead to heresy. Was Plato right in saying souls come
from their various stars preformed, and then return to
them? If so, what of FREE WILL? And if Heaven is
Justice, how have these souls sinned in being forced
against their wills? And if Heaven is truth, what of the
contradiction between Piccarda's statements and Beatrice's?*

*Beatrice resolves all of Dante's doubts. When she has
finished Dante asks if men may offer OTHER RECOM-
PENSE FOR BROKEN VOWS.*

A man given free choice would starve to death
　　between two equal equidistant foods,
　　unable to get either to his teeth.　　　　　　　　　　3

So would a lamb, in counterbalanced fear,
　　tremble between two she-wolves and stand frozen.
　　So would a hound stand still between two deer.　　6

If I stood mute, then, tugged to either side,
　　I neither blame myself, nor take my doubt—
　　it being necessary—as cause for pride.　　　　　　　9

I did not speak, but on my face, at once,
　　were written all my questions and my yearnings,
　　far more distinctly than I could pronounce.          12

And Beatrice did as Daniel once had done
　　when he raised Nebuchadnezzar from the wrath
　　that made him act unjustly in Babylon.               15

"I see full well how equal wish and doubt
　　tear you two ways," she said, "so that your zeal
　　tangles upon itself and cannot breathe out.          18

You reason: 'If the will that vowed stays true,
　　how can another's violence take away
　　from the full measure of bliss that is my due?'      21

And I see a second doubt perplex that thought
　　because the souls you see seem to return
　　to the stars from which they came, as Plato taught.  24

These are the questions that bear down your will
　　with equal force. Therefore, I shall treat first
　　the one whose venom has more power to kill.          27

Choose the most God-like of the Seraphim—
　　take Moses, or Samuel, or take either John,
　　or even Mary—not one is nearer Him,                  30

nor holds his seat atop the blessed spheres
　　in any heaven apart from those you saw;
　　nor has his being more or fewer years.              33

All add their beauty to the Highest Wheel,
　　share the sweet life, and vary in it only
　　by how much of the Eternal Breath they feel.        36

They showed themselves here not because this post
　　has been assigned them, but to symbolize
　　that they stand lowest in the Heavenly host.        39

So must one speak to mortal imperfection,
 which only from the *sensible* apprehends
 whatever it then makes fit for intellection.  42

Scripture in like manner condescends,
 describing God as having hands and feet
 as signs to men of what more it portends.  45

So Holy Church shows you in mortal guise
 the images of Gabriel and of Michael,
 and of the other who gave back Tobit's eyes.  48

For if Timaeus—as seems rather clear—
 spoke literally, what he says about souls
 is nothing like the truth shown to us here.  51

He says the soul finds its own star again,
 from which, as he imagines, nature chose it
 to give form to the flesh and live with men.  54

But it may be the words he uses hide
 a second meaning, which, if understood,
 reveals a principle no man may deride.  57

If he means that the blame or honor due
 the influence of each sphere returns to it,
 his arrow does hit something partly true.  60

This principle, misunderstood, once drove
 almost the whole world to attach to planets
 such names as Mars and Mercury and Jove.  63

The other doubt that agitates your mind
 is not as venemous, for not all its malice
 could drive you from my side to wander blind.  66

For mortal men to argue that they see
 injustice in our justice is in itself
 a proof of faith, not poisonous heresy.  69

But since the truth of this lies well within
 the reach of your own powers, I shall explain it,
 just as you wish. —If violence, to begin,   72

occurs when those who suffer its abuse
 contribute nothing to what forces them,
 then these souls have no claim to that excuse.  75

For the will, if it will not, cannot be spent,
 but does as nature does within a flame
 a thousand or ten thousand winds have bent.  78

If it yields of itself, even in the least,
 then it assists the violence—as did these
 who could have gone back to their holy feast.  81

If their whole will had joined in their desire—
 as whole will upheld Lawrence on the grill,
 and Mucius with his hand thrust in the fire,  84

just so, it would have forced them to return
 to their true way the instant they were free.
 But such pure will is too rare, we must learn!  87

If you have gleaned them diligently, then
 these words forever destroy the argument
 that would have plagued your mind time and again. 90

But now another pass opens before you,
 so strait and tortuous that without my help
 you would tire along the way and not win through. 93

I made you understand beyond all doubt
 that these souls cannot lie, for they exist
 in the First Truth and cannot wander out.  96

Later you heard Piccarda say that she
 who stood beside her kept her love of the veil;
 and it seems that what she said contradicts me. 99

Time and again, my brother, men have run
  from danger by a path they would not choose,
  and on it done what ought not to be done.        102

So, bending to his father's prayer, did he
  who took his mother's life. Alcmaeon I mean,
  who sought his piety in impiety.        105

Now weigh within your own intelligence
  how will and violence interact, so joining
  that no excuse can wipe out the offense.        108

Absolute will does not will its own harm,
  but fearing worse may come if it resists,
  consents the more, the greater its alarm.        111

Thus when Piccarda spoke as she did to you,
  she meant the absolute will; and I, the other.
  So both of us spoke only what was true."        114

—Such was the flowing of that stream so blest
  it flows down from the Fountain of All Truth.
  Such was the power that laid my doubts to rest.        117

"Beloved of the First Love! O holy soul!"
  I said then, "You whose words flow over me,
  and with their warmth quicken and make me
                       whole,        120

There is not depth enough within my love
  to offer you due thanks, but may the One
  who sees and can, answer for me above.        123

Man's mind, I know, cannot win through the mist
  unless it is illumined by that Truth
  beyond which truth has nowhere to exist.        126

In That, once it has reached it, it can rest
  like a beast within its den. And reach it can;
  else were all longing vain, and vain the test.        129

Like a new tendril yearning from man's will
    doubt sprouts to the foot of truth. It is that in us
    that drives us to the summit from hill to hill.        132

By this am I encouraged, by this bidden,
    my lady, in all reverence, to ask
    your guidance to a truth that still lies hidden:        135

can such as these who put away their veils
    so compensate by other good works done
    that they be not found wanting on your scales?"        138

Beatrice looked at me, and her glad eyes,
    afire with their divinity, shot forth
    such sparks of love that my poor faculties        141

gave up the reins. And with my eyes cast down
I stood entranced, my senses all but flown.

## Notes

1-9. DANTE'S DOUBT. The phrasing of this passage is difficult. Nor am I sure I have found the right rendering of all
the grammatical ambiguities. The intent, on the other hand, is
clear. Piccarda's account of herself has raised questions that, as
we shall see, tear Dante's understanding in two directions at
once. Beatrice, as usual, senses his self-division and resolves all in
the conversation that follows.

The difficulty of the phrasing is caused by the interplay of
the ideas "free choice" and "necessity." Dante follows Aquinas
in this: if the choices offered to a man are entirely equal, no
choice can be made and the man cannot act. Thus Dante
takes neither blame nor praise for his indecisive doubts since
he was unable to choose between them.

13. *as Daniel had done*: Nebuchadnezzar, King of Babylon,
condemned all his diviners to death because they could not
interpret a dream he had forgotten. Daniel first divined the
dream and then interpreted it, calming the fury of the king.
(*Daniel*, II, 1-45.)

19. *if the will that vowed stays true*: Dante is thinking of what Piccarda said. If her will to keep her vows never faltered, how can the fact that her brother's violence forced her to act against her will alter her just reward for the purity of her intentions (which, seemingly, should have earned her a higher place in Heaven).

24. *as Plato taught*: As Dante rendered the *Timaeus*, Plato taught that souls existed in the stars before they entered human bodies (Wordsworth's "Ode on the Intimations of Immortality" is a well-known treatment of this theme) and returned, at the body's death, to the same stars from which they had come. Such a doctrine, however, denies free will, the soul being pre-created to a fixed place in Heaven's order. And yet the souls of the Inconstant seem to return to the inconstant Moon. Thus one thought negates the other, leaving Dante's mind ensnared between the two.

27. *whose venom has more power to kill*: The doctrine within which lurks the greater danger of self-destroying heresy.

28-63. THE PLACE IN HEAVEN OF THE BLEST. Every soul in Heaven is equally a part of God. As Beatrice goes on to explain, all have their seats in the Empyrean. The various spheres in which *they appear to Dante* only symbolize the degree of their beatitude. It is necessary to use such symbols because the limited comprehension of mankind could not begin to grasp the truth in any other way. Thus, the Bible speaks of God as if he had a manlike body when he is in fact Essence. Beatrice's point is that every elect soul is equally in God. All have their place in one Heaven, all are eternal. They vary only in the degree of their beatitude, which is determined by their own ability to absorb the infinity of God's bliss.

36. *the Eternal Breath*: Recall from *Genesis* that it was God's breath that quickened the dust to life. The Eternal Breath, therefore, is the gift of life, and the difference in the beatitude of the blessed must be in the degree to which they are quickened to their Eternal life. The pallor of those moon-souls, as contrasted to the blinding radiance of those who appear higher, may also, perhaps, be taken as a measure of how much of the Eternal Breath is in them.

48. *the other*: Raphael, the third archangel. He cured Tobit of blindness (*Tobit*, XI, 2-17).

54. *to give form*: (The rest of this line, though implicit in Dante, is my own rhyme-forced addition.) The soul, in Scholastic teaching, is the *formative power*. (See *Purgatorio*, XXV, 40-42,

note.) The body is simply the matter upon which it works to impress its form.

61-63. *this principle*: That souls come down from the stars (or spheres, or planets) and return to them. *almost the whole world*: The exception was the Jews. All others imagined multiple gods (Mars, Mercury, and Jove, for example) whose names they attached to the planets. *Jove*: For Jupiter.

64-69. *the other doubt*: Of the justice of placing Piccarda and Constance among the Inconstant when they were forced to break their vows against their will. This doubt is not as venemous because it does not lead to heresy. The Council of Constantinople (540 A.D.) had denounced the doctrine of the *Timaeus* as heretical. But the church had not pronounced infallibly on the matter of Dante's second doubt. That second doubt, therefore, might lead Dante into error but not into heresy. It could not, therefore, drive him from Beatrice (Revealed Truth) to wander blind outside the church. *proof of faith*: To doubt a particular manifestation of divine justice implies a belief in its existence.

77. *as nature does within a flame*: The flame, that is to say, rises again.

81. *their holy feast*: Their convents and their vows.

83. *Lawrence*: In 258, during the reign of Valerius, St. Lawrence, then deacon of Rome, was ordered by the Roman Prefect to send him the treasure of the church. Lawrence sent him the poor and the oppressed, declaring that they were the one treasure. He was thereupon martyred. After many other tortures, he was roasted on a grill, but remained steadfast under torture. Jacobus de Voragine (*The Golden Legend*) reports him as saying to his torturer: "Thou hast roasted the one side, tyrant, now turn the other and eat."

84. *Mucius*: Mucius Scaevola, a young man of ancient Rome. He vowed to kill Porsenna and let his right hand be consumed by fire when its thrust missed the mark. Note that, as in the Whips and Reins of the Purgatory, Dante presents both a sacred and a classical example.

94. *I made you understand*: See III, 31-33.

96. *the First Truth*: God.

97-98. *she who stood beside her*: Constance.

105. *his piety*: To his father. *impiety*: To his mother. For Alcmaeon see *Purgatorio*, XII, 49-51 and note.

106-114.   The central idea of this passage is the difference between the Absolute and the Conditioned Will. The Absolute Will is incapable of willing evil. The Conditioned Will, when coerced by violence, interacts with it and consents to a lesser harm in order to escape a greater. All that Piccarda said was true of the Absolute Will, but all that Beatrice has said is true of the Conditioned Will.

113-115. *that stream*: Stands for both Beatrice and her discourse. *the Fountain of All Truth*: God. Dante's figure also expounds Beatrice's allegorical function as Revealed Truth (which flows from God, the Fountain of All Truth, and calms all doubt from the souls of those to whom it descends).

127. *In That*: In the truth of God, within which the soul may rest as instinctively as does a beast within its den.

# CANTO V

[4] BEATRICE COMPENSATION FOR BROKEN VOWS

ASCENT TO THE SECOND SPHERE    *Beatrice Discourses*

THE SECOND SPHERE: MERCURY    *The Seekers of Honor*
*The Emperor Justinian*

*BEATRICE EXPLAINS the SANCTITY OF THE VOW, its RELATION TO FREE WILL, THE LIMITED RANGE WITHIN WHICH VOWS MAY BE ALTERED, and the DANGERS OF EVIL VOWS.*

*When she has finished, she and Dante soar to the SECOND SPHERE. There a host of radiant souls gathers to dance homage around Beatrice and Dante. These are the SEEKERS OF HONOR, souls who were active in their pursuit of the good, but who were motivated in their pursuit by a desire for personal honor, a good enough motive, but the least of all good motives.*

*One soul among them addresses Dante with particular joy. In Canto VI this soul identifies itself as the radiance that in mortal life was the EMPEROR JUSTINIAN.*

"If, in the warmth of love, I manifest
  more of my radiance than the world can see,
  rendering your eyes unequal to the test,                3

do not be amazed. These are the radiancies
  of the perfected vision that sees the good
  and step by step moves nearer what it sees.             6

Well do I see how the Eternal Ray,
  which, once seen, kindles love forevermore,
  already shines on you. If on your way                   9

some other thing seduce your love, my brother,
   it can only be a trace, misunderstood,
   of this, which you see shining through the other.   12

You ask if there is any compensation
   the soul may offer for its unkept vows
   that will secure it against litigation."   15

So Beatrice, alight from Heaven's Source,
   began this canto; and without a pause,
   continued thus her heavenly discourse:   18

"Of all creation's bounty realized,
   God's greatest gift, the gift in which mankind
   is most like Him, the gift by Him most prized,   21

is the freedom he bestowed upon the will.
   All his intelligent creatures, and they alone,
   were so endowed, and so endowed are still.   24

From this your reasoning should make evident
   the value of the vow, if it is so joined
   that God gives His consent when you consent.   27

When, therefore, God and man have sealed the pact,
   the man divests himself of that great treasure
   of which I speak—and by his own free act.   30

What can you offer, then, to make amends?
   How can you make good use of what is His?
   Would you employ extortion to good ends?   33

This much will make the main point clear to you.
   But since the church grants dispensations in this,
   whereby what I have said may seem untrue;   36

you must yet sit at table, for the food
   you have just taken is crusty; without help
   you will not soon digest it to your good.   39

Open your mind to what I shall explain,
   then close around it, for it is no learning
   to understand what one does not retain.     42

The essence of this sacrificial act
   lies, first, in *what* one does, and, second, in *how*—
   the *matter* and the *manner* of the pact.     45

This second part cannot be set aside
   except by full performance; on this point
   what I said earlier stands unqualified.     48

Thus it was mandatory to sacrifice
   among the Jews, though the offering itself
   might vary, or a substitute might suffice.     51

The other—what I have called the *matter*—may
   be of the sort for which a substitution
   will serve without offending in any way.     54

But let no man by his own judgment or whim
   take on himself that burden unless the keys
   of gold and silver have been turned for him.     57

And let him think no change a worthy one
   unless what he takes up contains in it,
   at least as six does four, what he puts down.     60

There are, however, things whose weight and worth
   tip every scale, and for these there can be
   no recompense by anything on earth.     63

Let no man make his vow a sporting thing.
   Be true and do not make a squint-eyed choice
   as Jephthah did in his first offering.     66

He had better have cried, 'I had no right to speak!'
   than, keeping his vow, do worse. And in like case
   will you find that chief war leader, the great Greek     69

whose Iphigenia wept her loveliness,
   and made both fools and wise men share her tears
   hearing of such dark rites and her distress. 72

Be slower to move, Christians, be grave, serene.
   Do not be like a feather in the wind,
   nor think that every water washes clean. 75

You have the Testaments, both old and new,
   and the shepherd of the church to be your guide;
   and this is all you need to lead you true. 78

If cunning greed comes promising remission,
   be men, not mad sheep, lest the Jew among you
   find cause to point his finger in derision. 81

Do not be like the lamb that strays away
   from its mother's milk and, simple and capricious,
   fights battles with itself in silly play!"

                      84

—Thus Beatrice to me, just as I write.
   Then she turned, full of yearning, to that part
   where the world is quickened most by the True
                      Light. 87

Her silence, her transfigured face ablaze
   made me fall still although my eager mind
   was teeming with new questions I wished to raise. 90

And like an arrow driven with such might
   it strikes its mark before the string is still,
   we soared to the second kingdom of the light. 93

My lady glowed with such a joyous essence
   giving herself to the light of that new sky
   that the planet shone more brightly with her
                   presence. 96

And if the star changed then and laughed with bliss,
  what did I do, who in my very nature
  was made to be transformed through all that is?   99

As in a fish pond that is calm and clear
  fish swim to what falls in from the outside,
  believing it to be their food, so, here,   102

I saw at least a thousand splendors move
  toward us, and from each one I heard the cry:
  "Here is what will give increase to our love!"   105

And as those glories came to where we were
  each shade made visible, in the radiance
  that each gave off, the joy that filled it there.   108

Imagine, reader, that I had started so
  and not gone on—think what an anguished famine
  would then oppress your hungry will to know.   111

So may you, of yourself, be able to see
  how much I longed to know their names and nature
  the instant they had shown themselves to me.   114

—"O well born soul, permitted by God's grace
  to see the thrones of the Eternal Triumph
  while still embattled in the mortal trace,   117

the lamp that shines through all the vaults of Heaven
  is lit in us; if, therefore, you seek light
  on any point, ask and it shall be given."   120

—So spoke one of those pious entities.
  And my lady said: "Speak. Speak with full assurance.
  And credit them as you would deities!"   123

"I do indeed see that you make your nest
  in your own light, and beam it through your eyes
  that dazzle when you smile, o spirit blest.   126

But I know not who you are, nor why you are
   assigned here, to this sphere that hides itself
   from men's eyes in the rays of another star."      129

These were my words, my face turned to the light
   that had just spoken; at which it made itself
   far more resplendent yet upon my sight.            132

Just as the sun, when its rays have broken through
   a screen of heavy vapors, will itself
   conceal itself in too much light—just so,           135

in its excess of joy that sacred soul
   hid itself from my sight in its own ray,
   and so concealed within its aureole,                138

it answered me, unfolding many things,
the manner of which the following canto sings.

## Notes

9-12. *some other thing*: The light of God, once seen, kindles
eternal love and no soul so kindled can stray from it. Since
Dante's soul has already been so kindled, the only possible
error remaining to him is that he could mistakenly believe he
sees the light of God in some lesser object and so be seduced
by that lesser thing, not because his love is lacking, but because his understanding is.

15. *litigation*: At the bar of judgment.

16-18. An odd tercet. In it Dante pauses only to say
Beatrice did not pause but spoke and went on speaking. A
literal rendering (I have had to take liberties) would be: "So
Beatrice began this canto; and, like a man who does not in-
terrupt his discourse, continued her sacred process [of reasoning and explication] as follows:".

19-33. THE SANCTITY OF HOLY VOWS. Dante has asked
if a man may not, by other good works, make amends for an
unfulfilled vow. Beatrice replies that God's greatest gift to man
is his free will, and that a vow is a direct compact with God

wherein man, of his free will, offers that freedom back to God. Once God accepts, the man's will is no longer free for it has been given to God. How then is man free to will what is good, his will and freedom now belonging to God? To assert a free will that is no longer his is to seek to embezzle his way to the good.

23. *All his intelligent creatures*: Angels and men.

43. *this sacrificial act*: It need not, of course, be restricted to the vows taken for religious orders. One might, for example, vow to fast, or to go on a pilgrimage, or to give some or all of his goods to the poor, or to live in a specified way.

49-57. *Thus it was mandatory*: The law of the Jews absolutely required them to offer sacrifices to the Lord (the *substance* of the covenant) but allowed them some latitude in what might be sacrificed (the *manner*). The manner of the vow may be changed if its substance is kept, but the change must not be arbitrary (for man, having given away his will, may not choose at his own pleasure), and no man should make such a change without having submitted his case to church authority (whereby the gold and silver keys of papal authority are turned for him).

58-60. Sense of this tercet: Let no man think it worthy (even with church authority) to change the substance of his vow to a lesser thing. Rather, the new substance should be greater than the former at least as six is to four. It is always well to look for a special significance in Dante's use of numbers, but I know of none here. He seems to be using six-to-four simply as a reasonable ratio of increase.

61-62. *things whose weight and worth tip every scale*: A vow of chastity would involve such a thing, virginity being irreplaceable. A vow of a lifetime of service would, similarly, involve what is irreplaceable. By contrast, a man who vowed to make a gift of money to charity every year of his life, and who then loses all his money, might satisfy his vow by substituting labor, or even, if he grows infirm, prayer. Were he, on the other hand, to steal in order to keep his money vow, that would be an evil thing.

66. *Jephthah*: King of Israel. He fought the Ammonites and vowed that if he were victorious he would offer up to God the first thing he saw coming out of the door of his house. The first thing he saw was his daughter and he sacrificed her (*Judges*, XI).

67. *have cried, 'I had no right to speak!'* No right to speak such a vow. In so crying he would have renounced the vow, and better so, says Dante, than to do worse in the act of keeping it.

69-70. *the great Greek whose Iphigenia*: Agamemnon. Iphigenia was his daughter. Dante follows the legend in which Agamemnon vowed before the birth of Iphigenia that he would sacrifice to Artemis the loveliest creature the year brought forth. Rather than sacrifice Iphigenia, he did not keep his vow. Years later, however, when the Greek ships were becalmed at Aulis, the other Greek leaders, especially Menelaus, blamed their distress on the unkept vow and Agamemnon was finally persuaded to send for Iphigenia and to sacrifice her.

79. *cunning greed*: The greed of those who offer dispensations and other holy offices for money. To Dante such practices were damnable simony.

80. *lest the Jew among you*: The Jew could then point his finger in derision because his law was incorruptible in the matter of sacrifices.

86-87. To avoid a volume of scholarly disputation, let these lines be taken to mean that Beatrice turned to both the Sun (it was at the equator) and the Empyrean (thus toward the "True Light" in both senses) and that she and Dante ascended in the same way as before. In an instant, then, they soar to Mercury, their arrival signified by the increase in Beatrice's radiance.

94. *glowed with such a joyous essence*: Both the joy and the light are greater because she is now nearer God and has more of His essence breathed into her.

97-99. *the star*: Mercury. Dante regularly refers to planets as stars. Sense of these lines: "If the star could be so changed (being material), how could I not change, who was created with soul as my essence, hence born to be transformed through all there is, from dust to Godliness."

100 ff. THOSE WHO SOUGHT HONOR BUSILY (THE PERSONALLY AMBITIOUS). The souls in the sphere of Mercury worked, in their earthly lives, for honor and glory. On seeing the newcomers they burst into joyous revels (as in their heart's wish they had sought themselves to be honored by such revels? each giving what is most nearly of himself?). These souls sought the good actively and for good reason, but, in a sense, *for the least of all good reasons*. The light they give forth is so bright that they are often lost to Dante's sight in

their own radiance—a double felicity, first, as it describes the essence of their natures, and, second, because Mercury is so near the Sun that it is often hard to see because it is swallowed into the Sun's glow.

107-108. *each shade made visible, in the radiance*: The counterplay of "shade" and "radiance" seems to imply that the lineaments of these souls were traced upon the radiance that enclosed them.

114. *the instant they had shown themselves to me*: Note here and hereafter how regularly Dante speaks of the Paradisal souls as showing themselves rather than as being seen by him. (Cf. III, 109.) It is the nature of what belongs to Heaven to reveal itself of its own love and volition rather than to be apprehended by mortal means. There is also, of course, the fact that these souls are here only as symbolic manifestations, their real seat being in the Empyrean (IV, 28-63 and note).

117. *while still embattled*: Dante says, literally, "before your time in the militia is left behind." The essential point is that Heaven is the Eternal Triumph of which mortal life (for man) is the battle. Cf. the common phrase, "the church militant."

128-129. *this sphere that hides itself from men's eyes in the rays of another star*: The other star is the Sun. As noted above (note to 100 ff.) Mercury is often lost in the Sun's aura.

# CANTO VI

*Seekers of Honor: Justinian*
*The Roman Eagle*

*THE SPIRIT IDENTIFIES ITSELF as the soul of
THE EMPEROR JUSTINIAN and proceeds to recount
its life on earth, its conversion by AGAPETUS, and its
subsequent dedication to THE CODIFICATION OF
THE LAW.*

*It proceeds next to a DISCOURSE ON THE HIS-
TORY OF THE ROMAN EAGLE. It concludes by
identifying the spirit of ROMEO DA VILLANOVA as
one among the souls of the Second Heaven.*

"Once Constantine had turned the eagle's wing
    against the course of Heaven, which it had followed
    behind the new son of the Latian king,     3

two hundred years and more, as mankind knows,
    God's bird stayed on at Europe's furthest edge,
    close to the mountains out of which it rose.     6

And there, his wings spread over land and sea,
    he ruled the world, passing from hand to hand;
    and so, through many changes, came to me.     9

Caesar I was, Justinian I am.
    By the will of the First Love, which I now feel,
    I pruned the law of waste, excess, and sham.     12

Before my work absorbed my whole intent
    I knew Christ in one nature only, not two;
    and so believing, I was well content.     15

71

But Agapetus, blessed of the Lord,
  he, the supreme shepherd pure in faith,
  showed me the true way by his holy word.        18

Him I believed, and in my present view
  I see the truth as clearly as you see
  how a contradiction is both false and true.      21

As soon as I came to walk in the True Faith's way
  God's grace moved all my heart to my great work;
  and to it I gave myself without delay.        24

To my Belisarius I left my spear
  and God's right hand so moved his that the omen
  for me to rest from war was more than clear.     27

Of the two things you asked about before
  this puts a period to my first reply.
  But this much said impels me to say more      30

that you may see with how much right men go
  against the sacred standard when they plot
  its subornation or its overthrow.        33

You know what heroes bled to consecrate
  its holy destiny from that first hour
  when Pallas died to give it its first state.     36

You know that for two centuries then its home
  was Alba, till the time came when the three
  fought with the three and carried it to Rome.   39

What it did then from the Sabine's day of woe
  to good Lucretia's, under the seven kings
  who plundered the neighboring lands, you
                        also know,  42

and how it led the Chosen Romans forward
   against the powers of Brennus, and of Pyrrhus,
   and of many a rival state and warring lord.       45

Thence the fame of Torquatus, curly Quintius,
   and the Decii and Fabii. How gladly
   I bring it myrrh to keep it glorious.       48

It dashed to earth the hot Arabian pride
   that followed Hannibal through the rocky Alps,
   from which, you, Po, sweet river, rise and glide.    51

Under it triumphed at an early age
   Scipio and Pompey. Against the mountain
   that looked down on your birth it
                       screamed its rage.  54

Then as that age dawned in which Heaven planned
   the whole world to its harmony, Caesar came,
   and by the will of Rome, took it in hand.       57

What it did then from the Var to the Rhine is known
   to Isère, Arar, Seine, and every valley
   from which the waters of the Rhone flow down.    60

And what it did when it had taken flight
   from Ravenna and across the Rubicon
   no tongue may hope to speak nor pen to write.    63

It turned and led the cohorts into Spain;
   then to Dyrrachium; and then struck Pharsalus
   so hard that even the hot Nile felt the pain.    66

Antandros and the Simoïs, where it first saw light,
   it saw again, and Hector's grave, and then—
   woe to Ptolemy—sprang again to flight.       69

Like a thunderbolt it struck at Juba next;
   then turned once more and swooped down on your
                                       West
   and heard again the Pompeian trumpet vexed.     72

For what it did above its next great chief
   Brutus and Cassius wail in Cocytus;
   and Modena and Perugia came to grief.     75

For that, the tears still choke the wretched wraith
   of Cleopatra, who running to escape it,
   took from the asp her black and sudden death.     78

With him it traveled far as the Red Sea;
   and with him brought the world such peace that Janus
   was sealed up in his temple with lock and key.     81

But what this sign that moves my present theme
   had done before, all it was meant to do
   through the mortal realm it conquered—all
                        must seem     84

dim shadows of poor things, if it be scanned
   with a clear eye and pure and honest heart,
   as it appears in the third Caesar's hand;     87

for the Living Justice whose breath I here breathe in
   gave it the glory, while in that same hand,
   of avenging His just wrath at Adam's sin.     90

Now ponder the double marvel I unfold:
   later, under Titus, it *avenged*
   *the vengeance taken* for that crime of old!     93

And when the sharp tooth of the Lombard bit
   the Holy Church, victorious Charlemagne,
   under those same wings, came and rescued it.     96

Now are you truly able to judge those
   whom I accused above, and their wrongdoing,
   which is the cause of all your present woes.    99

One speeds the golden lilies on to force
   the public standard; and one seizes it
   for private gain—and who knows which is worse?   102

Let them scheme, the Ghibellines, let them plot and
                                 weave
   under some other standard, for all who use
   this bird iniquitously find cause to grieve!   105

Nor let the new Charles think his Guelfs will be
   its overthrow, but let him fear the talons
   that have ripped the mane from fiercer lions
                            than he.   108

Many a father's sinfulness has sealed
   his children's doom: let him not think his lilies
   will take the place of God's bird on His shield.   111

—This little star embellishes its crown
   with the light of those good spirits who were zealous
   in order to win honor and renown;   114

and when desire leans to such things, being bent
   from the true good, the rays of the true Love
   thrust upward with less force for the ascent;   117

but in the balance of our reward and due
   is part of our delight, because we see
   no shade of difference between the two.   120

By this means the True Judge sweetens our will,
   so moving us that in all eternity
   nothing can twist our beings to any ill.   123

Unequal voices make sweet tones down there.
  Just so, in our life, these unequal stations
  make a sweet harmony from sphere to sphere.    126

Within this pearl shines, too, the radiance
  of Romeo, whose good and beautiful works
  were answered by ingratitude and bad chance.    129

But the Provençals who worked his overthrow
  have no last laugh: he walks an evil road
  who finds his loss in the good that others do.    132

Four daughters had Count Raymond, each the wife
  of a Christian king, thanks to this Romeo,
  a humble man, a pilgrim in his life.    135

Envy and calumny so moved Raymond then
  that he demanded accounting of this just soul
  whose management had returned him twelve
                                     for ten.    138

For this he wandered, aged, poor, and bent,
  into the world again; and could the world
  know what was in his heart that road he went    141

begging his life by crusts from door to door,
much as it praises him now, it would praise him more.

## Notes

General Note: THE FIGURE OF JUSTINIAN. The glowing
spirit identifies itself as the soul of Justinian (482-565) who
became Emperor of Rome in 527.

He emerges, in his own account, as a luminous and mag-
nanimous spirit. A Christian, he subscribed to the Monophysitic
Heresy, which accepted the divine nature of Christ but rejected
his incarnation in mortal flesh. From this heresy he was
converted by Agapetus (Pope from 535-536). As soon as he

was converted, God's grace moved him to his great task of codifying the Roman Law, and to that work he gave himself wholly, leaving the conduct of his armies (which he had led with great success) to his general, Belisarius. So Dante sees him.

Another reading of history might have suggested several pits of Hell that might have claimed Justinian. Dante seems not to have known of the tyrannies of Justinian's reign, nor that the Justinian codification was the work of Tribonius, undertaken by him on Imperial command.

Whatever one's reading of history, one should note as part of Dante's structure that in *Inferno* VI he summarizes the condition of Florence, in *Purgatorio* VI the state of Italy, and here in *Paradiso* VI, the history of the Roman Empire.

1-3. *turned the eagle's wing*: The Imperial Eagle, standard and symbol of Rome. In 330 Constantine moved the seat of Empire to Byzantium. Thus the Roman eagle flew east "against the course of Heaven," which turns from east to west, but also against the will of heaven, for Dante believed God had decreed Rome to be the seat of His church and the Roman Empire to be its earthly arm.

He also believed that Constantine moved the seat of empire to Byzantium in order to give Rome to the church. This gift was the "Donation of Constantine" (see *Inferno*, XIX, 109-111 note) whereby the church (as Dante believed) grew rich and corrupt, hence, once more "against the course of Heaven."

The "new son of the Latian king" was Aeneas. He came from Troy (*with* the course of heaven), married Lavinia, daughter of the Latian king, and founded the line of the Roman Empire.

4. *two hundred years and more*: Byzantium became the imperial seat in 330. Justinian became emperor in 527. Thus the eagle had stayed at Europe's furthest edge for 197 years before it came to Justinian's hand. Some commentators argue the Dante meant the period from 330 to Justinian's military conquests in the east in 536. Such a reading brings the period to 206 years, justifying Dante's "two hundred years and more." It seems simpler, however, to assume that Dante made a mistake in his dates.

6. *close to the mountains out of which it rose*: The Trojan mountains. They are not far from Byzantium on a continental scale.

10-12. *Caesar I was*: On earth. But now only the name given him at the baptismal font is valid. *which now I feel*: May be taken to mean "now I am in Heaven" but the primary interpretation must be "now since my conversion."

*19-20. as closely as you see, etc.*: As a first principle of logic, a statement that contradicts itself contains both truth and falsehood. Of two contradictory terms only one can be true and the other must be false. Dante uses it here as an example of what is self-evidently true to human intellect. In Justinian's present state (informed by divine revelation) the duality of Christ's nature is as clear to him as is the nature of a logical contradiction to mortal intellect. (See also II, 45.)

*25. Belisarius*: Justinian's famous general was born 505, died 565. His successful campaigns against the Ostrogoths restored most of the Empire's authority over Italy. Dante seems not to have known that Justinian, in 562, in one of the endless intrigues of the Byzantine court, stripped "his" Belisarius of rank and had him imprisoned—an arrangement that became nearly standard as the Roman's soldier's pension plan.

*31-33. DENUNCIATION OF THE GUELFS AND GHIBEL-LINES.* Dante has asked to know (V, 126-127) the spirit's identity and why he was in the Sphere of Mercury. Lines 1-27 answer Dante's first question, but the nature of that reply moves Justinian to add a denunciation of both the Guelfs and the Ghibellines for opposing the true purposes of the Holy Roman Empire, whose history (and divine right) he then recounts. *with how much right*: None at all. *the sacred standard*: The Imperial Eagle. *when they plot its subornation*: The Ghibellines; they sought to suborn imperial authority to their own ends. *or its overthrow*: The Guelfs; they sought to end imperial authority and leave matters in the hands of local lords.

*36. Pallas*: Son of Evander, a Greek who had founded a kingdom on the present site of Rome. Evander joined Aeneas in fighting Turnus, king of the Rutulians. In the fighting Pallas was killed by Turnus. As a result of his victory, Aeneas acquired a kingdom that included the hereditary rights of Pallas. Thus Pallas died to give the eagle its first kingly state. Or so at least runs the Virgilian version followed by Dante.

THE HISTORY OF THE ROMAN EAGLE:

*37-39.* Following his victory over Turnus, Aeneas established his seat at Lavinium. His son, Ascanius, moved it from there to Alba Longa, called the Mother of Rome. There the eagle remained until in the seventh century B.C. the Curiatii (the three heroes of Alba) were vanquished by the three Horatii of Rome.

*40-42.* Expelled from Alba, Romulus established a base in Rome on the Palatine and recruited a band of raiders who carried out the raid on the Sabines (the often-painted Rape of the Sabine Women) in order to get wives. From this robber settlement grew the kingdom of Rome. Through a succession of seven kings it raided and looted its neighbors until Sextus, son of Tarquinius Superbus (the last of the Roman kings), violated Lucretia. When she died as a result of his attack, the people rose in anger, overthrew the king, and founded the Republic of Rome, in 510 B.C.

43-45. During the Republic, the Eagle was carried to many triumphs by Chosen Romans. Condensing almost three full centuries of history into nine lines, Dante cites the defeat of Brennus and his Gauls (circa 390 B.C.) and of Pyrrhus and his Greek invaders (280 B.C.).

46-48. From the Republican victories was born the fame of Torquatus (Titus Manlius Torquatus) who defeated (among others) the Gauls. In these battles one of the Fabii also distinguished himself. As did Lucius Quintius, called Cincinnatus because of an unruly lock of hair (from Latin *cincinnus*, a curl). The story of how he left the plow to become dictator of Rome and to conquer the Aquians in 485 B.C. is well known to schoolboys. Three generations of the Decii died in battle from 340 to 280 B.C., the last of these engagements being the defeat of the Greeks under Pyrrhus. And in 218 B.C. Quintus Fabius Maximus, the most notable of the Fabii, defeated Hannibal (see below).

Justinian recites these names and says he rejoices in anointing their fame with myrrh. (Myrrh was used by the ancients in embalming, as a means of preserving the body.) Note that Justinian, though on earth he was ambitious for his own glory, now rejoices in citing the glory of others.

49-51. It (the Eagle) defeated Hannibal in 218 B.C. Dante follows the custom of his times in referring to all inhabitants of north Africa as Arabs. The Po, here apostrophized, rises from the Alps.

52-54. Bracketing Scipio and Pompey, Justinian leaps from 218 to 81 B.C. In 218 Scipio Africanus, then seventeen, saved his father's life in battle against Hannibal at Ticinus. At twenty he defeated Hannibal's forces in Spain. And at thirty-three, by his successful invasion of Africa, brought about the destruction of Hannibal and of Carthage.

Pompey's first great victory (over Marius in 81 B.C.) occurred when he was twenty-five.

"The mountain that overlooked your [Dante's] birth" is Fiesole, and at Fiesole, according to Roman legend, the Eagle of the Republic overthrew Catiline.

55-60. These two tercets refer to the coming of Julius
Caesar (born 102 or 100 B.C.; assassinated March 15, 44 B.C.)
and to the Gallic Wars. In Dante's view of the Empire as the
seat God had chosen for His church, Caesar was serving
Heaven's plan in laying the foundation of Empire, for the
Empire would bring the whole world into the harmony that would
arise from unification under a single imperial rule.

Lines 58-60 describe the territory of the Gallic Wars (58-50
B.C.).

61-66. The Rubicon flows between Ravenna and Rimini. In
Caesar's time it marked the boundary between Italy and Gaul.
In crossing it (January 11, 49 B.C.), Caesar left his province
without permission of the senate, thus precipitating civil war.

64-66. Before the year was out Caesar struck Ilerda in Spain,
defeating Pompey's lieutenants. (Note that in this case the eagle
is striking against the eagle, for Pompey's cohorts also carried
the Roman standard.) In the next year Caesar laid siege to Pompey
in Dyrrachium (modern Durres in Albania), broke off, and then
engaged Pompey again at Pharsalus in Thessaly (August 9, 48
B.C.), this time winning a great victory. *even the Nile felt the
pain*: Because Pompey fled to Egypt and was killed there by
Ptolemy.

67-69. Antandros is a coastal town near Troy. The Simoïs is
a nearby river. Aeneas sailed from Antandros when he brought
the eagle to Italy. After Pompey's death, Caesar visited Troy.
Thus the Eagle saw its homeland again. From Troy ("Woe to
Ptolemy") Caesar moved to Egypt, defeated Ptolemy, and gave
Egypt to Cleopatra.

70-72. Led by Caesar, the Eagle next overthrew Juba, king
of Numidia (46 B.C.) under whom fourteen republican legions
had formed. In the next year he struck again at Spain ("on
your West") where Pompey's two sons had gathered a new army.

73-78. Augustus, Caesar's nephew, was "its next great chief."
After Caesar's murder led by Cassius and Brutus, Augustus
became the standard-bearer. He defeated Marc Antony at
Modena in 43 B.C., then formed an alliance with him, and the
two together finished Brutus and Cassius at Philippi in 42 B.C.
In 41 B.C. Augustus defeated Marc Antony's brother Lucius at
Perugia. And in 31 B.C. Augustus defeated Marc Antony at
Actium. Antony committed suicide soon after his defeat, and
Cleopatra did the same when she heard the news.

79-81. *him*: Augustus. *far as the Red Sea*: The limit of the
Empire. Augustus was now undisputed ruler of all Rome and

the Empire was at peace. *Janus*: The gates of his temple were always open in time of war. Now they were closed (as they had been only twice before) to indicate peace throughout the Empire. Thus the serene time was set for the birth of Christ, the Prince of Peace.

85-90. Tiberius was the third Caesar. The great glory given the eagle in his reign was the Crucifixion, for thereby the sin of Adam was wiped clean and the gates of Heaven were opened to redeemed mankind.

91-93. Under Titus, the fourth Caesar, Jerusalem was taken in a bloody conquest which Dante saw as a vengeance taken for a just vengeance. His argument would probably run that it was just to exact vengeance for Adam's sin and that God sent His only begotten son to mankind for that purpose. Yet, in exacting a vengeance upon the man, the Jews also offended the god, and it is just that they be made to suffer for that crime against God. Such would seem to be the basis for the prejudice against the Jew, and many vexed questions are, of course, involved: If God decreed the Crucifixion, had the Jews any choice? Are they more guilty than Pilate who simply washed his hands and let his soldiers drive the nails? What is free will in confrontation with a preordained act of God's will? Such questions must be referred to a quality of revelation unknown to footnotes.

94-96. Justinian now leaps ahead over six centuries. Desiderius, an eighth-century king of the Lombards, rose against the church but was overthrown by Charlemagne in 774 A.D. Charlemagne, as Emperor of the Holy Roman Empire, was still bearing the eagle standard.

97-98. *those whom I accused above*: The Guelfs and Ghibellines. See lines 31 ff.

100-102. *one speeds the golden lilies on to force the public standard*: The Guelfs. They urge the Lilies of France against the Eagle. *one seizes it for private gain*: The Ghibellines. They seek to pervert the Imperial standard to their own ends.

106. *the new Charles*: Charles II (The Lame) of Anjou, King of Naples and leader of the Guelfs.

109-111. *father's sinfulness . . . children's doom*: Justinian is pronouncing what may be a general sentiment, but he must certainly intend some reference to the woes that befell the house of Anjou, as Charles Martel (son of Charles the Lame) will amplify in VIII, 40-84.

112-114. Justinian has now answered Dante's first question (concerning his identity) and completed his additional remarks. He now addresses the second question (as to why he is in the sphere of Mercury and what sort of spirits are with him). He identifies this sphere as the manifest realm of the personally ambitious.

115-120. Dante's phrasing is especially dense in these lines and I have had to take more than usual liberties in order to bring it to rhyme. His point here may be stated as follows: "We of this sphere worked for the Good but did so in seeking honor for ourselves rather than for the one true motive, which is the love of God. When desire is so bent from the true good, it follows that the upward thrust toward God is lesser for being bent aside. Therefore we are low in Heaven. Yet part of our joy is in knowing that our station is well chosen, our reward being exactly equal to our merit."

121-123. *By this means*: By letting us recognize how exactly our present state corresponds to the merit we showed in our lives.

124. *down there*: On earth.

128. *Romeo*: Romeo da Villanova. He was born circa 1170 and became prime minister and chamberlain of Raymond Berenger IV, Count of Provence from 1209 to 1245. Dante follows the legend that Romeo, passing through Provence on his way back from a pilgrimage, attached himself to Raymond's court and soon achieved high station by his wise management of Raymond's affairs. Among his triumphs, Romeo negotiated the marriages of Raymond's four daughters, each to a king. Later the local nobles, envious of Romeo's position, accused him of mismanaging the treasury. When Raymond demanded an accounting, Romeo pointed to the increase in the treasury, and picking up his pilgrim's staff once more, left the court to wander as he had come.

131. *have no last laugh*: The nobles of Provence have committed the sin of envy and must suffer for it. They also have no last laugh in that Provence lost a good manager of the realm.

# CANTO VII

THE SECOND SPHERE: MERCURY

*Seekers of Honor: Justinian*

ASCENT TO THE THIRD SPHERE        *Beatrice Discourses*

*JUSTINIAN AND HIS COMPANIONS break into a HYMN TO THE GOD OF BATTLES and, dancing, disappear into the distance. Dante, torn by doubt, longs to ask how a just vengeance may justly be avenged, but dares not speak. Beatrice, sensing his confusion, answers his question before he can ask it.*

*She explains the DOUBLE NATURE OF THE CRUCIFIXION, and why the Jews, though blameless in the crucifixion of the man, were still guilty of sacrilege against the God. She then explains why God chose this means of redemption, and why that choice was THE GREATEST ACT OF ALL ETERNITY.*

*She then explains the difference between DIRECT AND INDIRECT CREATION and concludes by proving WHY THE RESURRECTION OF THE FLESH IS CERTAIN.*

"Osanna sanctus Deus Sabaoth
    superillustrans claritate tua
    felices ignes horum malachoth!"          3

—So, giving itself to its own harmony,
    the substance of that being, over which
    two lights were joined as one, appeared to me.     6

And all those souls joined in a holy dance,
    and then, like shooting sparks, gone instantly,
    they disappeared behind the veil of distance.      9

I stood, torn by my doubts. "Speak up. Speak up,"
   I said inside myself. "Ask the sweet lady
   who slakes your every thirst from the sweet cup."   12

But the awe that holds my being in its sway
   even at the sound of BEA or of TRICE
   kept my head bent as if I dozed away.   15

But she soon soothed my warring doubt and dread,
   for with a smile whose ray could have rejoiced
   the soul of a man tied to the stake, she said:   18

"I know by my infallible insight
   you do not understand how a just vengeance
   can justly be avenged. To set you right   21

I shall resolve your mind's ambivalence.
   Listen and learn, for what I shall now say
   will be a gift of lofty consequence.   24

Because he would not, for his own good, take
   God's bit and rein, the man who was not born,
   damning himself, damned mankind for his sake.   27

Therefore, for many centuries, men lay
   in their sick error, till the Word of God
   chose to descend into the mortal clay.   30

There, moved by His Eternal Love alone,
   he joined in His own person that other nature
   that had wandered from its Maker and
                                 been cast down.   33

Now heed my reasoning: so joined again
   to its First Cause, this nature (as it had been
   at its creation) was good and without stain.   36

But by its own action, when it turned its face
  from the road of truth that was its road of life,
  it was driven from the garden of God's grace. 39

If the agony on the cross, considering this,
  was a punishment of the nature thus assumed,
  no verdict ever bit with greater justice; 42

Just so, no crime to match this can be cited
  when we consider the Person who endured it
  in whom that other nature was united. 45

Thus, various sequels flow from one event:
  God and the Jews concurred in the same death;
  for it the earth shook and the heavens were rent. 48

You should no longer find it hard to see
  what is meant in saying that just vengeance taken
  was afterwards avenged by just decree. 51

I see now that your mind, thought upon thought,
  is all entangled, and that it awaits
  most eagerly the untying of the knot. 54

You think: 'I grasp the truth of what I hear.
  But why God chose this means for our redemption—
  this and no other—I cannot make clear.' 57

No one may grasp the hidden meaning of
  this edict, brother, till his inborn senses
  have been made whole in the sweet fire of love. 60

Truly, therefore, since so many sight,
  and so few hit, this target, I shall now
  explain exactly why this means was right. 63

That Good, which from Itself spurns every trace
  of envy, in Itself sends out such sparks
  as manifest the everlasting grace. 66

Whatever is uttered by Its direct expression
   thereafter is eternal; His seal once stamped,
   nothing can ever wipe out the impression.        69

Whatever is poured directly from Its spring
   is wholly free; so made, it is not subject
   to the power of any secondary thing.        72

The Sacred Fire that rays through all creation
   burns with most joy in what is most like It;
   the more alike, the greater Its elation.        75

All of these attributes endow the nature
   of humankind; and if it fail in one,
   it cannot help but lose its noble stature.        78

Sin is the one power that can take away
   its freedom and its likeness to True Good,
   whereby it shines less brightly in Its ray.        81

Its innate worth, so lost, it can regain
   only by pouring back what guilt has spilled,
   repaying evil pleasure with just pain.        84

Your nature, when it took sin to its seed,
   sinned totally. It lost this innate worth,
   and it lost Paradise by the same deed.        87

Nor could they be regained (if you heed my words
   with scrupulous attention) by any road
   that does not lead to one of these two fords:        90

either that God, by courtesy alone,
   forgive his sin; or that the man himself,
   by his own penitence and pain, atone.        93

Now fix your eye, unmoving, on the abyss
   of the Eternal Wisdom, and your mind
   on every word I say concerning this!        96

Limited man, by subsequent obedience,
  could never make amends; he could not go
  as low in his humility as once,                                  99

rebellious, he had sought to rise in pride.
  Thus was he shut from every means himself
  to meet God's claim that He be satisfied.                         102

Thus it was up to God, to Him alone
  in His own ways—by one or both, I say—
  to give man back his whole life and perfection.                 105

But since a deed done is more prized the more
  it manifests within itself the mark
  of the loving heart and goodness of the doer,                    108

the Everlasting Love, whose seal is plain
  on all the wax of the world was pleased to move
  in all His ways to raise you up again.                           111

There was not, nor will be, from the first day
  to the last night, an act so glorious
  and so magnificent, on either way.                               114

For God, in giving Himself that man might be
  able to raise himself, gave even more
  than if he had forgiven him in mercy.                            117

All other means would have been short, I say,
  of perfect justice, but that God's own Son
  humbled Himself to take on mortal clay.                          120

And now, that every wish be granted you,
  I turn back to explain a certain passage,
  that you may understand it as I do.                              123

You say: 'I see the water, I see the fire,
  the air, the earth; and all their combinations
  last but a little while and then expire.                         126

Yet all these were creations! Ought not they—
  if what you said of them before is true—
  to be forever proof against decay?'                         129

Of angels and this pure kingdom of the soul
  in which you are, it may be said they sprang
  full-formed from their creation, their beings whole.  132

But the elements, and all things generated
  by their various compoundings, take their form
  from powers that had themselves to be created.      135

Created was the matter they contain.
  Created, too, was the informing power
  of the stars that circle them in Heaven's main.      138

From the given potencies of these elements
  the rays and motions of the sacred lamps
  draw forth the souls of all brutes and all plants.     141

But the Supreme Beneficence inspires
  your life directly, filling it with love
  of what has made it, so that it desires                144

that love forever.—And from this you may
  infer the sure proof of your resurrection,
  if you once more consider in what way                  147

man's flesh was given being like no other
when He made our first father and first mother."

## Notes

1-3. The hymn sung by these spirits as they depart is
addressed to the God of triumphant armies (the God, as Dante
believed, who led the Roman Eagle) and is compounded of
Hebrew and Latin, the two languages of Heaven (though
*malachoth*—"kingdoms"—should properly be *mamlachoth*) and

may be rendered: "Hosannah, holy God of Sabaoth [of the armies], lighting from above with Your luster the blessed fires of these kingdoms!" The blessed fires (*felices ignes*) are the souls of heaven.

4-6. *its own harmony*: The harmony of the blessed voices. *two lights*: May stand, perhaps, for Justinian's double glory as Emperor and Lawgiver. *appeared to me*: Note, throughout the *Paradiso*, how Dante's phrasing suggests not that he saw the things of Heaven with his own senses, but that they were manifested to him by the blessed spirits as an act of love.

10 ff. DANTE'S DOUBT. Dante is torn between his thirst to know and his reluctance to ask. The question that fills him is "How can a just revenge be justly punished?" As usual, Beatrice (and her action in all such cases is certainly an allegory of her character as Divine Revelation) knows his wish before he can speak it and grants it before he can ask.

13-15. Intent of these lines: "But, as ever, the awe that overcomes my being if I hear so much as part of her name, made me unable to raise my head to speak and I kept it bent down like the head of a man who is dozing off while in an upright position".

25-51. THE CRUCIFIXION. Beatrice argues that the death of Christ was just because he had taken upon Himself both the nature and guilt of mankind. His expiation was just because the sin of His human nature was great. But since He was also a God, the pain inflicted upon His divinity was a sacrilege and demanded punishment. So ran the Scholastic argument Dante follows here.

26. *the man who was not born*: Adam.

29. *the Word of God*: Christ.

31-33. *Eternal Love*: The Holy Ghost. *His own person*: Christ, the Son. *that other nature*: Man. *Maker*: God the Father.

40. *considering this*: Considering what I have just said of the guilt of human nature and of the fact that Christ willingly assumed that guilt in His own person.

48. *earth shook . . . heavens were rent*: See *Matthew*, XXVII, 11-15.

66. *grace*: Dante says "beauty." The Scartazzini-Vandelli commentary offers the following interpretation of this tercet:

"The Divine Goodness, which rejects from Itself every trace of envy, being in Itself a single ardent flame, scintillates so that it shoots forth from Itself, like sparks, part of its Eternal Beauty, and by these (sparks) makes beautiful Its creatures. One must say *part* (of Itself) because a finite creature is not capable of the Infinite."

67-72. Dante is distinguishing here between "direct" (Godly) and "secondary" (angelic and human) creation. What God creates directly is eternal because nothing can wipe out the impression of His seal, and it is free because secondary creations have no power upon it. The point is further made in lines 130-144 below.

76. *all of these attributes*: The three Godly gifts are named above: immortality (lines 67-69), freedom (lines 70-72), and resemblance to God (lines 73-75). It follows that to lose any one these attributes is to fall from the first-created nobility (Adam's original state).

81. *it shines less brightly in Its ray*: Since God's fire rays forth most brightly in that which is most like God, and since sin makes man less like God, sin makes man shine less brightly in God's ray.

85-86. *seed . . . totally*: The seed is Adam. By his sin, all mankind fell from its first innate worth and lost Paradise.

97. *Limited man*: Man is limited by his mortal means. Within them, no depth of humility to which he could descend could be proportionate to the height he had sought in his rebellious sin. For man's sin was in seeking to become God, and there is no equivalent depth to which he could sink in recompense, for in sinning he had already damned himself to Hell.

104-105. *by one* (way): Mercy. *or both*: Mercy and Justice. Since man could not save himself, God could have forgiven him outright as an act of mercy. Or he could have created a man so perfect that he was capable of just expiation (that would have been the way of Justice). But in giving Himself through His own Son, He chose the double way that was both divine mercy and human justice. In the tercets that immediately follow Dante celebrates this choice as the supreme act of all eternity. *his whole life and perfection*: Because through Christ's redemption he could once more be received into Heaven and the whole life from which Adam's sin had excluded him.

114. *on either way*: On the way of mercy or on the way of justice.

122. *explain a certain passage*: Lines 67 ff. There Beatrice had explained that whatever God utters as His direct expression is eternal.

124-125. *water . . . fire . . . air . . . earth*: These were believed to be the four elements of which all things were compounded. Hence, they and their combinations make up all the material creation. These elements (seen as phenomena of the matter they contain, the matter itself being directly created) are the effects of certain directly created powers in nature, not as direct effects of God. As secondary effects, therefore, they are corruptible, whereas the soul of man, a direct creation, is eternal.

135. *powers that had themselves to be created*: Angels. God, of course, is the one power that did not Itself have to be created.

139-141. The four elements that give form to all matter (the matter being itself God-created and eternal but itself formless) derive their potencies from fixed (and first created) principles of nature which are ruled by angels. The stars in their courses then work upon these potencies and draw from them the sensitive and vegetative souls of beasts and plants (but not man's soul, which is God-created).

145-149. THE PROOF OF THE RESURRECTION OF THE FLESH. "From this," says Beatrice—from the principle declared in lines 67-68 that everything directly created by God is eternal, and from the fact that Adam and Eve were directly created by God—"you may infer the sure proof of your resurrection." There seems to be no explanation of Beatrice's reason for saying "your" (rather than "the" or "our") resurrection. As a co-descendant of Adam and Eve, she must herself expect the resurrection of her flesh on Judgment Day.

# CANTO VIII

THE THIRD SPHERE: VENUS

*The Amorous: Charles Martel*

*DANTE AND BEATRICE reach the Sphere of Venus, the Third Heaven. Instantly, a band of souls that had been dancing in the Empyrean descends to the travelers. These are the souls of the AMOROUS. As we learn in Canto IX, many of them, perhaps all, were so full of the influence of Venus that they were in danger of being lost to carnality. Through the love of God, however, their passion was converted from physical love to true caritas, and thus do they rejoice in Heaven.*

*Their spokesman is CHARLES MARTEL OF ANJOU. He identifies himself and prophesies dark days for the Kingdom of Naples because of the meanness of King Robert, his brother. Dante asks how it is that mean sons can be born of great fathers, and Charles answers with a DISCOURSE ON THE DIVERSITY OF NATURAL TALENTS, a diversity he assigns to the influence of the stars, as God provided them for man's own good as a social being, for only by diversity of gifts can society function. God had planned all these variations to a harmonious end. It is mankind, by forcing men into situations not in harmony with their talents, that strays from God's plan.*

The world, to its own jeopardy, once thought
    that Venus, rolling in the third epicycle,
    rayed down love-madness, leaving men distraught.  3

Therefore the ancients, in their ignorance,
    did honor not to her alone, but offered
    the smokes of sacrifice and votive chants  6

to Dione and to Cupid, her mother and son,
   and claimed that he had sat on Dido's lap
   when she was smitten by love's blinding passion.     9

From her with whom my song began just now
   they took the name of the star that woos the Sun,
   now shining at its nape, now at its brow.            12

I reached it unaware of my ascent,
   but my lady made me certain I was there
   because I saw her grow more radiant.                 15

And as a spark is visible in the fire,
   and as two voices may be told apart
   if one stays firm and one goes lower and higher;     18

so I saw lights circling within that light
   at various speeds, each, I suppose, proportioned
   to its eternal vision of delight.                    21

No blast from cold clouds ever shot below,
   whether visible or not, so rapidly
   but what it would have seemed delayed and slow       24

to one who had seen those holy lights draw nigh
   to where we were, leaving the dance begun
   among the Seraphim in Heaven on high.                27

And from the first who came, in purest strain
   "Hosannah" rang; so pure that, ever since,
   my soul has yearned to hear that sound again.        30

Then one of them came forward and spoke thus:
   "We are ready, all of us, and await your pleasure
   that you may take from us what makes you joyous.      33

In one thirst and one spiraling and one sphere
   we turn with those High Principalities
   to whom you once cried from the world down
                                      there:            36

*'O you whose intellects turn the third great wheel!'*
    So full of love are we that, for your pleasure,
    it will be no less bliss to pause a while."    39

I raised my eyes to the holy radiance
    that was my lady, and only after she
    had given them her comfort and assurance,    42

did I turn to the radiance that had made
    such promises. "Who are you?" were my words,
    my voice filled with the love it left unsaid.    45

Ah, how it swelled and grew even more bright,
    taking increase of bliss from my few words,
    and adding new delight to its delight.    48

So changed, it said: "My life there among men
    was soon concluded; had it lasted longer
    great evils yet to be would not have been.    51

The ecstasy that is my heavenly boon
    conceals me: I am wrapped within its aura
    as a silkworm is enclosed in a cocoon.    54

You loved me much, and you had reason to,
    for had I stayed below, you would have seen
    more than the green leaves of my love for you.    57

The left bank of the land washed by the Rhone
    after its waters mingle with the Sorgue's
    waited, in due course, to become my own;    60

as did that horn of Italy that lies
    south of the Tronto and Verde, within which
    Bari, Gaeta, and Catona rise.    63

Already on my brow there shone the crown
    of the land the Danube bathes when it has left
    its German banks. And though not yet my own,    66

beautiful Sicily, the darkened coast
   between the Capes of Faro and Passero,
   there on the gulf that Eurus lashes most,     69

(not dimmed by Typhoeus, as mythology
   would have men think, but by its rising sulfur)
   would yet have looked to have its kings,
                              through me,    72

from Charles and Rudolph, but that the bitter breath
   of a populace subjected to misrule
   cried out through all Palermo's streets 'Death!
                                 Death!'    75

And could Robert have foreseen how tyranny
   will drive men mad, he would have fled in fear
   from Catalonia's greedy poverty.     78

For some provision surely must be made,
   by him or by another, lest on his ship,
   already heavy laden, more be laid.     81

His nature, born to avarice from the loins
   of a liberal sire, would have required lieutenants
   who cared for more than filling chests with coins."    84

—"Sire, I hold dearer this felicity
   that fills me when you speak, believing it
   as visible to you as it is to me,     87

there where every good begins and ends.
   And this, too, I hold dear—that you discern it
   in looking on Him from whom all love descends.    90

You have given me joy. Now it is in your power
   to give me light. For your words leave me in doubt:
   how, if the seed is sweet, may the fruit be sour?"    93

Thus I. And he: "Could I make you recognize
   one truth of what you ask, then what is now
   behind your back, would be before your eyes.    96

The Good by which this kingdom you now climb
   is turned and gladdened, makes its foresight shine
   as powers of these great bodies to all time.    99

Not only does that Perfect Mind provide
   for the diversities of every nature
   but for their good and harmony beside.    102

And thus whatever arrow takes its arc
   from this bow flies to a determined end,
   it being aimed unerringly to its mark.    105

Else would these heavens you now move across
   give rise to their effect in such a way
   that there would be not harmony, but chaos.    108

This cannot be unless the intellects
   that move these stars are flawed, and flawed the first,
   which, having made them, gave them such defects. 111

—Should I expound this further?" he said to me.
   And I: "There is no need, for now I know
   nature cannot fall short of what must be."    114

And he: "Would man be worse off than he is,
   there on earth, without a social order?"
   "Yes!" I replied. "Nor need I proof of this."    117

"And can that be, unless men there below
   lived variously to serve their various functions?
   Your master, if he knows, answers you 'no.'    120

So point by point that radiant soul disputes.
   Now he concludes: "Your various aptitudes,
   it follows, therefore, must have various roots,    123

So one man is born Xerxes, another Solon;
    one Melchizedek, and another he
    who, flying through the air, lost his own son. 126

That ever-revolving nature whose seal is pressed
    into our mortal wax does its work well,
    but takes no heed of where it comes to rest. 129

So Esau parted from Jacob in the seed;
    and Romulus was born of such humble stock
    that Mars became his father, as men agreed. 132

Begotten and begetter, but for the force
    of overruling providence, the son's nature
    would always follow in the father's course. 135

—And now what was behind shines out before.
    But to make you understand how much you please me,
    I would wrap you in one corollary more: 138

what Nature gives a man Fortune must nourish
    concordantly, or nature, like any seed
    out of its proper climate, cannot flourish. 141

If the world below would learn to heed the plan
    of nature's firm foundation, and build on that,
    it then would have the best from every man. 144

But into holy orders you deflect
    the man born to strap on a sword and shield;
    and make a king of one whose intellect 147

is given to writing sermons. And in this way
your footprints leave the road and go astray."

## Notes

1. *to its own jeopardy*: Because in so believing it risked the
wrath that has often descended upon the idolatrous.

2. *epicycle*: Not to be confused with "sphere." The epicycle of Venus turns around the center line of the Third Sphere. Thus the planet keeps appearing in various positions around the sun, "now shining at its nape" (behind it, hence Venus as evening star), "now at its brow" (before it, hence Venus as morning star) as Dante says in line 12 below. In line 96 this epicyclic motion becomes allegorically significant. In line 135 this image theme is brought to rest. This sweetly managed development is a fine example of Dante's way with imagery.

3. *rayed down love-madness*: The rays of Venus, the pagans believed, drove men and women mad with love.

7. *Dione*: One legend has it that Venus was the daughter of Dione and Zeus. *Cupid*: He has many mythological manifestations. Dante is here taking him as the son of Venus by Mars or, more probably, by Mercury.

8-9. *had sat on Dido's lap*: When she was smitten by love for Aeneas, the passion that led to her death. (See *Inferno*, V, 61, 86.) Line 9 is my own rhyme-forced addition and does not occur in Dante.

10. *her*: Venus.

11-12. *that woos the Sun*: The apparent motion of Venus is from one side of the Sun to the other. See note to line 2, above.

19 ff. THE AMOROUS. These lights are the souls of the Amorous; not the pagan distortion of love-madness, but the Christian and divine radiance of *caritas*. Like all the souls of Heaven, they manifest themselves (at will) in their appropriate sphere, but they have their true place in the Empyrean among the Seraphim. They have been dancing there in their eternal joy when they become aware of Dante and Beatrice and, in a passion of *caritas*, descend to them at inconceivable speeds, still dancing and singing *Hosannah*.

22-24. *blast from cold clouds, etc*: Hot dry vapors colliding with cold wet clouds were believed to discharge visible or invisible blasts of wind at great speeds. Lightning was believed to be a blast of wind moving so fast that the friction of its motion caused it to ignite. But even such a rate of descent would have seemed laggard as compared to the descent of these souls when they see Dante and Beatrice. *below*: In earth's atmosphere.

31. *Then one of them*: Charles Martel (see below). He explains that all the souls of this sphere dance in perpetual bliss in the Empyrean, but that they are all so full of love and so eager to give joy to others, that to pause from bliss a while in order to give joy to others will seem no less bliss.

34. *In one thirst*: For God's love. *and one spiraling*: In one eternal circling of God's throne. *and one sphere*: In a round with the angels and powers of this third Heaven.

35-37. *those High Principalities*: The third heaven, we are to understand, is moved by Principalities (angels of a certain rank), or so Dante himself once addressed them in the words here quoted (from the *Convivio*). In IX, 61, however (see note), that function is assigned to Thrones. For the orders of angels see XXVIII.

40-84. CHARLES MARTEL. Born 1271, the first son of Charles II (The Lame) of Anjou. Crowned King of Hungary (though in title only) 1290. Died 1295. His conversation indicates that he and Dante had met on earth, probably when Charles visited Florence in 1294, and that Charles had intended to be Dante's royal patron. This Charles Martel must not be confused with the better known Charles Martel (Charles the Hammer), King of the Franks, who lived circa 688-741. The following dates may offer some useful points of reference in the maze of intrigue that marked the Kingdom of the Two Sicilies:

1268  Charles I of Anjou (French) defeats Conradin (German) at Tagliacozzo. (See *Inferno*, XXVIII, 17.)

1271  Charles Martel (grandson of Charles I) born.

1282  The Sicilian Vespers (Easter Day) in which most of the French (rulers of Sicily) were massacred in a popular uprising. In October of the same year Peter III of Aragon (Spanish) invaded Sicily and captured Messina, last French strongpoint. The House of Anjou is not totally driven from Sicily but retains the Kingdom of Naples (it and Sicily being the "Two Sicilies"). Soon after Peter's invasion, Pope Martin IV, anxious to defend the temporal rights of the Church in Sicily, declares a crusade against Aragon.

1284  Charles II (the Lame), father of Charles Martel, is captured in the Bay of Naples by the forces of Peter III of Aragon, and is held for ransom in Spain.

1286  Charles I dies while Charles II is still captive, and Charles Martel becomes regent at age 15.

1288  Charles II is released and takes over the rule of Naples. (Robert, Lodovico, and John, younger brothers of Charles Martel . . . are surrendered to Peter of Aragon as hostages for Charles' ransom, and they remain in Spain until 1295.)

1290   Charles Martel becomes titular King of Hungary.
1295   Charles Martel dies (before his father).

The warfare that followed the Sicilian Vespers continued for thirty years, spurred constantly by the Vatican, and involved not only the powers of Anjou and of Aragon, but of Valois and of Sicily, and of the Papal States, in various shifting alliances.

In lines 50-51, Charles points out that he died young, but declares that had he lived longer he might have averted the great evils of this long warfare by establishing harmony among the contesting forces. As becomes heavenly souls, Charles is a bit of an optimist: the intrigues of the various Popes who ruled from 1282 to 1303, and of their various secular allies, could hardly have been combed smooth by a stripling, but Charles seems to have had generous intentions toward Dante, and Dante repays him even more generously.

43. *the radiance that had made*: Charles. In line 33 he had promised to give Dante what would make him joyous.

48. *adding new delight to its delight*: Love of others is the delight and radiance of these souls. The thought of being able to give pleasure to Dante by answering his question makes the light of loving bliss swell and burn even more brightly.

51. *yet to be*: Charles is talking, of course, as of 1300. There were yet to be more than two years of war before the defeat of Charles of Valois in Sicily and the peace of 1303.

54. The silkworm in its cocoon was a common symbol of transfiguring rebirth. Note that the Sphere of Venus is the last in which the souls suggest any trace of human form or lineaments. The spirits higher up appear only as flames, until, in the Empyrean, something like their human forms reappears but mystically transfigured.

57. *more than the green leaves*: Charles stayed in Florence for three weeks on his visit of 1294, was warmly received by the Florentines, and responded warmly. Dante seems to have struck up a friendship with Charles and seems to have been promised Charles's love and patronage. Had Charles lived, Dante would have seen more than the promise (the green leaves) of Charles's love; he would have seen the fruit of it (active patronage).

58-60. *The left bank, etc.* The land so marked was Provence. Charles I (King of Naples and brother of the King of France) acquired it by marriage. It thus became attached to the crown of Naples, was passed on to Charles II, and would have passed on to Charles Martel as the firstborn son.

61. *that horn of Italy*: The territory so described was the former Kingdom of Naples, to which Charles was also heir. The Tronto and the Verde (now called the Garigliano) draw a nearly complete line across Italy. Together they were the main boundary between the Papal States to the north and the Kingdom of Naples to the south.

64-66. The Danube rises in Germany and flows east through Hungary. Charles Martel had the glow of the Hungarian crown on his brow, but the throne was occupied by Andreas III of Venice. Charles was King in title only. In 1310 Charles Robert, son of Charles Martel, became King of Hungary in fact as well as in title.

66-75. *And though not yet my own*: The passage is in Dante's denser style and complicated by the strange parenthesis about Typhoeus, a Titan associated with the fires and smokes of the earth's interior. He rose against Zeus, who (in the legend Dante follows) hurled him deep into the earth and piled Aetna upon him. Dante, in his paradisal freedom from the errors of mythology, explains that the smoke shrouds of Sicily are caused not by Typhoeus but by the burning sulfur of volcanoes.

The parenthesis understood, the gist of the rest of the passage is that Charles Martel, but for the overthrow of the French in the Sicilian Vespers, would have ruled Sicily and so continued in his sons the bloodlines of Anjou (on his side) and of Rudolph of Hapsburg (on his wife's side). *Faro*: Cape Faro, the northeast tip of Sicily. *Passero*: Cape Passero, the southeast tip. Dante calls them Pelorus and Pachynus. *Eurus*: The east wind. *the bitter breath . . . Palermo's streets*: The Sicilian Vespers. *misrule*: Of Charles I of Anjou.

76-78. *Robert*: Became King of Naples in 1309. He was one of the younger brothers of Charles Martel who remained in Spain from 1288 to 1295 as hostages for Charles II. In Catalonia, Robert made friends among the Spanish, who later became powerful in his government of Naples and who, in the greed of their poverty, oppressed the people. Charles is prophesying that Robert, a weak man, will reap a bad harvest from the seeds of misrule he has sown.

80. *on his ship*: Charles Martel may mean the "ship" of Robert's soul, already wallowing under the load of Catalonian avarice he has permitted, and which may damn him too; or he

may mean the "ship" of state of abused Naples, once destined
to be his own kingdom.

85-90.   The sense of this difficult passage depends on the
reader's awareness of "there where every good begins and ends."
I believe "there" is best understood as "the Empyrean" (the true
seat of these souls whose manifestations appear in the various
heavens). With "there" so understood, the passage may be para-
phrased: "Because I believe this felicity I feel is as clear to you
up 'there' as it is to me, it is the dearer to me. And it is also dear
to me that you discern my felicity (up 'there') by looking directly
upon God (to whom my joy is known) rather than by looking
merely into my heart."

93 ff. THE VARIATIONS OF PERSONAL ENDOWMENT.
Dante asks how sweet seed can bear sour fruit, i.e., how a noble
father can beget a mean son. Charles explains the central truth
whereby what is now behind Dante's back (hence, unseen) will
reveal itself to his eyes.

Obviously it would not be just for one family or bloodline to
inherit all the high qualities of mankind, as would be the case if
the sons of great fathers always inherited greatness. God does not
will it so.

Yet such would be the case were the qualities of the father
(the active male principle as discussed in *Purgatorio,* XXV, 37
ff.) transmitted to the children without any external force affecting the transmission. That external force is the influence of
the stars bearing on the hour of the individual's birth in order to
serve God's just and harmonious ends. For God created man as a
social being, and since society requires many different talents,
God assigns to the spheres the power to generate this necessary
diversity.

99. *these great bodies*: The heavenly bodies. Their influences
on mankind are powers granted them by God's providence. (Note
that Dante uses "providence" always in the sense of "pre-vision,"
i.e., foresight.)

109-111.   The argument here is *reductio ad absurdum.* The
heavenly bodies could produce chaos instead of harmony only if
the Intelligences that move each sphere were imperfect, and if
the First Intelligence (God) were also imperfect, having created
defective agents. Since these things cannot be, the argument is
false, and one must conclude that only harmony can flow from
the order of God's creation, all things interplaying to His ordained
ends.

114. *nature cannot fall short of what must be*: The universe, having been created and predestined to God's sure purpose, cannot do less than He predestined it to do.

117. *Nor need I proof of this*: Charles has just presented proofs of reason to support the truth of universal harmony. Dante is saying that on this point of the good of society to mankind he needs no such proofs, his own intellect being sufficient. In *De Monarchia* Dante discussed the nature of man as a civic being.

120. *Your master*: Aristotle. In the *Ethics* and elsewhere he expounds the various offices men in society must serve for the good of all.

120-123. The soul of Charles Martel has carried the disputation forward by deduction. Now it concludes: the various (and necessary) endowments required of social man could not follow from the single genetic source of the active (father) principle (which would reproduce itself without change) but must arise from various roots (the shifting influences of the heavenly bodies).

124-126. *Xerxes*: The Persian King. He is the type of the war-leader. *Solon*: Athenian lawgiver of the seventh century B.C., the type of the legislator. *Melchizedek*: As in *Genesis*, XIV, 18, "he was the priest of the most high God," hence, the type of the spiritual leader. *he who, flying . . . lost his own son*: Daedalus, the type of the artisan and mechanic.

127-129. *That ever-revolving nature*: The power of the ever-turning spheres. This nature (this rank of nature) impresses its influences upon mortals as a seal is pressed into wax, thus effecting its generalized purposes (the distribution of various gifts to mankind) but without regard to where its gift lodges.

130-132. *Esau . . . Jacob*: Though twins they were markedly different in character. "In the seed" is crucial here: Dante seems to imply that their genetic inheritance was identical. If so, only the diverse influences of the stars could have affected their differences. *Romulus*: His father was so humble that men were able to say he was born of Mars (as they could not have said had his father been sufficiently well known to have been remembered).

139-141. If a man's natural abilities (from his genetic inheritance and from the influences of the stars) sort well with the conditions into which he is born (as determined by Fortune, the agent of divine foresight), then the man prospers. But if his abili-

ties and his fortune are not so sorted, then, like a seed planted in
an unsuitable climate, his gift cannot achieve its full growth.

145-148. *into holy orders*: Charles's general sense is clear
enough here but he probably intends an additional reference to
his younger brother Lodovico who became Bishop of Toulouse.
*and make a king of one*: Here, in addition to the general sense,
Charles certainly intends a reference to his brother Robert, who
paid little attention to his duties as King of Naples, and who
composed a number of ornate sermons and other discourses.

# CANTO IX

The Amorous:
Cunizza, Folquet, Rahab

*CUNIZZA DA ROMANO next appears, lamenting the woes that have befallen her native Venetia and prophesying great grief to her countrymen for pursuing false fame on earth. Cunizza had begun her remarks by pointing out a soul who rejoices beside her in Heaven as one who pursued good ends. When she finishes speaking that soul identifies itself as FOLQUET, once BISHOP OF MARSEILLES. Folquet narrates his life and indicates that, like Cunizza, his amorous nature first led him to carnality but later filled him with passion for the True Love of God. Folquet then answers Dante's questions about the NATURE OF THE THIRD HEAVEN, identifies RAHAB, the Whore of Jericho, as the first soul to ascend to that sphere, and concludes with a DENUNCIATION OF BONIFACE VIII for neglecting the Holy Land and all things spiritual, and a further DENUNCIATION OF FLORENCE as a corrupt state and as the source of Papal corruption. A just vengeance, he prophesies, will not be long delayed.*

Fair Clemence, when your Charles, in speaking thus
   had shone his light into my mind, he told me
   of the schemes and frauds that would attack his
                            house. 3

But he said to me: "Say nothing. Let the years
   turn as they must." And so I can say only
   that they who wrong you shall find cause for tears. 6

Now to the Sun, the all-sufficing good,
   the eternal being of that sacred lamp
   had turned itself again to be renewed.     9

O souls deceived! ill-born impieties
   who turn your hearts away from the True Love
   and fix your eyes on empty vanities!     12

—And lo! another of those splendors now
   draws near me, and his wish to give me pleasure
   shows in the brightening of his outward glow.     15

The eyes of Beatrice, which, as before
   were fixed on me, saw all my wish and gave it
   the assurance of their dear consent once more.     18

"O blessed spirit, be pleased to let me find
   my joy at once," I said. "Make clear to me
   that you are a true mirror of my mind!"     21

Thereat the unknown spirit of that light,
   who had been singing in its depths, now spoke,
   like one whose whole delight is to delight.     24

"In that part of the sinful land men know
   as the Italy which lies between Rialto
   and the springs from which the Brenta and
                       Piave flow,   27

there stands a hill of no imposing height;
   down from it years ago there came a firebrand
   who laid waste all that region like a blight.     30

One root gave birth to both of us. My name
   was Cunizza, of Romano, and I shine here
   because this star conquered me with its flame.     33

Yet gladly I embrace the fate that so
  arranged my lot, and I rejoice in it,
  although it may seem hard to the crowd below.        36

This bright and precious jewel of our sky,
  whose ray shines here beside me, left great fame
  behind him on the earth; nor will it die             39

before this centenary is five times told.
  Now ask yourself if man should seek that good
  that lives in name after the flesh is cold.          42

The rabble that today spills through the land
  bound by the Tagliamento and the Adige
  think little of that, nor, though war's bloody hand  45

rips them, do they repent. But Paduan blood,
  having shunned its duty, shall soon stain the water
  that bathes Vicenza and drains into mud.             48

And there rules one who yet holds high his head,
  there where the Sile and the Cagnano join,
  for whom the net already has been spread.            51

And Feltro shall yet weep the treachery
  of its foul priest; no man yet entered Malta
  for a crime as infamous as his shall be.             54

Great would that ewer be that could hold at once
  the blood Ferrara will spill, and tired the man
  who set himself to weigh it ounce by ounce;          57

—all this the generous priest will freely give
  to prove his party loyalty; but then
  such gifts conform to how those people live.         60

On high are mirrors (you say 'Thrones') and these
  reflect God's judgment to us; so enlightened,
  we have thought it well to speak these prophecies."  63

Here she fell still and, turning, made it clear
  she was drawn to other things, joining once more
  the wheel of souls that dance through that
                                third sphere.   66

That other Bliss, he I had heard her say
  was precious to her, now showed himself to me
  like a fine ruby struck by the sun's ray.       69

Up there, joy makes those souls add light to light,
  as here it makes us laugh, while down below
  souls darken as they grieve through Hell's
                                long night.    72

"God sees all, and your insight, blessed being,
  makes itself one with His," I said, "and thus
  no thought or wish may hide beyond your seeing.  75

Why does your voice, then, which forever sings
  Heaven's delight as one with those Blest Flames
  who wrap themselves about with their six wings,  78

not grant my wish? Had I the intuition
  with which to read your wish as you read mine,
  *I* should not be still waiting for *your* question!"  81

"The greatest basin to which earth's waters flow
  —aside from the sea that girdles all the land—"
  his voice began when I had spoken so,          84

"extends so far against the course of the sun,
  between opposing shores, that at its zenith
  the sun must cross what first was its horizon.   87

I first saw light on that basin's shore between
  the Ebro and that river whose short course
  parts Tuscan from Genoese—the Magra, I mean.  90

Sunrise and sunset are about the same
  for Bougiah and my city, whose blood flowed
  to warm its harbor's waters when Caesar came.        93

My name—to such as knew it on the earth
  was Folquet; here eternally my ray
  marks all this sphere, as its ray marked my birth.   96

Dido did not burn hotter with love's rage,
  when she offended both Sichaeus and Creusa,
  than I, before my locks grew thin with age.          99

Nor she of Rhodopè who felt the smart
  of Demophoön's deception, nor Hercules
  when he had sealed Iole in his heart.                102

But none repents here; joy is all our being:
  not at the sin—that never comes to mind—
  but in the All-Ordering and All-Foreseeing.          105

Here all our thoughts are fixed upon the Love
  that beautifies creation, and here we learn
  how world below is moved by world above.             108

But that you may take with you from this sphere
  full knowledge of all it makes you wish to know,
  I must speak on a little further here.               111

You wish to know who is within this blaze
  you see in all its splendor here beside me,
  like purest water lit by the sun's rays.             114

Know, then, that in it Rahab finds her good;
  and that, one with our choir, she seals upon it
  the highest order of beatitude.                      117

Of all Christ's harvest, her soul was the one
  first summoned by this Heaven, on which the shadow
  the earth casts rests the point of its long cone.    120

It was fitting in every way that she should thus
    adorn one of these heavens as a palm
    of the high victory two palms won for us,    123

for she it was who helped win the first glory
    of Joshua's victory in the Holy Land
    (which seems to have slipped from the
                                Pope's memory).    126

Your Florence—which was planted by the One
    who first turned on his Maker, and whose envy
    has given men such cause for lamentation—    129

brings forth and spreads the accursed flower of gold
    that changes the shepherd into a ravening wolf
    by whom the sheep are scattered from the fold.    132

And so the Gospels and Great Doctors lie
    neglected, and the Decretals alone
    are studied, as their margins testify.    135

So Pope and Cardinal heed no other things.
    Their thoughts do not go out to Nazareth
    where the blessed Gabriel opened wide his wings.    138

But the Vatican, and the other chosen parts
    of Holy Rome that have been, from the first,
    the cemetery of those faithful hearts    141

that followed Peter and were his soldiery,
shall soon be free of this adultery."

## Notes

1-6. THE PROPHECY OF CHARLES MARTEL. On the
death of Charles Martel (1295) the throne of Naples passed to
his son Caroberto, but in 1309 Robert the Wise (younger brother
of Charles and, therefore, Caroberto's uncle) usurped the throne.

Thus the direct line of Charles Martel lost the crown of Naples. Robert and his followers, however, will yet have cause to weep in the disastrous consequences of their deceptions and of the suffering inflicted upon Robert's subjects by his Spanish lieutenants. Dante does not specify what will cause their tears, but the subsequent history of the Kingdom of Naples left generous provision for any amount of mourning.

There is no wholly satisfactory identification of the Clemence Dante here addresses. Charles' wife was named Clemence, but she died in 1295, and Dante's words seem clearly addressed to a living person. Charles' mother was also called Clemence, and she lived until 1323, but she was customarily known as Maria of Hungary, the daughter of Rudolph I of Hapsburg. And Charles had a daughter named Clemence, but if Dante intended the daughter, it seems odd to refer to the father as "her Charles."

8. *the eternal being*: Charles.

13. *another of those splendors*: Cunizza da Romano (*circa* 1198-*circa* 1279), younger daughter of Ezzolino II, Count of Onora, and the cruelest of the Ghibelline tyrants. He is in Hell with the Violent against their Neighbors (*Inferno*, XII, 110).

Cunizza was known as an outgoing woman, her tendencies attested by the fact that she had various lovers as well as three husbands. Sordello was one among her lovers (*Purgatorio*, VI, 58 ff.). Among other bad choices, she willed her estate to Alessandro and Napoleone, Counts of Mangone, two of the worst sinners in Hell (*Inferno*, XXXII, 41-60). There seems to be no way of knowing why Dante put her in Paradise. He must have credited her with a true contrition in her later years, and certainly he might have been moved to show that even a great sinner could find heaven's grace through repentance, but at best she would have been scheduled for more than twenty-one years in Purgatory. Her case may have been helped by the fact that in 1265 she manumitted a number of slaves who had been in bondage to her father and brothers.

15. *outward glow*: Dante regularly conceives the spirits of heaven as having an inner and an outer glow, of which only the outer is visible to him.

16. *as before*: As when Dante, with his eyes, asked of Beatrice's eyes their permission to talk to Charles Martel (VIII, 40-42).

19-21. Dante knows by now that the heavenly spirits know his thoughts without need for him to speak them, and that knowledge fills him with the expectation of joy. He asks Cunizza to give him that joy without delay, by demonstrating that she can address his unspoken thoughts.

22. *the unknown spirit*: Cunizza has not yet identified herself to Dante.

26-27. *Rialto*: The principal island of Venice, here taken for all of Venice. *the Brenta and Piave*: These rivers have their sources in the mountains north and northwest of Florence. The area so defined is la Marca Trivigiana whose principal city is Treviso.

29. *a firebrand*: Ezzolino (or Azzolino), Cunizza's brother.

33. The flame of Venus is, of course, love.

34-36. *the fate that so arranged my lot*: Cunizza's amorous nature was the force of fate that shaped her lot. The crowd below (mortal men) may think it painful for her to recall her natural amorousness and the loose life to which it led her. Yet that same fire of passion, properly directed to the love of God, was also the source of her blessedness.

37 ff. *This bright and precious jewel*: Folquet of Marseilles, a troubadour poet who became a Cistercian monk, and who was Bishop of Toulouse from 1205 to 1231. He was a leader (as he informs Dante in lines 123-142) in the atrocious crusade against the Albigensians. The fame he left on earth was written darkly enough in Albigensian blood, but Cunizza (and, through her, Dante) seems here to honor him as one who inveighed against the false passions of the people of Marca Trivigiana, exhorting them to seek the pure and lasting fame of an honored memory.

40. *this centenary*: The year 1300 was a Jubilee year (see *Inferno*, XVIII, 28-33, note). Dante is probably saying that five more such centenaries will pass before Folquet's fame dies.

43-48. CUNIZZA'S PROPHECY. The Tagliamento and the Adige are rivers. The land they bound is, approximately, the present Venetia. The Bacchiglione flows through this land a bit south of its center, passes by Vicenza and then Padua, and empties into the swamps behind Venice ("drains into the mud"). Dante's text can be variously interpreted but points clearly enough to the defeat of the Paduans outside Vicenza in 1314 by Dante's great patron, Can Grande della Scala. The duty the Paduans shunned was, in general, the observance of justice but, specifically, their allegiance to the empire as represented by Can Grande, the reigning Ghibelline.

49-51. Rizzardo da Cammino, Lord of Treviso ("where the Sile and Cagnano join"), was treacherously murdered in 1312 while playing chess. He was the son of "the good Gherardo" (*Purgatorio*, XVI, 124 and 138), the son-in-law of Judge Nin (*Purgatorio*, VIII, 53 *ff.*), and the husband of "my Giovanna" (*Purgatorio*, VIII, 71).

52-60. The Malta here referred to was a papal prison near Lake Bolsena. The worst of its criminals had yet to commit a crime as foul as the one that would be committed by Alessandro Novella, Bishop of Feltro, who accepted a group of Ghibelline refugees from Ferrara as his guests, and then (in July of 1314) turned them over to Pino della Tosa, one of the Spanish agents of Robert of Naples, to be beheaded. Thus the Bishop fell to his place in Ptolemea among those who were treacherous against their guests. (Sinners in that category, bear in mind, did not await their death to begin their damnation, but fell instantly into the ice of Cocytus, their earthly bodies being assumed by fiends.)

The blood of the Ferrarans would fill a great urn, but this generous priest (an irony) will give it gladly in duty to his party (Guelf), and be it said (another and a savage irony) such gifts of blood will suit the way the people of Marca Trivigiana live.

61. *Thrones*: There is no established creed concerning the hierarchy of the angels but Dante sets forth their orders. Cunizza's words indicate that Dante conceives the informing spirits of Venus (and probably of each of the spheres) to be Thrones. See also VIII, 35-37, note.

62-63. *so enlightened*: It is in the full illumination of God's judgment and wisdom that Cunizza has thought well to utter her prophecy. Clearly, however, she is the spokesman for all the spirits of this sphere.

64-66. To understand these lines, one should refer to VIII, 16-27 and 34-36, in which Dante describes how these souls dance their eternal delight in God.

67. *That other bliss*: Folquet. Dante does not yet know who he is, except as Cunizza referred to him in line 37 as "this bright and precious jewel."

70-71. *Up there*: In Heaven. *as here*: On earth.

73-81. Since the Heavenly Soul is one with God, it shares God's omniscience and no thought or wish may hide from it. Folquet, therefore, knows instantly what Dante is yearning to ask. Why then does he not speak at once? Had Dante the gift of

Paradisal omniscience, he declares, he would not have waited so long to gratify whatever wish Folquet may have. Dante's wish, of course, is to know the spirit's identity. *those Blest Flames . . . six wings*: The Seraphim. "Each one had six wings; with twain he covered his face, and with twain he covered his feet, and with twain he did fly" (*Isaiah*, VI, 2).

82-87. *the greatest basin . . . aside from the sea that girdles all*: The Mediterranean. Folquet conceives it as if he were standing in Spain; hence it extends against the course of the sun, from west to east. In common with most of his contemporaries Dante believed that the Mediterranean extended through 90° of latitude (it actually covers 42°): thus the sun at zenith over Jerusalem would have Gibraltar as its horizon, and moving west, would be at zenith over what was at first its horizon.

88-92. *the Ebro*: The Spanish river. *the Magra*: Runs south into the Mediterranean for a bit over 40 miles (its short course) between Tuscany and Liguria (whose capital city is Genoa). Marseilles lies about halfway between the two rivers and is in almost the same latitude as Bougiah (or Bougie) in Algeria (5° E.). Thus the two cities would see the sun rise and set at almost the same time.

92-93. *blood flowed . . . when Caesar came*: In 49 B.C., when Caesar left Brutus to defeat the forces of Pompey at Marseilles while he himself "swooped down on Spain." (*Purgatorio* XVIII, 102).

94. *to such as knew it*: Cunizza introduced (the unidentified) Folquet (38-39) as one who "left great fame behind him." Folquet is careful to speak of himself in far more modest terms.

95-96. *my ray marks all this sphere*: Folquet is now one with God. His radiance, therefore, is impressed upon Venus (influencing it) as powerfully as the influence of Venus impressed itself upon him at his birth.

97-99. *Dido*: See *Inferno*, V, 61-62, and note. Having conceived so violent a passion for Aeneas that she killed herself when he left, she wronged both Sichaeus, her dead husband, and Creusa, Aeneas's dead wife.

100-102. *she of Rhodopè . . . Demophoön*: Phyllis, daughter of King Sithon of Thrace (wherein rises Mount Rhodopè) was to marry Demophoön. When he did not arrive on the wedding day, she hanged herself and was changed into an almond tree. Demophoön (Ovid, *Heroides*, 2) narrates how the bridegroom arrived after a painful delay only to find that Phyllis had gone out on a limb.

101-102. *Hercules . . . Iole*: See *Inferno*, XII, 67, note. Folquet's three references are all to mythic figures who died painfully for love.

104. *not at the sin—that never comes to mind*: When the purified soul reaches the Terrestrial Paradise it is bathed in the waters of Lethe and the very memory of sin is taken from it (*Purgatorio*, XXXI, 91-102). Yet both Cunizza (30-36) and Folquet make the point that they do not regret their amorous natures, which once led them into carnality, because the same impulse later led them to the True Love. (See also *Purgatorio*, XXXIII, 91-102, and note.) There, Dante newly washed in Lethe, forgets that he was ever estranged from Beatrice, and she proves the sinfulness of his estrangement by the very fact that Lethe washed its memory from him.

One might argue that the pure soul forgets sin in what might be called the active sense, recalling its existence only in a passive and conceptual way that has no power upon it. After every subtlety, however, there remains an unresolvable contradiction in Dante's handling of this point, and the contradiction arises directly from the narrator's necessity. In whatever way these souls are conceived, Dante has to give them something to talk about, and the narrator has never existed who can sustain a conversation about mankind without bringing sin into it.

109-112. Folquet is mind-reading here, as directed to in lines 73-81. He has satisfied Dante's unspoken question about his identity and his place in Heaven. He now continues by answering Dante's next unspoken question. Note that he does not promise to explain the total mysteries of the Third Heaven but only to satisfy all the questions that arise in Dante's mind (which is yet incapable of conceiving the ultimate mystery).

115. *Rahab*: When Joshua sent spies before him into Jericho, Rahab, a harlot of that city, hid them from the king's men and helped them to escape. Thus she helped the people of Israel to regain the promised land, and immediately following the crucifixion her soul (which must have been in Limbo) was summoned by the Third Heaven, the first of its elected.

119-120. *shadow . . . rests the point of its long cone*: Some scholars of Dante's time believed that the cone of the earth's shadow came to a point in the third sphere.

121-126. *as a palm*: As a trophy. *two palms*: Of Christ when he was nailed to the cross. It is fitting that Rahab should be the heavenly trophy of Christ's victory for she had helped Israel win its promised land. It is a pity, Dante has Folquet say, that the Pope cares so little for the Holy Land (he had done nothing to reestablish Christianity there after Acre, the last Christian stronghold, fell to the Saracens in 1291).

127. *the One*: Satan was, of course, the first to turn on God, and it was Mars who founded Florence (*Inferno*, XIII, 143-150) but Dante's invective has a firm foundation in those church fathers who held that Mars and all the pagan gods were fiends.

130-132. *the accursed flower of gold*: The Florentine florin, a gold coin stamped with a lily. Dante's figure of a tree that bears magically evil flowers begins with "planted" in line 127. The power of gold transforms the shepherd (the Church, the Papacy in general, and Boniface VIII in particular) so that he preys on the sheep he should lead and guard.

132-135. *Great Doctors*: The Church Fathers, givers of doctrine. *the Decretals*: The volumes of canon law. Gregory IX ordered the compilation of the first five volumes in 1234 and Boniface VIII had a sixth added. The margins of the Decretals testify (by being worn and covered with annotations) how seriously they were studied, for they covered the temporal rights and privileges of the Church's vast power and wealth, and a knowledge of canon law could make a shyster's fortune.

138. *where . . . Gabriel opened wide his wings*: At the Annunciation.

# CANTO X

*Doctors of the Church*

THE FOURTH SPHERE: THE SUN
> *The First Garland of Souls:*
> *Aquinas*

*DANTE REVELS in the joy of God's creation and especially in the art shown by the placement of THE EQUINOCTIAL POINT. So rejoicing, he enters the SPHERE OF THE SUN, unaware of his approach until he has arrived.*

*A GARLAND OF TWELVE SOULS immediately surrounds him and Beatrice, the glory of each soul shining so brilliantly that it is visible even against the background of the Sun itself. These are TWELVE DOCTORS OF THE CHURCH, philosophers and theologians whose writings have guided the church in creed and canon law. Their spokesman, appropriately, is THOMAS AQUINAS. He identifies the souls in order around the ring.*

*When Aquinas has finished, the souls dance around Dante and Beatrice, raising their voices in harmonies unknown except to Heaven itself.*

Contemplating His Son with that Third Essence
   of Love breathed forth forever by Them both,
   the omnipotent and ineffable First Presence          3

created all that moves in mind and space
   with such perfection that to look upon it
   is to be seized by love of the Maker's grace.          6

Therefore, reader, raise your eyes across
   the starry sphere. Turn with me to that point
   at which one motion and another cross,         9

and there begin to savor your delight
   in the Creator's art, which he so loves
   that it is fixed forever in His sight.        12

Note how the wheel on which the planets ride
   branches from there obliquely: only thus
   may the earth that calls to them be satisfied.    15

For if these two great motions never crossed,
   the influence of the heavens would be weakened
   and most of its power upon the earth be lost.    18

For if its deviation were to be
   increased or lessened, much would then be wanting,
   both north and south, from the earth's harmony.    21

Stay on at table, reader, and meditate
   upon this foretaste if you wish to dine
   on joy itself before it is too late.        24

I set out food, but you yourself must feed!
   For the great matters I record demand
   all my attention and I must proceed.       27

Nature's majestic minister, the Sun,
   who writes the will of Heaven on the earth
   and with his light measures the hours that run,   30

now in conjunction (as I have implied)
   with Aries, rode those spirals whose course brings him
   ever earlier from the eastern side.       33

And I was with the Sun; but no more aware
   of my ascent than a man is of a thought
   that comes to mind, until he finds it there.    36

It is Beatrice, she it is who leads our climb
   from good to better, so instantaneously
   that her action does not spread itself through time.  39

How radiant in its essence that must be
   which in the Sun (where I now was) shows forth
   not by its color but its radiancy.                42

Though genius, art, and usage stored my mind,
   I still could not make visible what I saw;
   but yet may you believe and seek to find!      45

And if our powers fall short of such a height,
   why should that be surprising, since the sun
   is as much as any eye has known of light?     48

Such, there, was the fourth family of splendors
   of the High Father who fills their souls with bliss,
   showing them how He breathes forth and engenders.

                                       51

"Give thanks!" my lady said. "With all devotion
   give thanks to the Sun of Angels, by whose grace
   you have been lifted to this physical one!"    54

The heart of mortal never could so move
   to its devotion, nor so willingly
   offer itself to God in thankful love,        57

as mine did when these words had passed her lips.
   So wholely did I give my love to Him
   that she sank to oblivion in eclipse.        60

Nothing displeased, she laughed so that the blaze
   of her glad eyes pierced my mind's singleness
   and once again divided it several ways.     63

Splendors of living and transcendent light
   circle us now and make a glowing crown,
   sweeter in voice than radiant in sight.      66

Latona's daughter sometimes seems to us
  so banded when the vaporous air weaves round her
  the thread that makes her girdle luminous.          69

In Heaven's courts, from which height I have come,
  are many gems so precious and so lovely
  that they cannot be taken from the kingdom.         72

Of such those splendors sang. Who does not grow
  wings that will fly him there, must learn these things
  from the tidings of the tongueless here below.      75

When, so singing, those Sun-surpassing souls
  had three times turned their blazing circuit round us,
  like stars that circle close to the fixed poles,    78

they stood like dancers still caught in the pleasure
  of the last round, who pause in place and listen
  till they have caught the beat of the new measure.  81

And from within its blaze I heard one start:
  "Since the ray of grace from which true
                                love is kindled—
  and then by loving, in the loving heart             84

grows and multiplies—among all men
  so shines on you to lead you up these stairs
  that none descend except to climb again;            87

whoever refused your soul, it being thirsty,
  wine from his flask, would be no freer to act
  than water blocked from flowing to the sea.         90

You wish to know what flowering plants are woven
  into this garland that looks lovingly
  on the lovely lady who strengthens you for Heaven.  93

I was a lamb among the holy flock
  Dominic leads to where all plenty is,
  unless the lamb itself stray to bare rock.          96

This spirit on my right, once of Cologne,
  was my teacher and brother. Albert was his name,
  and Thomas, of Aquinas, was my own.                 99

If you wish, similarly, to know the rest
  let your eyes follow where my words shall lead
  circling through all this garland of the blest.     102

The next flame springs from the glad smile of Gratian
  who so assisted one court and the other
  that in him Heaven found good cause for elation.    105

The next to adorn our chorus of the glad
  was the good Peter who, like the poor widow,
  offered to Holy Church all that he had.             108

The fifth light, and the loveliest here, shines forth
  from so magnificent a love that men
  hunger for any news of it on earth;                 111

within it is that mind to which were shone
  such depths of wisdom that, if truth be true,
  no mortal ever rose to equal this one.              114

See next the taper whose flame, when formerly
  it burned in mortal flesh, saw most profoundly
  the nature of angels and their ministry.            117

Within the lesser lamp next on my right
  shines the defender of the Christian Age
  whose treatise led Augustine toward the light.      120

Now if your mind has followed on my praise
  from light to light, you are already eager
  to know what spirit shines in the eighth blaze.     123

In it, for having seen the sum of good,
    there sings a soul that showed the world's deceit
    to any who would heed. The bones and blood          126

from which it was cruelly driven have their tomb
    down there in Cieldauro: to this peace
    it came from exile and from martyrdom.              129

See next the flames breathed forth by Isidore,
    by Bede, and by that Richard whose
                                'Contemplations'
    saw all that a mere man can see, and more.          132

The next, from whom your eyes return to me,
    is the glory of a soul in whose grave thoughts
    death seemed to be arriving all too slowly:         135

it is the flame, eternally elated,
    of Siger, who along the Street of Straws
    syllogized truths for which he would be hated."     138

Then as a clock tower calls us from above
    when the Bride of God rises to sing her matins
    to the Sweet Spouse, that she may earn his love,    141

with one part pulling and another thrusting,
    *tin-tin*, so glad a chime the faithful soul
    swells with the joy of love almost to bursting—     144

just so, I saw that wheel of glories start
    and chime from voice to voice in harmonies
    so sweetly joined, so true from part to part        147

that none can know the like till he go free
where joy begets itself eternally.

## Notes

1-3. The idea of Trinity will hardly be contained in a footnote,
but note the essence of Dante's doctrine. The Father is the

Creator. The Son is Wisdom—the Word of God. Together, they eternally breathe forth the Third Essence of Love, the Holy Ghost. Note, therefore, that it is forever being born.

7-27. THE PERFECTION OF THE CREATION. Dante summons the reader to ponder the perfection of God's creation as exemplified by the point of the vernal equinox. It is at this point that the Sun's ecliptic crosses the celestial equator into the northern hemisphere. The two great circles intersect at an angle of 23° 27'.

These two circles are the "one motion and another." (The Sun is now at the vernal equinox.) The apparent equatorial (or diurnal) motion is from east to west. The apparent order in which the signs of the Zodiac appear along the ecliptic is from west to east. It follows, therefore, that the influences of the planets, following the zodiacal path, vary from north to south of the equator (see below, note to 32-33), striking the earth variously but in a fixed progression that is part of God's inscrutable plan. Were the courses of the equator and the ecliptic to run parallel, or were the angles between them to change, the influences of the spheres would be weakened, and earth that stands ever in need of those influences ("earth that calls on them") would lose the full good of their powers.

This is the mystical foretaste Dante offers the reader, bidding him to stay at table and feed himself (i.e., study God's ways) while Dante pursues his demanding theme.

31. *as I have implied*: In lines 8-9 ff., where he said the sun was at the vernal equinox, at which point it must be in Aries.

32-33. *those spirals*: The path of the Sun seems to be a spiral (as may be noted when it is drawn on a globe) from the Tropic of Capricorn (the southern limit of the sun's motion) to the Tropic of Cancer (the northern limit). These Tropics are the latitudes 23° 27' south and north respectively (the same angle at which the ecliptic crosses the equator). As the apparent spiral of the sun's course brings it toward the Tropic of Cancer, we see it rise earlier every day.

43-45. *Though genius, art, and usage stored my mind*: None of these resources of human understanding (reason) can make visible what faith alone can find.

48. *as much as any eye has known of light*: Dante (following Aristotle) sets the sun as the maximum of light the human eye can see and, therefore, the human mind can imagine. The sun-surpassing radiance of Heaven is, therefore, beyond human imagination.

49. *the fourth family*: The Fourth Sphere of the Blest.

51. *how He breathes forth and engenders*: Once more of the mystery of the Trinity. Through all Eternity God is conceived as creating the Son, in union with whom He eternally breathes forth the Holy Ghost.

52-54. *the Sun of Angels*: God. *this physical one*: The sun. As the sun lights man, so God lights the angels.

55-63. Note the allegorical possibilities. At the bidding of Beatrice (Revealed Truth) the man turns his mind so utterly to God that he forgets her until her joy in his absorption draws him back from single-minded devotion to an awareness of other (and necessarily lesser) things.

64. *transcendent*: Transcending the light of the sun.

67. *Latona's daughter*: The Moon. See *Purgatorio*, XX, 130-132, note. In vaporous air the moon seems girdled with light. Dante's figure conceives the vapors as weaving the thread (of light) that makes her glowing girdle.

72. *that they cannot be taken from the kingdom*: In one sense, no description can take the idea of them from heaven to mortal imagination. In a second, they are treasures Heaven reserves to itself because man is unworthy and incapable of them.

74-75. *must learn . . . from the tidings of the tongueless*: *i.e.*, not at all. Every human tongue is mute to speak the treasures of Heaven. One must go there himself (i.e., undertake the purification that leads to celestial sensibilities).

82-87. The speaker is Aquinas (see 97-99, note) and he has just announced nothing less than Dante's salvation.

89-90. *no freer to act than water*: Would not be acting according to his nature. The nature of the Celestial Soul is *caritas* and only an impediment outside itself can prevent it from giving love freely.

91-92. *what flowering plants*: What souls. *are woven into this garland*: Are in this company of souls that wreathe Beatrice round.

95. *Dominic*: St. Dominic, founder of the Dominican Order. He will be discussed at length in XII, 34 ff.

97-99. *Thomas Aquinas*: Aquinas (1227-1274), known as the "Doctor Angelicus," was author of the "Summa Theologica" (a principal source of Dante's learning), founder of Thomistic philosophy, and perhaps the most learned of Catholic theologians. He was not canonized until 1323, two years after Dante's death. Dante, therefore, was writing of Thomas, not of St. Thomas. As befits the modes of Heaven, Thomas does not mention his own name till he has identified the spirit on his right, a brother Dominican and his teacher. *Albert*: Albertus Magnus (circa 1200-1280), the "Doctor Universalis" who, with Aquinas, reestablished Aristotelian learning in Western thought. He was teaching in Cologne in 1248 when Aquinas went there to be his student. Albertus was canonized and proclaimed a Doctor of the Church in 1931.

100. *to know the rest*: Of the encircling souls.

103. *Gratian*: Or Gratianus. Twelfth-century scholar. It is for his "Decretum Gratiani" that Aquinas credits him with correlating and harmonizing civil and ecclesiastical law (the "one court and another").

107. *the good Peter*: Petrus Lombardus. Born early in the twelfth century, Bishop of Paris 1159, died 1160. Called "Magister Sententiarum" because of his "Sententiarum Libri IV," a compilation of scriptures and texts of the church fathers. In a sense, he did for doctrine what Gratianus did for canon law, and Dante typically puts the two side by side. *like the poor widow*: In his preface to "Sententiarum" Peter modestly compares himself to the poor widow in *Luke*, XXI, 1-4 who gave her two mites (all she had) to the treasury of the church.

109-114. *The fifth light*: Solomon. *so magnificent a love*: As expressed in the "Song of Songs" which was thought to be the wedding hymn of the Church and God. *men hunger for any news*: Of Solomon's final fate. *I Kings*, XI, 1-9 records the sins of Solomon's age and theologians of Dante's time debated whether he had been saved or damned. *if truth be true*: If Scripture (which is truth) be true. Hence: it certainly is true. *no mortal ever rose to equal this one*: Dante says, literally, "no second [equal] has risen." Adam, of course, knew God directly, and Christ was man-and-God. Both, therefore, surpassed Solomon. But Christ may be said to have descended and Adam to have issued from God, whereby they did not "rise." Whether or not Dante had these thoughts in mind, his words echo *I Kings* III, 12: "that there was none like thee before thee, neither after thee shall any arrive like unto thee." The exact phrasing of this line is important for it will be referred to several times in the next three Cantos.

115. *whose flame*: The soul of Dionysus the Areopagite, converted by St. Paul (*Acts*, XVII. 34) and wrongly believed in Dante's time to be the author of "The Celestial Hierachy."

119. *the defender of the Christian Age*: Dante may intend here Paulus Orosius, fifth-century Spanish priest whose *Historiarum Adversus Paganos* defended the effect of Christianity upon the Roman Empire. Or he may intend Marius Victorinus, fourth-century Roman, who became a Christian theologian, and whose example was believed to have contributed to the conversion of St. Augustine.

123. *what spirit shines in the eighth blaze*: Boethius. Anicius Manlius Severinus Boethius was born in Rome circa 470, studied in Greece, became consul of Theodoric the Ostrogoth in 510, later to be imprisoned by Theodoric in Pavia on charges of treason and magic, and executed in 524. His "De Consolatione Philosophiae," written in prison, is a work of pagan dignity that defends the joys of the good life without reference to any eternal reward. Despite its essential paganism, its influence upon the Middle Ages (and upon Dante) was enormous, among other reasons, as a source of late classical learning. In time the death of Boethius came to be thought of as a martyrdom. His remains were formally moved to a tomb in Pavia's Cieldauro (Church of St. Peter) in the eighth century, and though never canonized, he grew to be locally revered as St. Severinus.

130. *Isidore:* Of Seville (circa 560-636). Became Archbishop of Seville circa 600. Canonized St. Isidore, 1598. Designated a Doctor of the Church, 1722. His major work, "Etymologiae," was highly prized as an encyclopedia of medieval learning.

131. *Bede*: The Venerable Bede (circa 673-735). English Bible scholar and historian. The title of Venerable (the three orders of holiness are venerable, blessed, and saint, in mounting order) was conferred in the ninth century. Pope Leo declared him a Doctor of the Church in 1899.

131. *Richard*: Richard of St. Victor. Twelfth-century English mystic and theologian. Birthdate unknown; died circa 1173. He was called the Great Contemplater after one of his treatises, "De Contemplatione."

133. *from whom your eyes return to me*: Thus completing the round of the twelve doctors.

135. *death seemed to be arriving all too slowly*: In his eagerness to be done with the vanity of this world and to begin the eternal life.

137. *Siger*: Siger of Brabant. Born circa 1226. An outstanding Averroist philosopher, he taught philosophy at the University of Paris (which was then on *la rue de Feurre* or Street of Straws) and was cited for heresy in 1277 before the Grand Inquisitor of France (hence, "the truths for which he would be hated"). He fled to Orvieto to appeal his case to the Papal Court but was stabbed to death (circa 1283) by his secretary, probably in a mad fit.

140-141. *the Bride of God*: The Church. *the Sweet Spouse*: Christ.

# CANTO XI

*Doctors of the Church*
*The First Garland of Souls:*
*Aquinas*
*Praise of St. Francis*
*Degeneracy of Dominicans*

*THE SPIRITS complete their song and their joyous dance and once more gather around Dante and Beatrice.*

*Aquinas reads Dante's mind and speaks to make clear several points about which Dante was in doubt. He explains that Providence sent two equal princes to guide the Church, St. Dominic, the wise law-giver, being one, and St. Francis, the ardent soul, being the other. Aquinas was himself a Dominican. To demonstrate the harmony of Heaven's gift and the unity of the Dominicans and Franciscans, Aquinas proceeds to pronounce a PRAISE OF THE LIFE OF ST. FRANCIS. His account finished, he returns to the theme of the unity of the Dominicans and Franciscans, and proceeds to illustrate it further by himself lamenting the DEGENERACY OF THE DOMINICAN ORDER.*

O senseless strivings of the mortal round!
   how worthless is that exercise of reason
   that makes you beat your wings into the ground!    3

One man was giving himself to law, and one
   to aphorisms; one sought sinecures,
   and one to rule by force or sly persuasion;    6

one planned his business, one his robberies;
　　one, tangled in the pleasure of the flesh,
　　wore himself out, and one lounged at his ease;　　• 9

while I, of all such vanities relieved
　　and high in Heaven with my Beatrice,
　　arose to glory, gloriously received.　　12

—When each had danced his circuit and come back
　　to the same point of the circle, all stood still,
　　like votive candles glowing in a rack.　　15

And I saw the splendor of the blazing ray
　　that had already spoken to me, smile,
　　and smiling, quicken; and I heard it say:　　18

"Just as I take my shining from on high,
　　so, as I look into the Primal Source,
　　I see which way your thoughts have turned,
　　　　　　　　　　　　and why.　　21

You are uncertain, and would have me find
　　open and level words in which to speak
　　what I expressed too steeply for your mind　　24

when I said 'leads to where all plenty is,'
　　and 'no mortal ever rose to equal this one.'
　　And it is well to be exact in this.　　27

The Providence that governs all mankind
　　with wisdom so profound that any creature
　　who seeks to plumb it might as well be blind,　　30

in order that the Bride seek her glad good
　　in the Sweet Groom who, crying from on high,
　　took her in marriage with His blessed blood,　　33

sent her two Princes, one on either side
   that she might be secure within herself,
   and thereby be more faithfully His Bride.    36

One, in his love, shone like the seraphim.
   The other, in his wisdom, walked the earth
   bathed in the splendor of the cherubim.    39

I shall speak of only one, though to extol
   one or the other is to speak of both
   in that their works led to a single goal.    42

Between the Tupino and the little race
   sprung from the hill blessèd Ubaldo chose,
   a fertile slope spreads up the mountain's face.    45

Perugia breathes its heat and cold from there
   through Porta Sole, and Nocera and Gualdo
   behind it mourn the heavy yoke they bear.    48

From it, at that point where the mountainside
   grows least abrupt, a sun rose to the world
   as this one does at times from Ganges' tide.    51

Therefore, let no man speaking of that place
   call it *Ascesi*—'I have risen'—but rather,
   *Oriente*—so to speak with proper grace.    54

Nor was he yet far distant from his birth
   when the first comfort of his glorious powers
   began to make its warmth felt on the earth:    57

a boy yet, for that lady who, like death
   knocks on no door that opens to her gladly,
   he had to battle his own father's wrath.    60

With all his soul he married her before
   the diocesan court *et coram patre;*
   and day by day he grew to love her more.    63

Bereft of her First Groom, she had had to stand
   more than eleven centuries, scorned, obscure;
   and, till he came, no man had asked her hand:   66

none, at the news that she had stood beside
   the bed of Amyclas and heard, unruffled,
   the voice by which the world was terrified;   69

and none, at word of her fierce constancy,
   so great, that even when Mary stayed below,
   she climbed the Cross to share Christ's agony.   72

But lest I seem obscure, speaking this way,
   take Francis and Poverty to be those lovers.
   That, in plain words, is what I meant to say.   75

Their harmony and tender exultation
   gave rise in love, and awe, and tender glances
   to holy thoughts in blissful meditation.   78

The venerable Bernard, seeing them so,
   kicked off his shoes, and toward so great a peace
   ran, and running, seemed to go too slow.   81

O wealth unknown! O plenitude untried!
   Egidius went unshod. Unshod, Sylvester
   followed the groom. For so it pleased the bride!   84

Thenceforth this father and this happy lord
   moved with his wife and with his family,
   already bound round by the humble cord.   87

He did not grieve because he had been born
   the son of Bernardone; he did not care
   that he went in rags, a figure of passing scorn.   90

He went with regal dignity to reveal
   his stern intentions to Pope Innocent,
   from whom his order first received the seal.   93

Then as more souls began to follow him
   in poverty—whose wonder-working life
   were better sung among the seraphim—          96

Honorius, moved by the Eternal Breath,
   placed on the holy will of this chief shepherd
   a second crown and everflowering wreath.         99

Then, with a martyr's passion, he went forth
   and in the presence of the haughty Sultan
   he preached Christ and his brotherhood on earth;   102

but when he found none there would take Christ's
                               pardon,
   rather than waste his labors, he turned back
   to pick the fruit of the Italian garden.          105

On the crag between Tiber and Arno then, in tears
   of love and joy, he took Christ's final seal,
   the holy wounds of which he wore two years.       108

When God, whose loving will had sent him forward
   to work such good, was pleased to call him back
   to where the humble soul has its reward,          111

he, to his brothers, as to rightful heirs
   commended his dearest Lady, and he bade them
   to love her faithfully for all their years.      114

Then from her bosom, that dear soul of grace
   willed its return to its own blessed kingdom;
   and wished its flesh no other resting place.      117

Think now what manner of man was fit to be
   his fellow helmsman, holding Peter's ship
   straight to its course across the dangerous sea.   120

Such was our patriarch. Hence, all who rise
    and follow his command will fill the hold,
    as you can see, with fruits of paradise.    123

But his flock has grown so greedy for the taste
    of new food that it cannot help but be
    far scattered as it wanders through the waste.    126

The more his vagabond and distant sheep
    wander from him, the less milk they bring back
    when they return to the fold. A few do keep    129

close to the shepherd, knowing what wolf howls
    in the dark around them, but they are so few
    it would take little cloth to make their cowls.    132

Now, if my words have not seemed choked and blind,
    if you have listened to me and taken heed,
    and if you will recall them to your mind,    135

your wish will have been satisfied in part,
    for you will see how the good plant is broken,
    and what rebuke my words meant to impart    138

when I referred, a while back in our talk,
    to 'where all plenty is' and to 'bare rock.' "

## Notes

15. *rack*: Dante says "candellier," which may be taken to
mean candlestick, but equally to mean the candle-racks that
hold votive candles in churches. The image of the souls as
twelve votive candles in a circular rack is certainly apter than
that of twelve candles in separate candlesticks.

25-26. *leads to . . . all plenty*: X, 95. *no mortal ever*: X, 114.

28-42. INTRODUCTION TO THE LIFE OF ST. FRANCIS.
Compare the words of Bonaventura in introducing the life of
St. Dominic, XII, 31-45.

31. *the Bride*: The Church.

32. *crying from on high*: *Matthew*, XXVII. 46, 50; *Mark*, XV, 34, 37; *Luke*, XXIII, 46; and *John*, XIX, 26-30—all record Christ's dying cries upon the cross.

34. *two Princes, one on either side*: St. Dominic and St. Francis. Dominic, on one side (line 39 equates his wisdom with the cherubic), by his wisdom and doctrinal clarity made the church secure within itself by helping to defend it against error and heresy. Francis, on the other (line 37 ascribes to him seraphic ardor of love), set the example that made her more faithfully the bride of Christ.

43-51. ASSISI AND THE BIRTH OF ST. FRANCIS. The passage, in Dante's characteristic topophiliac style, is full of local allusions, not all of them relevant to St. Francis, but all describing the situation of Assisi, his birthplace. Perugia stands to the east of the upper Tiber. The Tiber at this point runs approximately north to south. Mt. Subasio, a long and many spurred crest, runs roughly parallel to the Tiber on the west. Assisi is on the side of Subasio, and it was from Assisi that the sun of St. Francis rose to the world, as "this one" (the actual sun in which Dante and Aquinas are standing) rises from the Ganges. The upper Ganges crosses the Tropic of Cancer, the line of the summer solstice. When the sun rises from the Ganges, therefore, it is at its brightest.

*the Tupino*: Skirts Mt. Subasio on the south and flows roughly west into the Tiber. *the little race*: The Chiascio [KYAH-show] flows south along the length of Subasio and empties into the Tupino below Assisi. *blessèd Ubaldo*: St. Ubaldo (1084-1160), Bishop of Gubbio from 1129. He chose a hill near Gubbio as a hermitage in which to end his days, but died before he could retire there. *Porta Sole*: Perugia's west gate. It faces Mt. Subasio. In summer its slopes reflect the sun's ray through Porta Sole; in winter, covered with snow, they send the cold wind. *Nocera* [NAW-tcheh-ra], *Gualdo* [GWAHL-doe]: Towns on the other side of (behind) Subasio. Their heavy yoke may be their subjugation by Perugia, or Dante may have meant by it the taxes imposed by Robert of Naples and his Spanish brigands.

51-54. It is such passages that certify the failures of all translation. *Ascesi*, which can mean "I have risen," was a common name for Assisi in Dante's day. *Oriente*, of course, is the point at which the sun rises. Let no man, therefore, call Assisi "I have risen" (i.e., a man has risen), but let him call it, rather, the dawning east of the world (a sun has risen).

55 ff. *yet far distant*: While he was still young. The phrasing continues the figure of the new-risen sun.

Francis, born Bernardone, was the son of a relatively prosperous baker and, early in life, assisted his father. In a skirmish between Assisi and Perugia he was taken prisoner and later released. On his return to Assisi (he was then twenty-four) he abandoned all worldly affairs and gave himself entirely to religious works.

*a boy yet*: Here, as in line 55, Aquinas is overdoing it a bit: twenty-four is a bit old for being a boy yet. *that lady*: Poverty. *his own father's wrath*: In 1207 (Francis was then twenty-five) he sold one of his father's horses along with a load of bread and gave the money to a church. In a rage, his father forced the church to return the money, called Francis before the Bishop of Assisi, and there demanded that he renounce his right to inherit. Francis not only agreed gladly but removed his clothes and gave them back to his father saying, "Until this hour I called you my father on earth; from this hour I can say in full truth 'our Father which art in Heaven.'"

*he married*: In his "Hymn to Poverty" Francis himself celebrated his union to Poverty as a marriage. He had married her before the diocesan court of Assisi, *et coram patre* (before the court, i.e., in the legal presence of, his father). The marriage was solemnized by his renunciation of all possessions.

64-66. *her First Groom*: Christ. *he*: St. Francis.

68. *Amyclas*: Lucan reported (see also *Convivio*, IV, 13) how the fisherman Amyclas lay at his ease on a bed of seaweed before Caesar himself, being so poor that he had nothing to fear from any man. Not even this report of the serenity Mistress Poverty could bring to a man, and not even the fact that she outdid even Mary in constancy, climbing the very cross with Christ, had moved any man to seek her in marriage.

79. *Bernard*: Bernard di Quintavalle, a wealthy neighbor, became the first disciple of Francis, kicking off his shoes to go barefoot in imitation of the master.

82-84. *unknown*: To men. Holy Poverty is the wealth none recognize, the plenitude none try. *Egidius . . . Sylvester*: The third and fourth disciples of Francis. Peter, the second disciple, seems not to have been known to Dante. *the groom*: Francis. *the bride*: Poverty.

87. *the humble cord*: Now a symbol of the Franciscans but then in general use by the poor as a makeshift belt.

88. *grieve*: At his humble origins.

93. *his order first received the seal:* In 1210. But Innocent III thought the proposed rule of the order so harsh that he granted only provisional approval.

96. *among the seraphim:* In the Empyrean, rather than in this Fourth Heaven.

97-99. *Honorius . . . second crown:* In 1223, Pope Honorius III gave his fully solemnized approval of the Francisan Order.

100-105. In 1219, St. Francis and eleven of his followers made a missionary pilgrimage to Greece and Egypt. Dante, whose facts are not entirely accurate, may have meant that pilgrimage; or he may have meant Francis's projected journey to convert the Moors (1214-1215) when Francis fell ill in southern Spain and had to give up his plans.

106-108. In 1224, on a crag of Mt. Alvernia (on the summit of which the Franciscans have reared a commemorative chapel), St. Francis received the stigmata in a rapturous vision of Christ. He wore the wound two years before his death in 1226, at the age of (probably) forty-four.

109-117. The central reference here is to Dame Poverty. *her bosom:* The bare ground of Poverty. *no other resting place:* Than in the bare ground.

119. *his fellow helmsman:* St. Dominic. *Peter's ship:* The Church.

121-132. THE DEGENERACY OF THE DOMINICANS IN DANTE'S TIME. Aquinas was a Dominican. As a master touch to symbolize the harmony of Heaven and the unity of Franciscans and Dominicans, Dante puts into the mouth of a Dominican the praise of the life of St. Francis. That praise ended, he chooses the Dominican to lament the degeneracy of the order. In XII, Dante will have the Franciscan, St. Bonaventure, praise the life of St. Dominic and lament the degeneracy of the Franciscans.

122. *his command:* The rule of the Dominicans. *will fill his hold:* With the treasures of Paradise. Dante is carrying forward the helmsman metaphor of lines 118-120, though the ship is now commanded by a patriarch. Typically, the figure changes at once to a shepherd-and-flock metaphor.

136. *in part:* In X, 95-96, in identifying himself as a Dominican, Aquinas said the Dominican rule "leads to where all plenty

s" unless the lamb itself stray to "bare rock." In lines 25-26, above, he refers to these words and also to his earlier statements (X, 114) about Solomon's wisdom (that "no mortal ever rose to equal this one"). What he has now finished saying about the degeneracy of the Dominicans will satisfy part of Dante's wish (about "plenty" and "bare rock"). The other part of his wish (about "no mortal ever rose to equal this one") will be satisfied later.

137. *the good plant*: Of the Dominican rule strictly observed.

# CANTO XII

---

*Doctors of the Church*
*The Second Garland of Souls:*
*Bonaventure*
*Praise of St. Dominic*
*Degeneracy of Franciscans*

*AS SOON AS Aquinas has finished speaking the wheel of souls begins to turn, and before it has completed its first revolution it is surrounded by a SECOND GARLAND OF TWELVE SOULS.*

*The spokesman of this second company is ST BONAVENTURE. In the harmonious balances of Heaven the Dominican Aquinas had spoken the praise of the life of St. Francis. In the same outgoing motion of love the Franciscan Bonaventure now speaks the PRAISE OF THE LIFE OF ST. DOMINIC. And as Aquinas had concluded by lamenting the degeneracy of the Dominican Order, so Bonaventure concludes his account with a LAMENT FOR THE DEGENERACY OF THE FRANCISCAN ORDER. He then identifies the other souls in his Garland.*

So spoke the blessed flame and said no more;
    and at its final word the holy millstone
    began revolving round us as before.

And had not finished its first revolution
    before a second wheel had formed around it,
    matching it tone for tone, motion for motion.

138

As a reflection is to the source of light,
   such is the best our sirens and muses sing
   to the chanting of those sheaths of pure delight.   9

As through thin clouds or mists twin rainbows bend
   parallel arcs and equal coloring
   when Juno calls her handmaid to attend—   12

the outer band born of the inner one,
   like the voice of that wandering nymph of
                      love consumed,
   as vapors are consumed by the summer sun—   15

whereby all men may know what God made plain
   in the pledge he gave to Noah that the waters
   of the great deluge would not come again—   18

just so, those sempiternal roses wove
   their turning garland round us, and the outer
   answered the inner with the voice of love.   21

And when the exalted festival and dance
   of love and rapture, sweet song to sweet song,
   and radiance to flashing radiance,   24

had in a single instant fallen still
   with one accord—as our two eyes make one,
   being moved to open and close by a single will—   27

from one of those new splendors a voice came;
   and as the North Star draws a needle's point,
   so was my soul drawn to that glorious flame.   30

Thus he began: "The love that makes me shine
   moves me to speak now of that other leader
   through whom so much good has been said of mine.  33

When one is mentioned the other ought to be;
   for they were militant in the same cause
   and so should shine in one light and one glory.   36

The troops of Christ, rearmed at such great cost,
   were struggling on behind the Holy Standard,
   fearful, and few, and laggard, and half lost,   39

when the Emperor who reigns eternally—
   of His own grace and not for their own merit—
   took thought of his imperiled soldiery;   42

and, as you have heard say, He sent His bride
   two champions by whose teachings and example
   the scattered companies were reunified.   45

In the land to which the West wind, soft and glad,
   returns each Spring to open the new leaves
   with which, soon, all of Europe will be clad,   48

at no great distance from the beat and bite
   of those same waves behind which, in its course,
   the sun, at times, hides from all mortal sight,   51

a fortunate village lies in the protection
   of the great shield on which two lions are,
   one subjugating and one in subjection.   54

Within its walls was born the ardent one,
   true lover and true knight of the Christian faith;
   bread to his followers, to his foes a stone.   57

His mind, from the instant it began to be,
   swelled with such powers that in his mother's womb
   he made her capable of prophecy.   60

And when he and his Lady Faith before
   the holy font had married and endowed
   each other with new gifts of holy power,   63

the lady who had spoken for him there
   saw, in a dream, the wonder-working fruit
   that he and his inheritors would bear.                    66

To speak him as he was, a power from Heaven
   was moved to give him the possessive form
   of His name unto Whom he was wholly given.                69

Dominicus he was called. Let him be known
   as the good husbandman chosen by Christ
   to help Him in the garden He had sown.                    72

A fitting squire and messenger of Christ
   he was, for his first love was poverty,
   and such was the first counsel given by Christ.          75

Often his nurse found him in meditation
   at night on the bare floor, awake and silent,
   as if he were saying, 'This is my vocation.'             78

O Felix his father in true 'felicity!'
   O mother truly Joan, 'whom God has graced!'
   —if the names can be translated literally!               81

Not as men toil today for wealth and fame,
   in the manner of the Ostian and Taddeo,
   but for love of the true manna, he soon became           84

a mighty doctor, and began to go
   his rounds of that great vineyard where the vine,
   if left untended, pales and cannot grow.                 87

Before that Seat where once the poor were fed
   and tended (now, through no fault of its own,
   but by its degenerate occupant, corrupted)               90

he did not ask the right to keep as pay
   three out of every six, nor a benifice,
   nor *decimas quae sunt pauperum Dei;*                     93

but license in the sick world there below
   to battle for that seed from which are sprung
   the four and twenty plants that ring you now.   96

Then, will and doctrine joined, and in the light
   of apostolic office, he burst forth,
   like a torrent from a mountain vein, to smite   99

the stumps and undergrowths of heresy.
   And where the thickets were least passable,
   there his assault bore down most heavily.   102

And from him many rivulets sprang to birth
   by which the Catholic orchard is so watered
   that its little trees spring greener from the earth.   105

If such was the one wheel of the great car
   in which the Church rode to defend herself
   and win in open field her civil war,   108

you cannot fail to see with a clear mind
   the excellence of that other, about whom,
   before I joined you, Thomas was so kind.   111

But the track its great circumference cut of old
   is so abandoned that the casks are empty,
   and where there once was crust, now
                      there is mold.   114

His family, that formerly used to go
   in his very footsteps, is so turned around
   that it prints toe on heel, and heel on toe.   117

Soon shall we see the harvest of these years
   of lazy cultivation, and hear the darnel,
   the storehouse shut against it, shed its tears.   120

Search our book leaf by leaf and you will see,
   I have no doubt, written upon some page:
   'I am today all that I used to be.'    123

But not at Casal' nor Acquasparta—there
   they come to keep our rule, and in the keeping
   one loosens it, one tightens it like a snare.    126

I am the life of Bonaventure, on earth
   of Bagnoregio, who in great offices
   always put back the things of lesser worth.    129

Illuminato and Augustine are here,
   two of the first-come of the barefoot poor.
   For the cord they wore God holds them ever dear.    132

The prior Hugo is here, and the deathless glow
   of Peter Mangiadore, and Peter of Spain
   whose light still shines in twelve small books
                               below.    135

And the prophet Nathan, and the eternal part
   of Chrysostom, and Anselm, and that Donatus
   who gladly turned his hand to the first art.    138

Rabanus is also here; and here beside me
   shines the Calabrian abbot Joachim
   whose soul was given the power of prophecy.    141

The ardent courtesy of my holy brother
   and his apt praise of one great paladin
   moved me to say this much about the other    144

in emulous and loving eulogy;
and so moved all these of my company."

## Notes

2. *the holy millstone*: The wheel of souls, called a millstone
here perhaps to suggest the ponderous turning of God's will (cf.

the expression "the mills of the Gods") but also to describe their motion, for a millstone moves slowly when it starts to turn, and this wheel of souls had not completed its first revolution before it was surrounded by another wheel.

5. *a second wheel*: Of twelve more splendors. In the heavenly hierarchy these are probably a grade inferior to the souls of the first wheel (line 13: "the outer band born of the inner one"). The inner band, moreover, revolves nearer the center of the sun (Divine Illumination). Lines 10-18 certainly suggest that the two wheels are complementary to one another. The total of twenty-four may suggest a reference to the books of the Old Testament. (See *Purgatorio*, XXIX, 64, note.)

10-18. The compounding of metaphors in this passage is characteristically Dantean. The twin rainbows were said to occur when Juno called her handmaiden (Iris) to attend her. Iris (the Rainbow) was the messenger of the Gods as well as being especially associated with Juno. Thus, when she attends her mistress she presents herself in a double splendor. Line 13 is based on Dante's belief that the outer band of a twin rainbow is a reflection of the inner band. This reflection is like the voice of Echo, an outer reflection of the inner (first) sound. Echo was the wandering nymph who wasted away for love of Narcissus (consumed by the fire of love as vapors are consumed by the Sun) until the gods changed her to a stone. The figure then shifts from classical mythology to the Bible, referring to *Genesis*, IX, 8-17, in which God made a pact with Noah and his sons, promising that the Deluge would not be repeated, and hung the rainbow in the sky as token of His pledge.

28. *one of those new splendors*: St. Bonaventure. A Franciscan, he eulogizes St. Dominic and laments the decay of the Franciscan order, just as Aquinas, a Dominican, has eulogized St. Francis and lamented the decay of the Dominican order. Later, Bonaventure will identify the other souls of his circle (lines 130 *ff.*).

St. Bonaventure (1221-1274) was born Giovanni di Fidanza at Bagnoregio (now Bagnorea) near Lake Bolsena. He was a scholar saint and a leading theologian. He became Minister General of the Franciscan Order in 1257 and was created Cardinal Bishop of Albano in 1273. Much of his scholarship was carried out in France, where he died during the sessions of the second Council of Lyons. He was canonized in 1482 by Sixtus IV and pronounced sixth (Doctor Seraphicus) among the Doctors of the Church by Sixtus V in 1587.

31-45. INTRODUCTION TO THE LIFE OF ST. DOMINIC. Compare the words of Aquinas in introducing the Life of St. Francis (X, 28-42).

32. *that other leader*: St. Dominic.

33. *through whom*: The phrasing is obscure. Dante probably means that the earlier praise of St. Francis (Bonaventure's leader) is due to Dominic because his rule taught Aquinas such loving praises.

37-39. *rearmed*: By the blood of martyrs when persecution had all but scattered it. *the Holy Standard*: The Cross.

43. *as you have heard said*: In XI, 32 *ff*. *His bride*: The Church.

46-51. The land here referred to is Spain. In the sea beyond it, according to Dante's geography, the sun hides from all mortal sight when it is midnight in Jerusalem. For Dante, all of the earth's land area consisted of an arc of 180° from India to Spain with Jerusalem at the center, the other 180° of the earth's circumference being water. Thus, when the sun was at its furthest point from Jerusalem it shone only upon the watery wastes, hidden from the eyes of mortals.

52-54. *a fortunate village*: Calahorra, birthplace of St. Dominic, lies on the Ebro about 60 miles due south of the Bay of Biscay where it washes the westernmost point of the Spanish-French border. *the great shield*: Of the house of Castile. It is quartered and contains on one side a castle above a lion and on the other a lion above a castle, thus one lion is subjugating the castle and the other is being subjugated by it.

55 *ff*. LIFE OF ST. DOMINIC (1170-1221). Not all of the details Dante offers in his account of St. Dominic have a historic base. Dominic may have been born of an ancient family named Guzman, but little is known of his origins. He was an austere but undeviating man of mercy and with whole faith in pure doctrine. Beginning as an Augustinian, Dominic sought to overcome the heresies of the Albigensians, partly in defense of the pure faith and partly to save them from the terrors of the crusade that eventually destroyed them in a hideous blood bath. He founded the Dominican Order with the special purpose of saving the Albigensians from destruction in this world and damnation in the next. In 1215 he won provisional papal approval of his order from Innocent III, and, in 1216, full confirmation by Honorius III. He died in Bologna in 1221 and was canonized in 1234. Unlike Francis, who dreaded learning as a corruptive

force and praised the holy ignorance of the rude and simple mind, Dominic labored for purity of doctrine and founded his order for missionary scholars who were to go forth and preach the pure faith. Thus the founding principles of the two great orders were in many senses opposed and yet complementary.

The notes that follow comment on Dante's version of the life of St. Dominic, not on the historical record:

58-60. The mind and soul form at the instant of conception and take on the gifts assigned by the influences of the spheres. While still in the womb, Dominic was said to be so gifted that his mother foresaw the Dominican Order in a dream of giving birth to a black and white dog. Black and white are the Dominican colors, and *"Domini canes"* translates "hounds of the Lord."

61-66. Dominic married the faith at the Baptismal font, each bringing to the other a dowry of strength and of holy purpose. Following his baptism, his godmother is supposed to have dreamed that he had a star on his forehead, a sign that he would bring God's light to man.

67-75. "Dominic" is the possessive form of Latin *"Domine"* (the Lord). Note the triple use of "Christ" to rhyme with itself. Dante has not so rhymed before in the "Comedy." He will again in XIV, XIX, and XXXII. He will not rhyme "Christ" with any other word because none is fit to be joined with that holy name. In a *tenzone* against Forese (who appears in *Purgatorio,* XXIII) the younger Dante had once made use of what he probably came to think of as a sacrilegious rhyme on "Christ." This later device may be his way of making amends.

75-81. As noted above, little is known about Dominic's parents. The details of their names, like the tales of Dominic's prenatal powers, are the stuff of pious folk tales.

82-87. *the Ostian*: Enrico di Susa, who became Bishop of Ostia in 1271. *Taddeo*: Probably Taddeo d'Alderotto, a Florentine physician born circa 1215. The first was a successful scholar of canon law, the second of medicine. Both acquired money and fame as a result of their secular studies. Dominic, on the other hand, studied only for the true manna of spiritual knowledge in order that he might labor in the vineyard (the Church) in which the vines wither and grow pale if they are neglected.

88-96. Because of a decree against the founding of new Orders, Dominic had to plead for many years before he could win approval from the papal seat which is now (i.e., as of 1300) corrupted by Boniface VIII. Dominic did not ask permission to dispense church wealth (withholding two or three of every six coins for himself), nor for a benefice, nor for *decimas quae sunt pauperum Dei* (the tithes that belong to God's poor). He asked only for license to combat heresy, and thus to defend the seed of the true faith from which are sprung, as plants of the everlasting tree, the twenty-four doctors that surround Dante as Bonaventure speaks.

97-102. The reference here is to Dominic's years of labor against the Albigensian heresy. He joined a mission for that purpose as early as 1203. In 1206 he opened in France a mission house dedicated to saving Albigensian women from their heresy. In 1208 Innocent III declared a crusade against the Albigensian plain-folk (they were anti-church and, among other major points of doctrine, denied the Resurrection). In seven years of savage warfare and massacres the Albigensians were wiped out. Thus, when Dominic was allowed in 1215 to found his Order of Preaching Friars, he had already been laboring for at least twelve years to wipe out heresy, not by the sword, but by winning the heretics back to the faith through his preachments.

106-111. *If such was the one . . . the excellence of that other*: Since the car (the chariot) must have two equal wheels if it is to work properly, the excellence of the one wheel (Dominic) testifies to the excellence of the other (Francis), about whom Aquinas spoke in XI.

112 ff. LAMENT FOR THE DECLINE OF THE FRAN-CISCAN ORDER. Bonaventure now laments the decline of his Franciscans as Aquinas earlier lamented the decline of the Do-minicans. The core of this metaphor has changed from the chariot of war to the two-wheeled cart in which peasants haul grapes from the vineyard. The circumference of this great wheel (the Franciscan order) no longer turns in its former track, going back and forth from the vineyard to the winery. Hence the grapes (souls? good works?) are not brought in, and in the barrels (salvation? rectitude? the church?) where once there used to gather the crust of sediment left by good wine, there is now only the mold that forms in empty barrels.

117. *toe on heel, and heel on toe*: Instead of walking, as the first disciples did, in the footsteps of St. Francis, the decayed Franciscans walk backward in them, leaving their toe prints on the heel of the true tracks, and their heel prints on the toes; hence, walking in the other direction.

118-120. *the harvest . . . of lazy cultivation*: Bonaventure's moral point and its symmetrical response to Aquinas's lament for the decline of the Dominican Order are clear enough, but historically, the original rule of St. Francis was so harsh that it was, in effect, banned by the church. Its severity had, in fact, caused a schism within the order even before the death of St. Francis. One group sought to modify the rule of absolute poverty. The other (the Zealots or Spiritual Franciscans from whom stemmed the Penitentes) insisted on the rule to the point of open conflict with church authority. In 1318, in fact, four of the Spirituals were burned for heresy when they refused to modify the original rule of St. Francis.

There is an odd irony in the history of the Franciscans. The piety, fervor, and absolute poverty of the early monks made its impression upon a pious people, who began to make rich gifts to the order. Inevitably, an administrator had to appear, and so the monks of poverty had to acquire stewards and accountants. St. Bonaventure sought to resolve this conflict by teaching that all the property given to the friars was the property of the church but was held for their use (*usus pauperis*) in their life and work.

This schism was the lazy cultivation that made a bad harvest inevitable. Given the nature of Bonaventure's teaching, the bad harvest (the darnel) would be those Franciscans who risked excommunication by insisting, against direct papal orders, on the unmitigated rule (though he would, of course, include those Franciscans who observed the modified rule too slackly). Darnel or rye grass or black caraway springs up among the cultivated grains. Its hard seeds, ground up with the edible grains and so eaten as bread, can cause nervous disorders. It (the damned souls?) must be weeded out carefully (by good cultivation) and kept out of the good grain, the storehouse (the order? the church? heaven?) shut against it.

121-123. *our book*: Used figuratively for the Franciscan Order. *some page*: Some brother, some member of the Order.

124-126. *Casal*: The Franciscan monastery at Casale in Monferato. Ubertino di Casale (1259-1338) was general of the chapter and, favoring the Spirituals, so tightened the rule that he was forced to leave the Order. *Acquasparta*: In Todi. From this monastery Matteo d'Acquasparta rose to be general of the Order in 1287 and cardinal in 1288. Under him the Franciscan rule was substantially relaxed.

THE SOULS OF THE SECOND GARLAND:

130. *Illuminato and Augustino*: Two of the early brothers. Illuminato accompanied St. Francis on his mission to the East. Augustino joined the order in 1210.

133. *The prior Hugo*: Hugo of St. Victor (1096?-1141). Born in Saxony, he went to the monastery of St. Victor in Paris in 1115, where he taught philosophy and theology. In 1133 he was made prior and given charge of all studies.

134. *Peter Mangiadore*: Of Troyes (1110-1179?), Dean of the Cathedral of Troyes, 1147-1164. His *Historia Scholastica* was long the standard work on Bible history. *Peter of Spain*: Became John XXI in 1276, died in 1277. He was born in Lisbon circa 1226. Among the twelve books here referred to was his well-known summary of logical principles, *Summulae logicales*.

136. *the prophet Nathan*: See *II Samuel*, XII. Nathan spoke out against the sins of King David.

137. *Chrysostom*: The name in Greek means "Golden Mouth," a tribute to his oratorical power. He was John of Antioch (344?-407), Metropolitan of Constantinople. Like Nathan, he denounced the sins of the ruler. He was exiled for his pains by the Empress Eudoxia. *Anselm*: Born in Aosta, Lombardy, circa 1033. As Archbishop of Canterbury (from 1093) he fought the king on the question of the recognition of the Pope. Forced into exile in 1103, he returned to Canterbury in 1107, and died there in 1109. *Donatus*: Lived in Rome about the middle of the fourth century. He wrote commentaries on Terence and Virgil (the latter of which may have been what recommended him to Dante for his place here) and a book on grammar that was widely used in Dante's time. Grammar is "the first art" (first of the seven liberal arts that make up the trivium and quadrivium of the classical curriculum).

139. *Rabanus*: Rabanus Maurus (776?-856). Became Archbishop of Mainz in 847. Bible scholar, poet, and author of *De clericorum institutione*, a manual for clerics.

140. *Joachim*: Of Fiore (1132?-1202). A Cistercian mystic whose doctrines were especially popular among the Spiritual Franciscans who opposed Bonaventure. There is no historic evidence of his prophetic gift, and some of his preachments were specifically condemned by the Lateran Council in 1215 and by Alexander IV in 1256.

142-144. *my holy brother*: St. Thomas. *one great paladin*: St. Francis. *the other*: St. Dominic. The paladins were the twelve great champions who surrounded Charlemagne.

# CANTO XIII

---

THE FOURTH SPHERE: THE SUN   *The Intellect of the Faith:*
*Theologians and Doctors of the Church:*
*Aquinas*

*THE TWENTY-FOUR blessed spirits, moved by the
concluding words of Bonaventure, manifest themselves
as a mystical constellation while ringing forth a hymn of
praise that fills all Heaven.*

*When the hymn has been sung Aquinas speaks again.
He has read Dante's mind and addresses its perplexity,
explaining WHY NONE EVER ROSE TO EQUAL
SOLOMON'S WISDOM. He concludes with a WARN-
ING AGAINST HASTY JUDGMENT.*

If you would understand what I now write
   of what I saw next in that Heaven, imagine
   (and hold the image rock-fast in your sight)    3

the fifteen brightest stars the heavens wear
   in their living crown, stars of so clear a ray
   it pierces even the mist-thickened air;    6

imagine that Wain that on our heaven's breast
   lies night and day, because the tiller's turning
   causes no part of it to sink to rest;    9

imagine the bright mouth of the horn one sees
   flower from the axle star, around which spins
   the first wheel—and imagine all of these    12

forming two constellations, each a wreath
  (like that the daughter of King Minos made
  when through her limbs she felt the chill of death) 15

and imagine, last, that one wreath has its rays
  inside the other, and that both are turning
  around one center but in opposite ways. 18

So might you dimly guess (if mankind could)
  what actual stars, joined in their double dance,
  circled around the point on which I stood; 21

though such experiences outrun our knowing
  as the motion of the first and fastest heaven
  outruns the low Chiana's sluggish flowing. 24

There they sang no Bacchic chant nor Paean,
  but Three Persons in One Divine Nature
  and It and human nature in One Person. 27

The song and circling dance ran through their measure,
  and now those holy lights waited on us,
  turning rejoiced from pleasure to new pleasure. 30

The silence of these numina was broken
  by the same lamp from which the glorious life
  of God's beloved pauper had been spoken. 33

It said: "Since one sheaf has been thrashed my brother,
  and the good grain of it has been put by,
  sweet love invites me now to thrash the other. 36

Into that breast, you think, from which was carved
  the rib that went to form the lovely cheek
  for whose bad palate all mankind was starved, 39

and into that the lance pierced when it made
  such restitution for the past and future
  that every guilt of mankind was outweighed, 42

as much of wisdom's light, to the last ray,
   as human nature can contain, He breathed
   by whose power they were clad in mortal clay.      45

And, therefore, you were puzzled when I came
   to the fifth light and said no mortal ever
   had matched the wisdom sheathed within its flame. 48

Now open your eyes to what I shall say here
   and see your thought and my words form one truth,
   like the center and circumference of a sphere.      51

All things that die and all that cannot die
   are the reflected splendor of the Form
   our Father's love brings forth beyond the sky.      54

For the Living Light that streams forth from the Source
   in such a way that it is never parted
   from Him, nor from the Love whose mystic force    57

joins them in Trinity, lets its grace ray down,
   as if reflected, through nine subsistant natures
   that sempiternally remain as one.      60

From thing to thing to the last least potencies
   the ray comes down, until it is so scattered
   it brings forth only brief contingencies;      63

and these contingencies, I would have you see,
   are those *generated things* the moving heavens
   bring forth from seeds or not, as the case may be. 66

The wax of these things, and the powers that press
   and shape it, vary; thus the Ideal seal
   shines through them sometimes more and
                        sometimes less.      69

So trees of the same species may bring forth
 fruit that is better or worse; so men are born
 different in native talent and native worth. 72

Were the wax most ready and free of every dross,
 and were the heavens in their supreme conjunction,
 the light of the seal would shine through
        without loss: 75

but nature scants that light in all it makes,
 working in much the manner of a painter
 who knows the true art, but whose brush
        hand shakes. 78

But if the Fervent Love move the Pure Ray
 of the First Power to wield the seal directly,
 the thing so stamped is perfect in every way. 81

So once a quickening of the dust of earth
 issued the form of the animal perfection;
 so once the Virgin Womb quickened toward birth. 84

Therefore I say that I am one with you
 in the opinion that mankind was never,
 nor will be, what it once was in those two. 87

Having said this much, I must yet go on
 or you would ask: 'How then can it be said,
 no mortal ever rose to equal this one?' 90

But to make clear what yet seems not to be,
 think who he was, and what it was that moved him
 to answer when God said, 'What shall I give thee?' 93

I speak these words that you may understand
 he was a king, and asked the Lord for wisdom
 in governing his people and his land, 96

and not to know the number and degree
   of our motor-angels, nor if a premised 'may'
   can ever conclude, in logic, 'this must be,'     99

nor if there is prime motion, nor if in the space
   of a semicircle a non-right triangle
   may be drawn with the diameter as its base.     102

Hence you may see that when I spoke before
   of unmatched wisdom, it was on royal prudence
   that the drawn arrow of my intention bore.     105

Note well that I said 'rose' when I spoke of it.
   Thus you will see I spoke only of kings,
   of whom there are many, though so few are fit.     108

Such were my words, and taken in this light
   they are consistent with all that you believe
   of our first father and of our Best Delight.     111

And lead weights to your feet may my words be,
   that you move slowly, like a weary man,
   to the 'yes' and 'no' of what you do not see.     114

For he is a fool, and low among his kind,
   who answers yea or nay without reflection,
   nor does it matter on which road he runs blind.     117

Opinions too soon formed often deflect
   man's thinking from the truth into gross error,
   in which his pride then binds his intellect.     120

It is worse than vain for men to leave the shore
   and fish for truth unless they know the art;
   for they return worse off than they were before.     123

Of this, Parmenides and Melissus bear
   their witness to all men, along with Bryson,
   and others who set out without knowing where;     126

so Arius, Sabellius, and their schools
  who were to Scripture like a mirroring sword,
  distorting the straight faces to mislead fools.  129

Men should not be too smug in their own reason;
  only a foolish man will walk his field
  and count his ears too early in the season;  132

for I have seen a briar through winter's snows
  rattle its tough and menacing bare stems,
  and then, in season, open its pale rose;  135

and I have seen a ship cross all the main,
  true to its course and swift, and then go down
  just as it entered its home port again.  138

Let Tom and Jane not think, because they see
  one man is picking pockets and another
  is offering all his goods to charity,  141

that they can judge their neighbors with God's eyes:
for the pious man may fall, and the thief may rise."

## Notes

1-24. THE DANCE OF THE TWO GARLANDS. The passage,
though in Dante's most elliptical style, presents the basically
simple image of the two garlands of souls transformed into twin
constellations in the form of two concentric wheels revolving in
opposite directions around the point on which Dante is standing.

To envision the glory of the twenty-four stars (twelve and
twelve), the reader is invited to pick the fifteen brightest stars
from anywhere in heaven (4-6), to add to them the seven stars
of the Big Dipper (7-9), and to add the two bright stars from
the mouth of the Little Dipper (10-12).

All these are to be imagined as forming into the two circles,
each like the Corona Borealis, which, according to legend, was
made from the bridal wreath of Ariadne (daughter of King
Minos) when, abandoned by Theseus, she is found by Dionysus
and is taken to heaven to become his wife (13-15).

Put all these imaginings together and you may glimpse perhaps a shadow of the actual experience, for such things surpass mortal understanding by as much as the speed of the Primum Mobile surpasses the flow of the Chiana, a Tuscan river that, in Dante's time, wound sluggishly through swamplands that have since been drained (19-24).

8. *the tiller*: The Pole. It turns all the stars. Those of the Big Dipper, however, are so close to it that they never set, but lie night and day at the Celestial North Pole ("our heaven's breast").

25. *Paean:* Specifically a hymn to Apollo, though used generally for any pagan hymn.

30. *pleasure to new pleasure*: From the pleasure of praising God to the pleasure of serving Him in an act of *caritas*.

31. *numina*: A numen (pl. numina) is a divine spirit or a god conceived as a person.

32. *the same lamp*: St. Thomas Aquinas.

33. *God's beloved pauper*: St. Francis.

34-36. At the end of XI, Thomas had finished explaining his use of "where all plenty is." He paused in XII for Bonaventure to give the counterpoint to his Franciscan eulogy and Dominican lament. That first sheaf of understanding, then, has been thrashed (the grains of truth extracted from the straw). Now he is moved by love to thrash the second sheaf, separating from Dante's error (the straw) the truth about the wisdom of Solomon, and of Aquinas's earlier words (X, 114) "no mortal ever rose to equal this one."

38. *the lovely cheek*: Cheek, in conjunction with rib and breast, results in a somewhat anatomically strewn figure of speech, but is meant to stand here as a synecdoche for Eve, the part standing for the whole, while specifically referring to the part of her that contained the sinful palate.

40. *and into that*: That breast (of Christ).

47. *the fifth light*: Solomon. (See X, 109-114.)

48 ff. THE WISDOM OF SOLOMON. Aquinas proceeds to explain why "no mortal ever rose to equal this one" in wisdom, for Aquinas's statement had perplexed Dante, who had immediately concluded (as we shall see) that Aquinas was implying that Solomon was wiser than Christ and than Adam, though that could not be.

Aquinas parses the question in meticulous Scholastic detail in order to clear Dante's misconception, explaining, in essence, that though Adam and Christ-the-man were wiser than Solomon, containing more of the light of God, they were *direct* creations of God, whereas Solomon was a *secondary* creation, arising from Nature. Thus, Solomon sprang from the earth ("rose"), whereas Adam and Christ-the-man sprang directly from God and were apart from mortal creation.

53. *Form*: The Platonic Form. Idea.

55-58. *the Living Light*: The Son, as the Wisdom of mankind. *the Source*: The Father as Creator. *the love*: The Holy Ghost.

59-60. *nine subsistant natures*: The nine orders of angels that attend the heavenly spheres.

61-63. *thing*: Actuality. (It. *atto*.) The Scholastic term for "that which actually exists." *potency*: That which does not exist but that has the power of coming into being. *contingency*: What could exist (what could have actuality) but does not.

66. *from seeds or not*: See *Purgatorio*, XXVIII, 69, and 109-120, and note, for Dante's theory of wind-sown generative "virtues."

67-69. *the wax*: The matter that is available for the formation of contingencies. The term is used here metaphorically. It is not part of Scholastic terminology. *the powers that press*: The influences of the heavens. "Press" continues the "seal-in-wax" metaphor. *the Ideal Seal*: A metaphoric equivalent of the Ideal Form of Plato, here, the Divine Concept. It is perfect and unchangeable but, descending through the constant changes of the Spheres to the flux of matter, it is transmitted and received in a necessarily diminished way. Thus the Divine Idea shines through all things, and through some more than through others, but never perfectly.

79-81. The rendering of the original lines is much disputed, but their general sense is clear. Secondary creation, as Aquinas has explained, is never entirely perfect. Direct creation, on the other hand, is necessarily so. In lines 52-60 Aquinas explained direct creation as the ray of the Father and of the Son conjoined in Trinity. Here the force of the periphrasis is to cite all the Trinity in One, the Fervent Love being the Holy Ghost, the Pure Ray being the Son, and the First Power being the Father.

83. *the animal perfection*: The perfection of animal existence (as contrasted, perhaps, to angelic existence). In its ideal form

this perfection was embodied in Adam and in Christ-the-man, as direct creations.

86. *in the opinion*: Which Aquinas has read in Dante's mind.

88. *those two*: Adam and Christ-the-man.

90. *this one*: Solomon.

91. *but to make clear what yet seems not to be*: Aquinas knows everything that passes in Dante's mind. Thus, he not only instructs but knows instantly how much of the instruction has registered; the perfect, if supernatural, teacher.

93. *'What shall I give thee?'*: After Solomon went to Gideon and offered up a thousand burnt offerings, the Lord appeared in a dream and asked what gift he would choose. Solomon asked for the wisdom with which to rule his people. *I Kings*, III 4-14.

97-102. THE WISDOM SOLOMON DID NOT SEEK. Aquinas cites a number of propositions that engaged medieval learning. *motor-angels*: The angels that moved the spheres. How many they were, and of what degree (e.g., Principalities or Thrones) provided the subject of many disputations. *may . . . this must be*: Any qualification of the premise must, logically, be reflected in the conclusion. The premise "x may be" can never lead to the conclusion "x must be," but logicians kept trying in ingenious ways to derive a "must be" from a "may be." *if there is prime motion*: Prime motion would be uncaused motion. The learned question here would be whether or not such motion can exist. *semicircle . . . non-right angle*: Euclid demonstrated that any triangle whose base is the diameter of a circle and whose apex is on the circumference of that circle must be a right triangle. Medieval mathematicians, however, tried to theorize a non-right triangle to these specifications.

Hence, all these examples are of the wisdom required for playing abstract and learned games, as opposed to the wisdom Solomon sought in order to deal justly with God's people.

Earlier in his life, Dante himself had sometimes been drawn to metaphysical hair-splitting. Here he is renouncing all such, as he had earlier renounced his overreliance on natural philosophy, in order to seek the greater truths of faith.

103-108. The reference here is, once again, to X, 109-114: "No mortal ever rose to equal this one." Aquinas is explaining that the "arrow of his intention" was sighted only upon the qualities of royal prudence. It was in that order of wisdom (and not, for example, in metaphysical speculation) that Solomon was unequaled.

And that specific intent, Aquinas adds, Dante may see for himself if he will recall that Aquinas had said "rose" to equal. That usage could apply only to kings, one gathers, since only kings may be said to "rise" above the masses of mankind. In another sense, neither Christ-the-man and Adam, being direct creations, could have "risen."

Such fine-spun parsing of a construction that could have had several meanings may leave the modern reader uneasy and lead him to miss the point. Dante conceives these spirits as direct participants in God's omniscience and infallibility. Their every word, therefore, is exactly chosen and must be studied meticulously.

It is not their words that lack clarity but Dante's understanding that lacks vision. Their very use of language, for that matter, is a concession to Dante, akin to their willingness to manifest themselves to him, not as they ultimately are, but in the closest approximation that Dante can grasp. Since their knowledge is a direct ray from God, their understanding is reflected from one to the other, through God, with no need of words.

1-11. *our first father*: Adam. *our Best Delight*: Christ.

112 ff. AQUINAS REPROACHES DANTE. Dante had jumped to a conclusion. Because he failed to understand what Aquinas had said, he concluded that Aquinas had contradicted the truth in speaking of Solomon. Now that the contradiction has been resolved, Aquinas warns him not to be in a hurry to decide "yes" or "no" in matters that surpass his understanding.

117. *on which road*: Whether the road of affirmation or of denial.

123. *worse off*: Because they will have left their ignorance only to fall into error.

124-126. THE FOOLISH PHILOSOPHERS. All three of the philosophers here mentioned were refuted by Aristotle in the *Organon* (*Sophistici Elenchi*, I, 10) and that is probably all Dante knew of them. Parmenides taught that all things come from and return to the Sun. Melissus, a disciple of Parmenides, taught that there is no motion in the universe but only an appearance of motion. Bryson labored devotedly and at great length to square the circle.

127-129. THE HERETICAL PHILOSOPHERS. Arius, an Alexandrian priest (died in 336) taught that the Son, having been created by the Father, could not be one with Him. Sabellius advanced the Monarchian heresy that there is no real distinction between Father and Son and that the Trinity was merely a succession of modes in which a single person appears. Little is known about him except that he was probably born in Libya and that he died about 265.

139-143. *Tom and Jane*: Anyone in general. (Dante says: "*donna Berta o ser Martino*.") It is easy for people in general, observing that one man acts sinfully and another piously, to conclude that the sinful man will be damned and the pious one saved. But that could be a hasty judgment. No man should let himself believe that he can foresee another's fate with the eyes of Divine Omniscience. The pious man may fall from grace (as even Solomon turned to idolatry in his old age and risked damnation) or a thief may repent and win his seat in heaven.

# CANTO XIV

*THOMAS AQUINAS has finished speaking. Now, anticipating the wish Dante has not yet realized is his own, Beatrice begs the double circle of Philosophers and Theologians to explain to Dante the state in which the blessed will find themselves after the RESURRECTION OF THE FLESH. The radiant spirit of SOLOMON answers.*

*As Solomon finishes his discourse and the souls about him cry "Amen!" Dante becomes aware of a THIRD CIRCLE OF SOULS, higher and more radiant even than the first two. Its radiance dawns slowly and indistinctly at first, and then suddenly bursts upon him. Only then does he realize that he and Beatrice have been ascending and that he has entered the FIFTH SPHERE, MARS. The souls he had seen in the third great circle are those of the WARRIORS OF GOD. There Dante beholds, shining through the Sphere of Mars (in about the way the rays of a star sapphire shine within the stone), the VISION OF CHRIST ON THE CROSS.*

"The water in a round vessel moves about
   from center to rim if it is struck from within,
   from rim to center if it is struck from without."   3

—Such was the thought that suddenly occurred
   to my rapt mind when the immortal ray
   of Thomas had pronounced its final word,   6

occasioned by the likeness to the flow
   of his speech and my lady's, she being moved
   to speak when he had done, beginning so:   9

"There is another need this man must find
   the holy root of, though he does not speak it,
   nor know, as yet, he has the thought in mind.   12

Explain to him if the radiance he sees flower
   about your beings will remain forever
   exactly as it shines forth in this hour;   15

and if it will remain so, then explain
   how your restored eyes can endure such brilliance
   when your beings have grown visible again."   18

As dancers in a country reel flush brighter
   as they spin faster, moved by joy of joy,
   their voices higher, and all their gestures lighter—   21

so at my lady's prompt and humble plea
   the sacred circles showed yet greater joy
   in their dance and in their heavenly harmony.   24

Those who mourn, here, that we must die to gain
   the life up there, have never visualized
   that soul-refreshing and eternal rain.   27

That One and Two and Three that is eternal,
   eternally reigning in Three and Two and One,
   uncircumscribed, and circumscribing all,   30

was praised in three great paeans by each spirit
   of those two rings, and in such melody
   as would do fitting honor to any merit.         33

And I heard, then, from the most glorious ray
   of the inner circle, a voice as sweetly low
   as the angel's must have sounded to Mary, say:   36

"Long as the feast of Paradise shall be,
   so long shall our love's bliss shine forth from us
   and clothe us in these radiant robes you see.     39

Each robe reflects love's ardor shining forth;
   the ardor, the vision; the vision shines down to us
   as each is granted grace beyond his worth.     42

When our flesh, made glorious at the Judgment Seat,
   dresses us once again, then shall our persons
   become more pleasing in being more complete.   45

Thereby shall we have increase of the light
   Supreme Love grants, unearned, to make us fit
   to hold His glory ever in our sight.       48

Thereby, it follows, the vision shall increase;
   increase the ardor that the vision kindles;
   increase the ray its inner fires release.     51

But as a coal, in giving off its fire,
   outshines it by its living incandescence,
   its form remaining visible and entire;     54

so shall this radiance that wraps us round
   be outshone in appearance by the flesh
   that lies this long day through beneath the ground; 57

nor will it be overborne by so much light;
   for the organs of the body shall be strengthened
   in all that shall give increase of delight."    60

And "Amen!" cried the souls of either chain
  with such prompt zeal as to make evident
  how much they yearned to wear their flesh again;    63

perhaps less for themselves than for the love
  of mothers, fathers, and those each soul held dear
  before it became an eternal flame above.           66

And lo! all round me, equal in all its parts,
  a splendor dawned above the splendor there
  like a horizon when the new day starts.            69

And as, at the first coming on of night,
  new presences appear across the sky,
  seeming to be, and not to be, in sight;            72

so did I start to see Existences
  I had not seen before, forming a ring
  around the other two circumferences.               75

Oh sparkling essence of the Holy Ghost!
  How instantly it blazed before my eyes,
  defeating them with glory, their function lost!    78

But Beatrice let herself appear to me
  so glad in beauty, that the vision must lie
  with those whose glory outdoes memory.             81

From her I drew again the power of sight,
  and looked up, and I saw myself translated,
  with her alone, to the next estate of light.       84

I was made aware that I had risen higher
  by the enkindled ardor of the red star
  that glowed, I thought, with more than usual fire.  87

With all my heart, and in the tongue which is
  one in all men, I offered God my soul
  as a burnt offering for this new bliss.            90

Nor had the flame of sacrifice in my breast
   burned out, when a good omen let me know
   my prayer had been received by the Most Blest;   93

for with such splendor, in such a ruby glow,
   within two rays, there shone so great a glory
   I cried, "O Helios that arrays them so!"          96

As, pole to pole, the arch of the Milky Way
   so glows, pricked out by greater and lesser stars,
   that sages stare, not knowing what to say—       99

so constellated, deep within that Sphere,
   the two rays formed into the holy sign
   a circle's quadrant lines describe. And here     102

memory outruns my powers. How shall I write
   that from that cross there glowed a vision of Christ?
   What metaphor is worthy of that sight?           105

But whoso takes his cross and follows Christ
   will pardon me what I leave here unsaid
   when *he* sees that great dawn that rays forth
                         Christ.   108

From arm to arm, from root to crown of that tree,
   bright lamps were moving, crossing and rejoining.
   And when they met they glowed more brilliantly.  111

So, here on earth, across a slant of light
   that parts the air within the sheltering shade
   man's arts and crafts contrive, our mortal sight   114

observes bright particles of matter ranging
   up, down, aslant; darting or eddying;
   longer and shorter; but forever changing.         117

And as a viol and a harp in a harmony
   of many strings, make only a sweet tinkle
   to one who has not studied melody;               120

so from that choir of glories I heard swell
   so sweet a melody that I stood tranced,
   though what hymn they were singing, I
                         could not tell.     123

That it was raised in lofty praise was clear,
   for I heard "Arise" and "Conquer"—but as one
   may hear, not understanding, and still hear.     126

My soul was so enraptured by those strains
   of purest song, that nothing until then
   had bound my being to it in such sweet chains.     129

My saying so may seem too bold at best,
   since I had not yet turned to those dear eyes
   in which my every yearning found its rest.     132

But think how the living seals of every beauty
   grow stronger toward their heights, and though
                       I had not
   turned to those others yet in love and duty,     135

reason may yet dismiss the charge I bring
   against myself in order to dismiss it;
   and see the holy truth of what I sing;     138

for my sacred pleasure in those sacred eyes
can only become purer as we rise.

## Notes

1-9. Dante and Beatrice are standing in the center of a double circle of souls that forms, so to speak, a rim around them. The rim suggests to Dante the flow of ripples in a round basin filled with water. If the basin is struck from the outside, the ripples flow toward the center, growing smaller. In Dante's fancy, the sound of Thomas's voice had flowed in this way, from rim to center. Now Thomas falls still and Beatrice speaks from the center, her voice seeming to flow outward like ripples from the center to the rim.

10-18. *another need*: To know the truth of the resurrection of the flesh. Dante has not spoken this thought. He does not yet know, in fact, that it is forming in his mind, but Beatrice knows he is about to think to ask how it will be after the Day of Judgment if these souls retain their superhuman radiance after they have resumed their bodies (grown visible again). How will their restored human eyes be able to bear such radiance both within and without?

22. *prompt*: Beatrice entered her plea in Dante's behalf even before he knew it was what he wished. It hardly seems possible to be prompter.

27. *rain*: Of light.

35. *a voice*: Solomon.

36. *as the angel's must have sounded*: At the Annunciation.

40. *robe*: In which each spirit is clad.

40-42. As ever in Dante, many degrees of being exist within each category. The brilliance in which these souls are robed is in proportion to (reflects) the degree of ardor (of *caritas*) that burns in each. That intensity, in turn, reflects the intensity of each soul's beatific vision. And the vision is granted to each soul by God's grace, in proportion to the worth of the individual soul. But that grace is more than even such great souls as these can merit: it is God's gift to man beyond man's merit.

67-81. THE THIRD RING OF SOULS. There is no way of assigning an exact symbolism to this third ring of souls, though three of anything is a natural unity in Dante. The third circle appears above the other two and outshines even their glory. The third circle appears dimly and slowly at first, then bursts upon Dante's vision just as he and Beatrice soar into the next higher heaven (of Mars). The third circle is also identified as the "sparkling essence of the Holy Ghost" (line 76). It is reasonable, then, to think of the earlier two circles of Philosophers and Theologians as being identified with the Father and the Son, the law and the wisdom of the Trinity, surmounted and encompassed by its ardor. So interpreted, the shining of the third circle becomes a first view of the souls of the Sphere of Mars, the heaven of God's warriors; and the two spheres (of the Sun and of Mars) combine into a symbolism of the Trinity.

82-84. *from her*: Divine Revelation restores Dante's vision. *translated*: The ascent, despite the slow dawning of the vision of the Third Circle of Souls, is here presented as being instantaneous. *with her alone*: With Beatrice, leaving the spirits of the Fourth Heaven behind. *to the next estate*: The Fifth Heaven, the Sphere of Mars.

88-90. Dante waits for no prompting from Beatrice but offers his soul in thanks to God, offers it as wholly as if it were a burnt offering sent aloft in the consuming fire (ardor of soul) of sacrifice. *the tongue which is one in all men*: The tongue of true prayer. Men may phrase it in different languages, but its essence is always the same.

94. ff. THE VISION OF CHRIST ON THE CROSS. Embedded in the Sphere of Mars (much like the rays of a star sapphire but with a magnitude on the order of the Milky Way) a cross forms on the Heaven of Mars, and in a ruby glow (the redness of Mars and the blood of Christ's sacrifice are both indicated here), Christ himself shines forth.

96. *Helios*: Greek for "sun" and specific to Apollo. Dante is praising God for the glory in which he arrays His vision.

100. *that sphere*: Mars.

102. *a circle's quadrant lines*: A quadrant is one fourth of a circle. The lines that describe the four quadrants form a cross within a ring.

103-108. *Christ . . . Christ . . . Christ*: Dante never rhymes "Christ" with anything but itself, no word being worthy of being so paired.

109. *that tree*: The Cross.

111. *And when they met they glowed more brilliantly*: The lights Dante sees are souls. Their radiance is the flame of *caritas* within them. Whenever two or more meet there their love of one another flares the brighter.

112-117. THE FIGURE OF MOTES IN A RAY OF SUN. Having begun his figure on a galactic scale, Dante shifts to the scale of earthly particles dancing in a ray of sun that strikes across a darkened room. The shift is dramatic and the figure of motes in sunlight not only apt in itself but apt again to set the scale of the galactic vision, the souls, in their enormous dimension, being so far from Dante that they are seen as motes.

127-140. DANTE'S RAPTURE. Hitherto. Dante has found his bliss in Beatrice, and it has been to her eyes that he has turned as each new vision awed him. Here, however, he is so enraptured by the vision of the cross and by the power of the music, that he has not turned to Beatrice. He has even declared that nothing in all that has gone before has filled him with such bliss.

Shall he then be accused of ignoring Beatrice? Of neglecting her, his ardor cooled? He brings the charge against himself only that he may dismiss it. His joy in her can only become purer and more intense as they ascend to the heights of the glorious mystery.

In one allegorical sense, of course, there is the perfect beauty, beyond even Divine Revelation, of the thing revealed. The Heavenly Soul, subsumed into the body of God, becomes its own revelation. In that sense, even Beatrice must be outgrown, as Virgil was, though the comparison is questionable, the one relation being finite and the other infinite. Beatrice cannot be outgrown: she has her place in God, as Dante is aspiring to his. When she does leave him at the height of Heaven, it is to reassume her throne in God. She does not disappear but takes her place, and as Dante grows closer to God he grows closer to Beatrice. Thus, to look away from Beatrice toward God, is to turn the more closely to Beatrice.

131. *those dear eyes*: Of Beatrice.

133-135. *living seals*: The Heavens. Their influences stamp themselves, as a signet does in wax, upon the souls of men. *those others*: The eyes of Beatrice.

# CANTO XV

*The Warriors of God*
                                                        *Cacciaguida*

*THE SOULS OF THE GREAT CROSS stop their
singing in order to encourage Dante to speak, and one
among them descends to the foot of the cross like a
shooting star, glowing with joy at the sight of Dante. It
is, as Dante will discover, CACCIAGUIDA, Dante's own
great-great-grandfather.*

*Cacciaguida addresses Dante as "Blood of mine," and
though he already knows Dante's thoughts, he begs his
descendant to speak them for the joy of hearing his
voice.*

*Dante does as he is bid, and Cacciaguida, in answer
to Dante's request, identifies himself, gives an AC-
COUNT OF ANCIENT FLORENCE, and explains how
he followed CONRAD in the Crusades, BECAME A
KNIGHT, and died in battle passing from MARTYR-
DOM TO BLISS.*

Good will, in which there cannot fail to be
    the outgoing love of right (just as we find
    self-seeking love in all iniquity),                          3

stopped the sweet trembling harp, and let fall still
    the blessed viol, upon whose many strings
    the Hand of Heaven plays Its sacred will.                    6

How shall those beings not heed a righteous prayer
    when, to encourage me to speak my wish,
    they stopped with one accord, and waited there?             9

Justly they mourn in their eternal wasting
   who, in their love for what does not endure,
   stripped off the hope of this love everlasting.    12

As through the pure sky of a peaceful night
   there streaks from time to time a sudden fire,
   and eyes that had been still move at the sight,    15

as if they saw a star changing its post
   (except that none is gone from where it started,
   and blazed its little while, and soon was lost)—    18

so, in a trail of fire across the air,
   from the right arm to the foot of the great cross,
   a star streaked from the constellation there.    21

Nor did that gemstone leave its diadem.
   Like fire behind an alabaster screen,
   it crossed those radiant ranks, still one with them.    24

Just so did the shade of ancient Ilium
   (if we may trust our greatest muse) go forth
   to greet Aeneas in Elysium.    27

*"O sanguis meus, o superinfusa*
   *gratia Dei, sicut tibi, cui*
   *bis unquam coeli ianua reclusa?"*    30

So spoke that radiance as I stared wide-eyed.
   Then I turned my eyes back to my blessed lady,
   and between those two souls I stood stupefied,    33

for such a fire of love burned in her eyes
   that mine, I thought, had touched the final depth
   both of my Grace and of my Paradise.    36

Then, radiating bliss in sight and sound,
   the spirit added to his opening words
   others I could not grasp: they were too profound.    39

Nor did the spirit's words elude my mind
  by his own choice. Rather, his thoughts took place
  above the highest target of mankind.                42

And when the bow recovered from the effect
  of its own ardor, and its words arced down
  nearer the target of our intellect,                45

the first on which my straining powers could feed
  were: "Praised be Thou, O Triune Unity
  which showeth me such favor in my seed!"        48

Continuing: "The sight of you assuages
  a long dear hunger that grew within this lamp
  from which I speak, as I perused the pages      51

of the Great Book where neither black nor white
  can ever change. I give thanks to this spirit
  whose love gave you the wings for this high flight.  54

You believe that what you think rays forth to me
  from the Primal Intellect, as five and six,
  if understood, ray forth from unity.            57

And for that reason you do not inquire
  who I may be, nor why I am more joyous
  than the other spirits of this joyous choir.    60

And you are right: for here in Paradise
  greatest and least alike gaze in that Mirror
  where thoughts outsoar themselves before they rise.  63

But, that the Sacred Love in which I wake
  to the eternal vision, and which fills me
  with a sweet thirst, you may the sooner slake,  66

let your own voice, assured, frank, and elated,
  sound forth your will, sound forth your soul's desire,
  to which my answer is already fated!"            69

I turned to Beatrice and while I still
    sought words, she heard, and smiled such glad assent
    the joy of it gave wings to my glad will.        72

Thus I began: "When the First Equipoise
    shone forth to you, love and the power to speak love
    became in each of you an equal voice;        75

because the Sun that warmed and lighted you
    contains its heat and light so equally
    that though we seek analogies, none will do.        78

But mortal utterance and mortal feelings—
    for reasons that are evident to you—
    have no such equal feathers to their wings.        81

I, then, being mortal, in the perturbation
    of my unequal powers, with heart alone
    give thanks for your paternal salutation.        84

I do indeed beseech you, holy flame,
    and living topaz of this diadem,
    that you assuage my hunger to know your name."        87

"O leaf of mine, which even to foresee
    has filled me with delight, I was your root."
    —So he began in answer to my plea.        90

And then: "The first to take your present surname
    (whose soul has crawled the first round of the
                                mountain
    a century and more), he who became        93

father of your grandfather, was my son.
    You would do well, by offering up good works,
    to shorten his long striving at his stone.        96

Florence, within her ancient walls secure—
    from them she still hears *tierce* and *nones* ring
                                 down—
    lived in sweet peace, her sons sober and pure.          99

No golden chains nor crowns weighed down her spirit,
    nor women in tooled sandals and studded belts
    more to be admired than the wearer's merit.          102

A father, in those days, was not terrified
    by the birth of a daughter, for marriage and
                        marriage portion
    had not escaped all bounds on either side.          105

No mansions then stood uninhabited.
    No Sardanapalus had yet arrived
    to show what may be done in hall and bed.          108

Montemario had not yet been outshone
    by your Uccellatoio, which having passed it
    in the race up, shall pass it going down.          111

Bellincion Berti, with whom I was acquainted,
    went belted in leather and bone; and his good wife
    came from the mirror with her face unpainted.          114

I have seen the lords of Vecchio and of Nerli
    content to wear plain leather, and their wives
    working the spindle and distaff late and early.          117

Fortunate they! And blest their circumstance!
    Each sure of her own burial place; none yet
    deserted in her bed because of France.          120

One watched the cradle, babbling soft and low
    to soothe her child in the sweet idiom
    that is the first delight new parents know.          123

Another, spinning in her simple home,
   would tell old tales to children gathered round her,
   of Troy, and of Fiesole, and of Rome.       126

A Cornelia or Cincinnatus would amaze
   a modern Florentine as a Cianghella
   or a Lapo would have startled men in those days. 129

To so serene, so fair a townsman's life,
   to a citizenry so wedded in good faith,
   to such sweet dwelling, free of vice and strife,       132

Mary gave me—called in the pain of birth—
   and in your ancient Baptistry I became
   a Christian—and Cacciaguida, there on earth.       135

Moronto and Eliseo my brothers were.
   My wife came from the valley of the Po.
   The surname you now bear derives from her.       138

I served with Conrad in the Holy Land,
   and my valor so advanced me in his favor
   that I was knighted in his noble band.       141

With him I raised my sword against the might
   of the evil creed whose followers take from you—
   because your shepherds sin—what is yours by right. 144

There, by that shameless and iniquitous horde,
   I was divested of the flesh and weight
   of the deceitful world, too much adored       147

by many souls whose best hope it destroys;
and came from martyrdom to my present joys.

## Notes

4-6. Dante does not say "harp" and "viol" but "lyre" and
"strings." I take him to be referring to XIV, 117, and repeat the

phrasing of that line to reinforce the reference. In any case, it is the spirits themselves who are the instruments, and it is God's Will (the Hand of Heaven) that plays upon them. Now, however, as an act of heavenly *caritas,* they have foregone the bliss of their singing and wait silently to be the more readily at Dante's service.

7-12. Since *caritas* is the essence of Heaven, it is the joy of the blessed to hear and to grant righteous prayers. It is fitting, therefore, that the damned mourn forever, having deliberately cast from themselves, for the sake of temporal satisfactions, the everlasting love that would have received them with such eager joy.

22-24. The soul whose glory Dante sees flashing like a falling star is compared first to a gem on a ribbon or diadem, and then to a fire moving behind an alabaster screen. The soul does not leave the blessed company, but moves through it, so rapidly and so brightly that it seems to be a falling star. Dante is standing at the foot of the great cross. Thus, the spirit approaches him from within it, remaining inside the cross, but at the point closest to Dante.

25-27. *Ancient Ilium:* Anchises, i.e., "the ancient king of Ilum." Aeneid, VI, 684 ff., narrates the meeting of Anchises and Aeneas in the Elysian Fields. *Muse:* For "poet." Virgil.

28-30. "O blood of mine! O ever abundant grace of God poured over you! To whom was the gate of Heaven ever thrown open twice, as it is to you?" *twice:* Now, while Dante is still in the flesh, and again after his death. St. Paul was borne up in a dream to the Third Heaven, but Dante has come in the flesh. The speaker is Cacciaguida (cah-cha-GWEE-da), Dante's great-great-grandfather. The details of Cacciaguida's life are best presented piecemeal, in the notes to the conversation that follows. Note, however, that Cacciaguida lived in the middle and later twelfth century when the spoken language was still basically Latin. The reference to Virgil and to the *Aeneid* makes it doubly felicitous that he begin his remarks in Latin.

31-36. Dante is astonished by the fact that this new soul addresses him as "Blood of mine!" He turns to Beatrice (Revelation) and sees her eyes light with such bliss that he believes he has experienced the final joy of Heaven. Beatrice, of course, is radiant with her foreknowledge of Dante's pleasure when he learns the identity of the new soul.

37-39. *in sight and sound:* By the sight of his radiance and by the quality of his voice. *added to his opening words:* some commentators have taken this phrasing to signify that Cacciaguida continued in Latin. He may have done so but that can hardly be Dante's point, for Latin would have posed no problem of understanding. There is, rather, a much richer point to be made. Cacciaguida left the earth about a century before this meeting. His long absorption into the Divine Intellect has given him infinite insights and has made natural to him modes of thought beyond mortal understanding. He must learn, therefore, to adjust his speech to Dante's understanding, and he begins by overshooting it.

What he has been absorbed into is, of course, omniscience, and omniscience, one might argue logically enough, would have no need to learn by trial and error. Yet, as a touch of characterization, his first inability to speak on Dante's level is masterful.

42. *target*: Not only does his thought exist at a higher level than any arrow of human thought could reach, but higher even than man could think of placing the target.

48. *seed*: Line of descent.

52. *the Great Book*: Of fate. *black nor white*: To alter the black would be to change what is written. To alter the white would be to add to or subtract from what is written. If neither can be changed, no least change is possible.

53. *this spirit*: Beatrice.

55. Dante is asserting, as a principle of mathematics, that all numbers (Five or Six, for example) derive from One. So all knowledge derives from the Primal Thought, which is unity.

62. *the greatest and least alike*: All souls in Paradise brim full of the most bliss they can achieve or conceive, and all are united in the body of God. Yet, as everywhere in Dante, degrees of difference are meticulously observed. Perhaps this state of things will seem contradictory to human reason, but we are here dealing with revelation. And certainly one can accept the premise that God's grace, while giving to each its fill, gives one soul a greater capacity than another.

63. *where thoughts outsoar themselves before they rise*: I have had to yield to a rhyme-forced metaphor. Dante's text, rendered literally, would read: "In which, before you think it, your thought outspreads itself."

64-69. Cacciaguida knows Dante's wish and what the answer will be, but has a sweet thirst to hear Dante's voice: an understandable grandfatherly sentiment.

73-87. DANTE'S REPLY TO CACCIAGUIDA. Cacciaguida has

asked that Dante speak in his "own voice, assured, frank, and elated." In one sense, then, he has asked the poet Dante to rejoice Heaven with the power of poetry. Dante replies with a passage so superbly balanced that the temptation to cite it as an example of Dante's highest style is counterbalanced only by the fact that he achieves such heights so regularly.

*The First Equipoise*: God, in whom all attributes co-exist equally, as light and heat co-exist in the sun. When the spirits of the Blessed are subsumed into the body of God, they, too, share this fullness of equal powers. Thus, their feelings of love and their ability to express those feelings are equal to one another in their fullness. Mortal man's powers of feeling, on the other hand, outrun his powers of utterance. In the perturbation of his unequal powers, therefore, Dante can give thanks only with his heart. Thus, hearing Cacciaguida address him as *"sanguis meus"* (his "paternal salutation") he is more deeply moved than he has power to express.

88-89. *"O leaf of mine . . . I was your root"*: Dante seems not to have known his lineage prior to Cacciaguida, who here describes himself as the root of the family tree of which Dante is the present leaf. The metaphoric tree can foresee little continuity from a leaf, and certainly "branch of mine" might have promised more for the future. In "leaf," Dante may have meant to express his transcience and smallness as compared to Cacciaguida's eternal glory. *foresee*: Dante uses *"aspettando"* (awaiting). But since Heavenly souls can foresee what they wait for—and rhyme demanding—I have thought this rendering reasonable.

91-96. *present surname*: The surname Alighieri (then Aldighiero) is thus identified as having originated with Cacciaguida's son. The name occurs in a Florentine document of 1189. This Aldighiero (father of Bellincione, who fathered Dante's father) was still alive in 1201 though his date of death is not known. "A century and more," therefore, is a bit too long. *first round of the mountain*: Of Purgatory. The ledge of the Proud. Pride may have been a hereditary failing of the Alighieri, or Dante may be further recognizing his own weakness. (Cf. *Purgatorio*, XIII, 133-138.)

97. *her ancient walls*: The original Roman walls. In 1173 a new ring of walls was completed, and others were added in 1284.

98. *from them . . . tierce and nones*: The church called La Badia was built on the old Roman walls. This church rang all the canonical hours (including *tierce* and *nones*).

103-105. In Dante's time, Florentine girls were married in

childhood, before they were ten in some cases, and with such enormous dowries that it was said a man with one daughter was impoverished and a man with two ruined. *on either side*: The marriage custom escaped all bounds of moderation, on one side because the girls were too young, and on the other because the dowry demands were too great.

106. *no mansions then stood uninhabited*: Mansions might be empty because wealthy Florentines kept great suites and halls for ostentatious display, rather than to live in; or because dissolute living had destroyed ancestral fortunes and hereditary palaces had to be closed for lack of maintenance; or because the owners (like Dante) had been forced into exile. Dante probably intends all of these reasons, for all are part of the degeneracy he has Cacciaguida lament.

107-108. *Sardanapalus*: King of Assyria from 667 to 626 B.C. He is cited as the type of the luxurious and libertine debauché of the harem. *in hall and bed*: i.e., "indoors" (by way of debauchery and of riotously expensive display).

109-111. *Montemario*: (Mon-teh-MAHR-i-o): A hill with a commanding view of Rome. *Uccellatoio* (Oo-tchell-ah-TOY-oh): A hill with a similar view of Florence. The splendor of the view from the Uccellatoio had not yet outdone the view from Montemario, but just as Florence is rising faster than Rome, so will she plunge to ruin faster.

112-113. *Bellincion Berti*: A nobleman of some importance, honorary citizen of Florence, and father of "the good Gualdrada" (see *Inferno*, XVI, 38, note). *belted in leather and bone*: i.e., simply—a leather belt with a bone clasp rather than ornamented stuff with a jeweled clasp.

115. *Vecchio* (VEH-kyo): *Nerli* (NEHR-lee): Both were Guelf lords of Cacciaguida's time and leading citizens of Florence.

119. *sure of her own burial place*: As Dante was not, having been exiled. As, by implication, few later Florentines could be, since any of them might find himself banished.

120. *because of France*: In both of two possible senses. Florentine bankers and merchants often traveled to France, hence they were often out of town. But in France, too, they learned vices for which they abandoned their wives even when they were back in Florence.

122. *the sweet idiom*: Baby talk.

127-129. Dante is contrasting a man and woman of decayed

Florence to a man and woman of republican Rome. *Cornelia*: Daughter of Scipio Africanus and mother of the Roman paragons, the Gracchii. Dante saw her in Limbo (*Inferno*, IV, 128). *Cincinnatus*: See VI, 46-48, note. *Cianghella*: (Chan-GHELL-ah) A Florentine woman married to a lord of Imola. She died about 1330, having acquired a reputation for a sharp tongue, a haughty extravagance, and an easy bed. *Lapo*: Lapo Saltorello. A Florentine poet and lawyer noted for his extravagant living. He and Dante were banished in the same decree of March 10, 1302.

133-134. *Mary . . . called in the pain of birth*: Sense: Cacciaguida's mother, in the throes of her birth pains, cried out a plea to the Virgin Mary, who thereupon granted him life and sweet dwelling in ancient Florence. *Baptistry*: Of San Giovanni. See *Inferno*, XIX, 17-18, and note.

136-138. There is no historic record of any of the persons here mentioned.

139. *Conrad*: Dante says "the Emperor Conrad." (Conrad III, reigned 1137-1152.) He went crusading in 1147 and was defeated at Damascus. He never visited Florence, however, whereas Conrad II (reigned 1024-1039) knew Florence well. Conrad II crusaded against the Saracens in Calabria. Dante has probably run the two Conrads into one.

143-144. *the evil creed*: Islam. *because your shepherds sin*: See *Inferno*, XXVII, 82 ff. Because of bad popes (such as Boniface VIII) the Holy Land, which Dante held to be rightfully Christian, was left to Islam. In Dante's view, a proper pope would have called for a crusade and hacked it free of unGodly hands.

149. *from martyrdom to my present joys*: To call a death in battle a "martyrdom" may be stretching the meaning of the word. In any case, Cacciaguida, having died fighting for the faith—for God—seems to have mounted directly to his place in Heaven. (Cf. the Islamic belief that true believers who die in battle mount instantly to heavenly bliss.)

# CANTO XVI

---

*The Warriors of God: Cacciaguida*

*DANTE THRILLS WITH PLEASURE on learning that his ancestor had been elevated to knighthood, and feeling the power of pride of ancestry even in Heaven, in which there is no temptation to evil, he has a new insight into the family pride in which mortals glory. Moved by pride, Dante addresses Cacciaguida with the formal "voi," an affectation at which Beatrice, half amused, admonishes him with a smile.*

*Dante then asks Cacciaguida for details of his birth and ancestry and of THE HISTORY OF EARLY FLORENCE. Cacciaguida, as if to warn Dante away from pride of ancestry, dismisses the question of his birth and of his forebears as a matter best passed over in silence, and proceeds to a detailed account of the lords and people of Florence in the days when her bloodlines and traditions had not been diluted by the arrival of new families. It is to this "mongrelization" of the Florentines that Cacciaguida attributes all the subsequent degeneracy of Florence.*

O trivial pride of ours in noble blood!
   that in possessing you men are possessed,
   down here, where souls grow sick and lose

                         their good,   3

will never again amaze me, for there, too,
   where appetite is never drawn to evil—
   in Heaven, I say—my own soul gloried in you!   6

You are a mantle that soon shrinks and tears.
    Unless new cloth is added day by day,
    time will go round you, snipping with its shears!    9

I spoke again, addressing him with that "*voi*"
    whose usage first began among the Romans—
    and which their own descendants least employ—    12

at which my Lady, who stood apart, though near,
    and smiling, seemed to me like her who coughed
    at the first recorded fault of Guinevere.    15

"You are my father," I started in reply.
    "You give me confidence to speak out boldly.
    You so uplift me, I am more than I.    18

So many streams of happiness flow down
    into my mind that it grows self-delighting
    at being able to bear it and not drown.    21

Tell me, then, dear source of my own blood,
    who were your own forefathers? when were you born?
    and what transpired in Florence in your boyhood?    24

Tell me of St. John's sheepfold in those days.
    How many souls were then within the flock,
    and which of them was worthy of high place?"    27

As glowing coals fanned by a breath of air
    burst into flames, so did I see that light
    increase its radiance when it heard my prayer.    30

And as its light gave off a livelier ray,
    so, in a sweeter and a softer voice—
    though not in the idiom we use today—    33

it said: "From the day when *Ave* sounded forth
    to that in which my mother, now a saint,
    being heavy laden with me, gave me birth,    36

this flame had come back to its Leo again
  to kindle itself anew beneath his paws
  five hundred times plus fifty plus twenty plus ten.   39

My ancestors and I were born in the place
  where the last quarter of the course begins
  for those who take part in your annual race.   42

Of my fathers, be content with what you have heard.
  Of who they were and whence they came to Florence
  silence is far more fitting than any word.   45

Of men who could bear arms there were counted then,
  between Mars and the Baptist, the fifth part
  of what may be mustered there from living men.   48

But the citizenry, now mongrelized by the blood
  of Campi, of Certaldo, and of Figghine,
  was pure then, down to the humblest
                                      planer of wood.   51

Oh how much better to have been neighbors of these
  of whom I speak, and to have Trespiano
  and Galuzzo still fixed as your boundaries,   54

than to have swallowed them and to bear the stink
  of the yokel of Aguglione, and of Signa's boor
  who still has eyes to swindle and hoodwink.   57

Had the world's most despicable crew not shown
  a hard stepmother's face and greed to Caesar
  but been a loving mother, one who is known   60

as a Florentine, and who trades in goods and debt,
  would be back in Simifonti, where his grandsire
  once gypsied in the streets for what he could get.   63

Montemurlo would still be owned by its own counts,
 the Cerchi would be in the parish of Acone,
 and in Valdigreve, still, the Bondelmounts.          66

It has always been a fact that confusion of blood
 has been a source of evil to city-states,
 just as our bodies are harmed by too much food;    69

and that a bull gone blind will fall before
 a blind lamb does. And that one sword may cut
 better than five has been proved in many a war.    72

If you will think of Luni and Urbisaglia,
 how they have passed away, and how, behind them,
 are dying now Chiusi and Sinigaglia,               75

it should not be too hard to comprehend,
 or strange to hear, that families dwindle out,
 when even cities come at last to an end.           78

All mankind's institutions, of every sort,
 have their own death, though in what long endures
 it is hidden from you, your own lives being short. 81

And as the circling of the lunar sphere
 covers and bares the shore with never a pause,
 so Fortune alters Florence year by year.           84

It should not, therefore, seem too wondrous strange
 to hear me speak of the good Florentines
 whose fame is veiled behind time's endless change. 87

I knew the Ughi, the Catellini, the line
 of the Greci, Filippi, Ormanni, and Alberichi—
 illustrious citizens, even in decline.             90

I knew those of Sannella, and those of the Bow,
 and the Soldanieri, Ardinghi, and Bostichi;
 as grand as they were ancient, there below.        93

Not far from the portal that now bears the weight
   of such a cargo of new iniquity
   as soon, now, will destroy the ship of state,    96

once lived the Ravignani, from whom came
   Count Guido Guerra, and whoever else
   has since borne Bellincione's noble name.    99

The della Pressa were already furnished
   with knowledge of how to rule, and Galigaio
   had his gold hilt and pommel already burnished.    102

Great already were the lands of the vair,
   Sacchetti, Giuochi, Fifanti, Barucci, and Galli,
   and of those who blush now for the stave affair.    105

The trunk that bore the many-branched Calfucci
   had grown already great; already called
   to the curule were Sizii and Arrigucci.    108

How great I have seen them who are now undone
   by their own pride! And even the balls of gold—
   in all great deeds of Florence, how they shone!    111

So shone the fathers of that gang we see
   in the bishop's palace when your See falls vacant,
   fattening themselves as a consistory.    114

That overweening and presumptuous tribe—
   a dragon to all who run from it, a lamb
   to any who stand and show a tooth or bribe—    117

were coming up, though still so parvenu
   Donato was hardly pleased when his father-in-law
   made him a relative of such a crew.    120

The Caponsacchi had come down by then
   from Fiesole to market; the Infangati
   and Giudi were established as good townsmen.    123

And here's an astonishing fact, though little known:
  in ancient times a gate of the inner wall
  was named for those of the Pera, now all gone.   126

All those whose various quarterings display
  the staves of the great baron whose name and worth
  are kept alive every St. Thomas' Day   129

owe him the rank and privilege they enjoy,
  though one who binds those arms with a gold fringe
  makes common cause today with the hoi polloi.   132

Gualterotti and Importuni were then well known.
  And Borgo would still be a peaceful place
  had it not acquired new neighbors from
                              Montebuon'.   135

The line from which was born your grief and strife
  because of the righteous anger that ruined you,
  and put an end to all your happier life,   138

was honored in itself and its allies.
  O Buondelmonti, what ill you did in fleeing
  its nuptials to find comfort in other ties!   141

Many would still be happy whom we now pity,
  had God seen fit to let the Ema drown you
  on the first day you started for the city.   144

But it was fitting that to the broken stone
  that guards the bridge, Florence should offer a victim
  to mark the last day's peace she has ever known.   147

With such as these, and others, my first life's years
  saw Florence live and prosper in such peace
  that she had, then, no reason to shed tears.   150

With such as these I saw there in my past
  so valiant and so just a populace
    that none had ever seized the ensign's mast    153

and hung the lily on it upside down.
Nor was the red dye of division known."

## Notes

1. *in noble blood*: Pride of birth into a family with patents of nobility.

6. *my own soul gloried in you*: On hearing that Cacciaguida had been knighted by (whichever) Conrad. The point is curiously made. Despite the statements of many of Dante's commentators, who were probably working backward from Dante's own claim rather than from any historical record, there is no recorded evidence either that Cacciaguida had been knighted, or even that he had served in the crusades. Dante may be following a family legend, or he may be inventing his own claim to nobility, the latter an oddly uncelestial act of pride. Dante, in any case, hastens to disclaim any real merit in the possession of noble ancestry unless the descendants labor to maintain the family's true nobility of soul.

10-12. *voi*: The second person plural. It seems to have come into use as the deferential form of address to a single person in about the third century A.D., but Dante is following the popular belief of his time that it was first used in addressing Caesar when he assumed all the high offices of the Republic and so became, in effect, many personages in one. English does not distinguish between "*tu*" (you-singular) and "*voi*" (you-plural) except perhaps in the dialect of the southern states where "you" (singular) and "you-all" (plural) is standard. *least employ*: The modern Romans, always a mannerless lot, made the least use of this polite or deferential form. The "you" that begins each of the three sentences in lines 16-18 is this "*voi*."

13-15. Beatrice notes Dante's foible in using the "*voi*" form and admonishes him with a half-amused smile that reminds him of the wife of Mallehaut (see *Inferno*, V, 124-134, and notes) who coughed when she first saw Guinevere with Launcelot.

25. *St. John's sheepfold*: Florence. John the Baptist was its patron saint.

34. *Ave*: Hail. The first word spoken to Mary by the Angel of the Annunciation.

37-39. *this flame*: Mars. *its Leo*: Astrologers asserted various special connections between Mars and Leo. Both were classified as "hot and dry." And Leo is the constellation of the Lion, the warlike and heraldic beast perhaps closest to the god of war.

39. THE DATE OF CACCIAGUIDA'S BIRTH. The Annunciation took place on March 25. Scartazzini cites a text of Dante's time that sets the Martian year at 686.94 days. That figure multiplied by 580 and divided by the 365.2466 days of the earth year (as Scartazzini asserts, my mathematics floundering in his wake) yields as a birthdate January 25, 1091. Even Scartazzini does not complicate his computations by entering a correction for various calendar reforms. In any case, Cacciaguida is thought to have died when he was about 56.

40-42. The annual race was run in Florence on June 24, the Feast of St. John. "Quarter" here signifies "quarter of a town," as in "Latin Quarter." Scholars disagree as to the course of the race and the exact quarter Dante had in mind. Porta San Piero is generally favored by the commentators.

43. *Of my fathers*: This much in answer to Dante's first question, and also as a rebuke to Dante for his pride of ancestry, but note, too, that this answer covers Dante's own ignorance of his remoter ancestry.

47. *between Mars and the Baptist*: To be between Mars and the Baptist signifies, in effect, to be in Florence, the statue of Mars on the Ponte Vecchio and the Baptistry of St. John marking two of the limits of Florence in Cacciaguida's time. In 1300 Florence had a population of about 70,000, of which (according to a doubtful estimate by Scartazzini) about 30,000 were able to bear arms.

50. *of Campi, of Certaldo* (tchehr-TAHL-doh) *and of Figghine* (fee-GHEE-neh): All are nearby places a self-righteous Florentine would think of as the backwoods. Florence was on the main highway of invasion from the north. Inevitably, therefore, many tribal strains were joined in its people. Dante is seldom temperate in his views of outsiders.

52-57. *those of whom I speak*: In line 50. *Trespiano*: A crossroads village now at the edge of Florence, but in Cacciaguida's time an hour's walk away on the road to Bologna. *Galuzzo*: A village at about the same distance on the road to Siena. *the yokel of Aguglione* (ah-goo-LYOW-neh): Baldo

d'Aguglione. His family name traces to a "backwoods" castle in
Val di Pesa, but he became a power in Florence. He was probably involved in the swindles Dante cites in *Purgatorio*, XII,
100-105. On September 3, 1311 he issued a decree recalling a
number of Florentine exiles but left Dante's name off the list,
whereby, of course, he put himself on Dante's list to be
registered as a stink in Heaven. *Signa's boor*: Fazio dei
Morubaldini of Signa (SEE-nyah), a hamlet near Florence.
Fazio was a lawyer of Dante's time with a considerable reputation as a grafter, swindler, and barrator.

58-59. *crew*: The clergy. *Caesar*: Here as a symbol of temporal
government. Sense: Had the church been a loving mother in
temporal affairs.

60. *one who is known*: Dante may have had a specific person
in mind but many Florentines, old-line and parvenu, traded as
merchants and pawnbrokers. Dante seems to charge all such evil
commerce to the influx of new families that resulted from the
political scheming of the church.

62. *Simifonti*: A castle and town in Valdessa captured by
Florence in 1202.

64. *Montemurlo*: A castle between Pistoia and Prata. It
formerly belonged to the counts Guidi (see *Inferno*, XXX, 76-
77). In 1254, unable to defend the castle against the Pistoians,
the counts sold it to Florence.

65. *the Cerchi* (TCHEHR-kee); *Acone* (ah-CON-eh): is in
Val di Sieve. In Dante's time, the Cerchi had become leaders
of the White Party in Dante's own soi-disant ancestral quarter
of Porta San Piero.

66. *Valdigreve*: South of Florence where the Buondelmonti
had a castle called Montebuoni. In 1135 the castle was taken
from them by the Florentines and they were forced to move into
Florence, where they became powerful in Borgo Sant' Apostolo.

67. *confusion of blood*: The admixture of new blood lines to
those of an old established population.

73-75. Cacciaguida is citing examples of dead or enfeebled
cities; the first two are already dead, the second two are dying.
*Luni*: An ancient city on the Magra at the northern boundary
of Tuscany, already a ruin in Dante's time. *Urbisaglia* (oor-bee-
SAH-lyah): In the March of Ancona; not quite dead in Dante's
time. *Chiusi* (KYOO-zee): Ancient Clusium. In Val di Chiana.
*Sinigaglia* (see-nee-GAH-lyah): On the coast north of Ancona.
Both were ravaged by malaria in Dante's time, but both have
survived their prophesied extinction.

84. *so Fortune alters Florence*: Now raising her on the flood, now letting her down on the ebb. Fortune, of course, is Dame Fortune.

88-90. *Ughi* (OO-ghee), *etc.*: Cacciaguida lists six solid old families of the first half of the eleventh century and says they were illustrious even in their decline. In 1300 these families had finished declining and were extinct, at least as influential voices in Florentine affairs.

91. *those of the Bow*: The family dell' Arca. They and the other four families here cited were numerous and powerful in Cacciaguida's time, In Dante's time the dell' Arca clan was extinct; the Soldanieri, a Ghibelline clan, still existed but had been banished; and the descendants of the other three clans had lost power and social standing.

94. *the portal*: Of San Piero, where the Cerchi ruled in Dante's time (see line 65) showing the destruction of Florence.

97-99. *Ravignani . . . Count Guido Guerra . . . Bellincione*: Bellincione (bell-een-TCHOE-neh) Berti dei Ravignani (rah-vee-NYAH-nee) was praised in XV, 112-114. Count Guido Guerra VI was praised in *Inferno*, XVI, 37-39, though he is damned among the sodomites. He was a great grandson of Bellincione, who was the father of the Good Gualdrada. Through another daughter, his name descended to many members of the Adimari family (see Filippo Argenti, *Inferno*, VIII, 32, note, and note to line 119 below).

100. *della Pressa*: An emergent family (in Cacciaguida's time) who had been elected to govern some of the nearby territories of Florence. Their descendants were charged with betraying the Florentines at Montaperti (for which see *Inferno*, X, 86, and note to 32-51).

101. *Galigaio* (gal-ee-GUY-oh): A noble family of Porta San Piero, here said to have been already of the knighthood ("gold hilt and pommel") in Cacciaguida's time, but reduced to the rank and file by 1300.

103. *vair*: A fur, usually of a small squirrel. Represented in heraldry by rows of little bells. It appeared on the arms of the Pigli (PEE-lyee), a family of Porta San Pancrazio.

104. A continuation of the early eleventh-century Florentine social register.

105. *those who blush now for the stave affair*: The Chiaramontesi of Porta San Piero. See *Purgatorio*, XII, 100-105, note.

106. *Calfucci* (kahl-FOO-tchee): Were collateral with the Donati. Dante's wife, Gemma, was a Donati.

108. *the curule*: A chair in which only the highest officers of Rome might sit. Here used to indicate highest rank. *Sizii* (see-TZEE-yee) *and Arrigucci* (ah-ree-GOO-tchee): Neither family was extinct by Dante's time, but the first was nearly so, and the second much reduced.

110. *balls of gold*: From the arms of the Lamberti. Mosca, one of this line, is in the Bolgia of the Sowers of Discord (*Inferno*, XXVIII, 106, and note).

112. *so shone the fathers of that gang we see*: As the Lamberti once shone in every great deed of Florence so shone (in evil deeds) the Visdomini and the Tosinghi, hereditary patrons and defenders of the episcopal see and palace. Whenever the see fell vacant, they were in charge of episcopal affairs until a new bishop was elected. Dante here accuses them of forming themselves into a private consistory in order to fatten themselves on the resources of the see.

115. *That . . . tribe*: The Adimari. Dante had special reasons for disliking them. When Dante was banished, Boccaccio Adimari took over his forfeited estates and resisted every effort to rescind the decree of banishment.

119. *Donato . . . his father-in-law*: Bellincione married the good Gualdrada to Umbertino Donati of the family of the Counts Guidi. He then married another daughter to the upstart Adimari, thus relating the two families. The Donati refused to acknowledge kinship.

121-123. *Caponsacchi . . . Giudi . . . Infangati*: Three Ghibelline families, once well established, but much diminished by Dante's time. Is it only coincidence that these three names mean, at root, Head-in-a-sack, Judases (or Jews), and Covered-with-mud? Could Dante be suggesting that these Johnny-come-latelies were as outlandish as their names in comparison with the old line Florentines?

125. *the inner wall*: The first (Roman) wall of the city. Cacciaguida is saying that Dante would know the long-vanished della Pera family was an ancient one, but not that it traced back to the very founding of Florence.

127-132. Hugh of Brandenburg, known in Italy as Ugo il Grande, marchese di Toscano, was the Imperial Vicar of Tuscany. Thus he was the voice of Imperial authority and order (see note to *Purgatorio*, VI, 100) and Tuscany's chief Ghibelline.

His arms bore seven staves, which are variously reproduced in the arms of "all those" families he raised to knighthood and fortune (among them the Giandotti, Pulci, della Bella, and Neri). He died on St. Thomas' Day, 1006, and it is still part of the festival of St. Thomas to offer solemn prayers to Ugo in the Abbey he built in Florence. *though one who binds those arms*: Giano (DJAH-no) della Bella. He was exiled in 1295 and was no longer making common cause with the hoi polloi. But Dante, though he had to become a Guelf once there were no more Ghibellines in Florence, still has his only political hope in the party of the Emperor and will not miss a chance to condemn the great Ghibelline families that identified themselves with the cause of vulgar independence.

133. *Gualterotti and Importuni*: Guelf families of Borgo Santo Apostolo, great in Cacciaguida's time, but common workingmen in Dante's.

136. *new neighbors from Montebuon'*: The Buondelmonti. Cacciaguida goes on to describe the grief and disorder they brought to Florence. Their houses were next to those of the Gualterotti and Importuni.

136-138. *The line*: Of the Amidei. A great family related to the Lamberti and allied to many noble families of Florence. Despite the fact that it was of much higher rank, it betrothed one of its daughters to Buondelmonte dei Buondelmonti, who broke off the nuptials in order to marry a daughter of the Donati. The Amidei, in "righteous anger" at this affront by a man of lower rank, held a council of war. It was at this council that Mosca dei Lamberti (*Inferno*, XXVIII, 106, and note) declared, "A thing done has an end." As a result Buondelmonti was murdered at the foot of the statue of Mars in 1215. As a result of that murder Florence, previously united, became divided into Guelf and Ghibelline factions, and was plunged into civil war, thereby ending its "happier life."

143. *the Ema*: A river bounding the lands from which the Buondelmonti were dispossessed before they came to Florence.

145-147. *the broken stone*: The mutilated statue of Mars. It is fitting, says Cacciaguida in bitter irony, that Florence should mark its return to the rule of Mars by offering up the blood of a victim at the foot of the mutilated statue of its first pagan patron.

153-154. Cacciaguida means that the Florentines had never been defeated in war. It was a custom to mock the vanquished by flying their captured flags upside down on the mast. The lily was, of course, the emblem of France.

155. The ancient standard of Florence bore a white lily on a red field. In 1251 the Guelfs changed their standard to a red lily on a white field, the Ghibellines preserving the original. Thus there were two Florentine standards and division had dyed the lily red. The "red dye," of course, is also the blood spilled in war.

# CANTO XVII

*The Warriors of God: Cacciaguida*

*BEATRICE AND CACCIAGUIDA already know
what question is burning in Dante's mind, but Beatrice
nevertheless urges him to speak it, that by practicing
Heavenly discourse he be better able to speak to men
when he returns to Earth. So urged, Dante asks
Cacciaguida to make clear the recurring DARK PROPH-
ECIES OF DANTE'S FUTURE.*

*Cacciaguida details DANTE'S COMING BANISH-
MENT FROM FLORENCE, identifies the patrons
Dante will find, and assures Dante of his future fame.
He warns Dante not to become bitter in adversity, assuring him that the Divine Comedy, once it becomes
known, will outlive the proudest of the Florentines and
bring shame to their evil memories for ages to come.*

Like him who went to Clymene to learn
   if what he had heard was true, and who makes fathers
   unwilling to yield to their sons at every turn—   3

such was I, and such was I taken to be
   by Beatrice and by the holy lamp
   that, earlier, had changed its place for me.   6

Therefore my lady: "Speak. And let the fire
   of your consuming wish come forth," she said,
   "well marked by the inner stamp of your desire;   9

not that we learn more by what you say,
  but that you better learn to speak your thirst,
  that men may sooner quench it on your way."          12

"Dear root of my existence, you who soar
  so high that, as men grasp how a triangle
  may contain one obtuse angle and no more,          15

you grasp contingent things before they find
  essential being, for you can see that focus
  where all time is time-present in God's mind.          18

While I was yet with Virgil, there below,
  climbing the mountain where the soul is healed,
  and sinking through the dead world of its woe,          21

dark words of some dark future circumstance
  were said to me; whereby my soul is set
  four-square against the hammering of chance:          24

and, therefore, my desire will be content
  with knowing what misfortune is approaching;
  for the arrow we see coming is half spent."          27

—Such were the words of my reply, addressed
  to the light that had spoken earlier; and with them
  as Beatrice wished, my own wish was confessed.          30

Not in dark oracles like those that glued
  the foolish like limed birds, before the Lamb
  that takes our sins away suffered the rood;          33

but in clear words and the punctilious style
  of ordered thought, that father-love replied,
  concealed in and revealed by his own smile:          36

"*Contingency*, whose action is confined
  to the few pages of the world of matter,
  is fully drawn in the Eternal Mind;          39

but it no more derives *necessity*
  from being so drawn, than a ship dropping
                          down river
  derives its motion from a watcher's eye.                    42

As a sweet organ-harmony strikes the ear,
  so, from the Primal Mind, my eyes receive
  a vision of your future drawing near.                       45

As Hippolytus left Athens, forced to roam
  by his two-faced and merciless stepmother,
  just so shall you leave Florence, friends, and home. 48

So is it willed, so does it already unfold,
  so will it soon be done by him who plots it
  there where Christ is daily bought and sold.                 51

The public cry, as usual, will blame you
  of the offended party, but the vengeance
  truth will demand will yet show what is true.                54

All that you held most dear you will put by
  and leave behind you; and this is the arrow
  the longbow of your exile first lets fly.                    57

You will come to learn how bitter as salt and stone
  is the bread of others, how hard the way that goes
  up and down stairs that never are your own.                  60

And what will press down on your shoulders most
  will be the foul and foolish company
  you will fall into on that barren coast.                     63

Ingrate and godless, mad in heart and head
  will they become against you, but soon thereafter
  it will be they, not you, whose cheeks turn red.             66

Their bestiality will be made known
  by what they do; while your fame shines the brighter
  for having become a party of your own.                    69

Your first inn and first refuge you shall owe
  to the great Lombard whose escutcheon bears
  the sacred bird above, the ladder below.                   72

In such regard and honor shall he hold you,
  that in the act of granting and requesting,
  what others do late, shall be first between you two.   75
With him you will see another, born of this star
  and so stamped by the iron of its virtues

  that he shall be renowned for deeds of war.             78

The world has not yet noticed him: these spheres
  in their eternal course above his youth
  have turned about him now only nine years.            81

Before the Gascon sets his low intrigue
  to snare high Henry, men will start to speak
  of his disregard of money and fatigue.                     84

The knowledge of his magnanimities
  will spread so far that men will hear of it
  out of the mouths of his very enemies.                     87

Look you to him and his great works. The fate
  of many shall be altered by his deeds,
  the rich and poor exchanging their estate.              90

And write this in your mind but remain silent
  concerning it . . ."—and he said things about him
  to astonish even those who shall be present.          93

Then added: "Son, these are the annotations
  to what was told you. These are the snares that hide
  behind a few turns of the constellations.                  96

But do not hate your neighbors: your future stretches
   far beyond the reach of what they do
   and far beyond the punishment of wretches."          99

—When, by his silence, that blessed soul made clear
   that he had finished passing his dark shuttle
   across the threads I had combed for him there,        102

I then, as one who has not understood
   longs for the guidance of a soul that sees,
   and straightway wills, and wholly loves the good:      105

"Father, I do indeed see time's attacks
   hard spurred against me to strike such a blow
   as shall fall most on him who is most lax.             108

And it is well I arm myself with foresight.
   Thus, if the dearest place is taken from me,
   I shall not lose all place by what I write.            111

Down through that world of endless bitter sighs,
   and on the mountain from whose flowering crown
   I was uplifted by my lady's eyes,                      114

and then through Heaven from ray to living ray,
   I have learned much that would, were it retold,
   offend the taste of many alive today.                  117

Yet if, half friend to truth, I mute my rhymes,
   I am afraid I shall not live for those
   who will think of these days as 'the ancient
                                times.' "     120

The light in which my heaven-found treasure shone
   smiled brighter in its rapture, coruscating
   like a gold mirror in a ray of sun;                    123

then answered me: "A conscience overcast
   by its own shame, or another's, may indeed
   be moved to think your words a bitter blast.   126

Nevertheless, abjure all lies, but match
   your verses to the vision in fullest truth;
   and if their hides are scabby, let them scratch!   129

For if your voice is bitter when first tested
   upon the palate, it shall yet become
   a living nutriment when it is digested.   132

This cry you raise shall strike as does the wind
   hardest at highest peaks—and this shall argue
   no little for your honor, as you will find.   135

Therefore you have been shown—here in these spheres,
   there on the mount, and in the valley of woe—
   those souls whose names most ring in mortal ears;   138

for the feelings of a listener do not mark
   examples of things unknown, nor place their trust
   in instances whose roots hide in the dark;   141

nor will men be persuaded to give ear
   to arguments whose force is not made clear."

## Notes

1-3. *him who went to Clymene*: Phaeton, son of Clymene and
Apollo. Epaphus had told him Apollo was not his father and the
boy had run to his mother to be reassured. Phaeton makes all
fathers chary of yielding too readily to their sons by his example
in persuading Apollo to let him drive the chariot of the Sun.
Apollo consented but Phaeton was not strong enough to control
the horses. They bolted and the Sun was about to burn Earth
and sky when Zeus stopped the chariot with a thunderbolt,
killing Phaeton. Thus the reluctance Phaeton teaches fathers is
for the good of the sons.

6. *changed its place*: In descending to the foot of the cross.

7-12. The mixed metaphor with which Beatrice opens is once again based on the impress of a signet in wax. Here the fire is the wax and inner desire the signet. She and Cacciaguida (and all the heavenly souls) already know Dante's mind and their knowledge of it cannot be increased by his speaking, but by encouraging him to discourse on a heavenly level, Beatrice is preparing him the better to speak his soul's need when he returns to earth, in order that men may be moved to the good he urges.

13-18. Sense of this passage: "You grasp the future as easily as men grasp a problem in geometry, for your sight is fixed upon God's mind, in which all time is one and present." *root*: Dante uses *"piota,"* which may mean "root, soil around a root, sod, turf, or sole of the foot."

16. *contingent things*: Contingency, in Scholastic terminology, is "that which could or could not exist." Contingency is dependent upon the action of *necessity* (that which must necessarily exist). Contingent being is possible, finite, and secondary. Necessary being is certain, infinite, and primary.

29. *to the light*: To Cacciaguida.

31-32. *that glued the foolish like limed birds*: Bird-lime, a highly viscous substance, is spread on boughs and used to trap birds much as flies are trapped on fly paper. Dante compares the sayings of pagan oracles to that lime, in which the pagan world let itself be trapped before the Lamb of Christ suffered to set men free of such traps.

36. *his own smile*: "Smile" is used here for "gladness of spirit"—a regular usage in the *Paradiso*. That gladness is revealed to Dante by the brightening of the flame that hides Cacciaguida from Dante's view. Thus he is both concealed in and revealed by the brighter shining of his bliss.

37-42. Divine foreknowledge of *contingency* does not confer *necessity* because man is given free will. The nature of free will within the workings of omniscient prevision is a point of faith and must be referred to the mysteries rather than to reason.

46. *Hippolytus*: Son of Theseus and the Amazon Antiope. He rejected the advances of his stepmother, Phaedra, and she, accusing him of what she herself wanted, turned Theseus against him. Theseus not only drove him from home but called on Poseidon for vengeance and Poseidon sent a bull from the sea to kill Hippolytus as he was driving his chariot along the shore. Ovid tells the story in *Metamorphoses*, XV, 487 ff. Through

Cacciaguida, Dante is, of course, protesting that the charges brought against him were as false and self-seeking as Phaedra's against Hippolytus.

Dante, as a high official of Florence and a leader of the Whites, was charged, vaguely and inconclusively, with grafting. The "Anonimo Fiorentino," a nearly contemporary fourteenth-century commentary, says that part of the charge brought against Dante was his "opposition to the Holy Mother Church," which in this case is, clearly enough, another way of saying "opposition to the politics of Pope Boniface VIII."

50-51. *him who plots it*: Boniface VIII, if not in person and with Dante specifically in mind, then through his corrupt agents and evil policies. *where Christ is daily bought and sold*: Rome, i.e., the Vatican.

52-53. *you of the offended party*: Both Dante and his party, the Whites.

53-54. *the vengeance truth will demand*: Truth will take its vengeance by punishing those who are guilty. In so doing, it will bear witness to what is true. Throughout this passage (from line 46) Boniface VIII is compared to Phaedra. (See *Inferno*, XII, 12-18, and note.) For the force of the comparison it is well to bear in mind that Phaedra was born of a foul beast (the Minotaur) and a queen so lecherous that she crept into a wooden cow in order to be taken by the bull. Phaedra later committed suicide, overcome by her guilt, her death clearing the name of Hippolytus. Hippolytus, curiously enough, survived a shift of legend and appears in Catholic hagiography as St. Hippolytus or St. Hippolyte.

62. *the foul and foolish company*: Dante seems to be alluding to his own party, the Whites. As a fallen leader, he seems to feel his party has betrayed him. In any case there seems to be nothing to hope for from political parties. In line 69 Cacciaguida praises him for having become his own party of one.

63. *that barren coast*: Of exile.

65-66. *soon thereafter . . . cheeks turn red*: The same sort of machinations that led to Dante's banishment led Florence into foolish wars and bloody internal disorders that left the Florentines with more than enough reasons for blushing. The Whites in particular suffered many humiliations and bloody defeats.

69. *A party of your own*: In 1266 the Ghibellines were driven forever from Florence (see *Inferno*, X, 32-51, note).

The Guelfs, thereupon, divided into Whites and Blacks, and Dante became a member of the Whites' ruling council. At the end of 1301 the Blacks elected a new *podestà*, and on January 27, 1302, while Dante was on a mission to Rome, the Blacks published a decree fining him 5,000 florins and banishing him for two years. On March 10, not having appeared to pay his fine, Dante was banished permanently, and sentenced to death if he returned. In 1303, the Whites, joined now with the remnants of the Ghibellines, were gathering forces for an assault on Florence, and Dante was their ambassador at the court of Bartolomeo della Scala, Lord of Verona. At that time Boniface VIII died, and was succeeded by Benedict XI, who sent a cardinal to Florence to negotiate a settlement. With that hope in view, Dante remained affiliated with the Whites. The Blacks, however, resisted all negotiation, and the Whites prepared an attack that was repulsed with heavy losses at La Lastra, above Florence, July 20, 1304. Dante seems to have felt that the internal bickerings of the Whites had caused the carnage, and it was probably after La Lastra that he withdrew, damning Blacks and Whites together, to become a one-man party of his own.

71 ff. THE SCALIGERI (DELLA SCALA). The ancient noble family of the Scaligeri (its German branch was named Scaliger) ruled over Verona and later acquired the office of Imperial Vicar of Tuscany. Alberto died in 1301 and was succeeded, in order, by his three sons: Bartolomeo, died 1304; Alboino, died 1311; Francesco (Can Grande), who shared power with Alboino beginning in 1308, became sole lord of Verona in 1311, and died in 1329. (Dante died in 1331.) Francecso was Dante's great patron and the lord on whom Dante based some of his hope of peace and order in Italy. (See *Inferno*, I, 95, and note.) *the great Lombard*: Francesco. *the sacred bird*: The eagle. The arms of the Scaligeri displayed a ladder (*scala*) below an eagle.

73-75. Others ask first and give later. But between Bartolomeo and Dante (as, note, among the souls of Heaven) the giving shall be first and any request (of service from the other) shall come late, the service having already been freely offered.

76. *another*: Can Grande. He won no particular renown as a warrior. "Of war" (line 78) does not occur in Dante. It is my own rhyme-forced addition. Yet to be stamped by the influence of Mars, praised by one of the warriors of God, and to be hailed, as Dante may have intended, as the Greyhound that shall hunt down and destroy evil, can only be appropriate to a warrior, even when the war record is missing. Perhaps Dante was still hoping ahead from the time of (as distinct from time "in") the writing, for Can Grande was then in power.

81. *nine years*: Earth years. Cacciaguida does not say nine "times." Nine Martian years would equal about seventeen earth years and Can Grande was nine years old on March 9, 1300. (Note that March is "Mars month.")

82-83. *the Gascon . . . high Henry*: The Gascon is Clement V (see *Inferno*, XIX, 77-79, and note. Also *Purgatorio*, XXXII, 149-150). He succeeded Boniface VIII to the Papal throne in 1305, and to the baptismal font of Hell in 1314. Henry VII of Luxembourg, Emperor 1308-1313 (see *Purgatorio*, VII, 96, and note), was the main prop of Dante's hopes for a general peace and for the end of his exile. Clement invited him to Rome with fair promises but threatened to excommunicate him in 1312. "Before," therefore (line 82), means "before 1312." By that time Can Grande was twenty-one, had been joint lord of Verona for four years, and sole lord for one. *men will start to speak*: Dante says, literally, "sparks of his virtue will appear."

92-93. *him*: Can Grande. *those who shall be present*: To bear witness to the astonishing things Cacciaguida prophesies to Dante while enjoining him not to repeat them.

96. *a few turns*: Probably intended as daily rather than annual revolutions. At the Easter season of 1300 Dante was less than two years from his banishment.

108. *on him who is most lax*: Who has least foreseen and forearmed himself.

110. *the dearest place*: Florence.

112. *that world*: Hell.

113. *flowering crown*: The Earthly Paradise.

# CANTO XVIII

---

*BEATRICE COMFORTS DANTE, who is pondering the bitter and the sweet of Cacciaguida's prophecy, then instructs him to turn back to Cacciaguida, who proceeds to name among the souls who form the Cross of Mars THE GREAT WARRIORS OF GOD. They flash like shooting stars along the arms of the cross. Finished, Cacciaguida reascends to his original place in the right arm and the whole choir resumes its hymn.*

*Dante turns back to Beatrice, sees her grow yet more beautiful, and knows they have made the ASCENT TO THE SIXTH SPHERE. He sees the pale glow of Jupiter replace the red glow of Mars and in that silvery sheen he sees THE VISION OF EARTHLY JUSTICE, a spectacular arrangement of lights that spell out a message, letter by letter, and then form as an EAGLE (The Empire) ornamented by glowing lilies (France).*

*Moved by this vision of Justice, Dante prays that these souls of Heavenly Justice will visit their wrath upon the corrupt Pope, who, like a money-changer in the temple, denies the sacraments of God's people by excommunication and interdiction, in order to sell back to them what is rightfully theirs. So, for the love of money does the successor of Peter and Paul betray holy office.*

Now that holy mirror rejoiced alone,
   rapt in its own reflections; and I tasted
   the bitterness and sweetness of my own.                    3

My guide to God said: "Turn your thoughts along
   a happier course. Remember I dwell near
   the One who lifts the weight of every wrong."             6

I turned to the loving sound of my soul's aid,
   and the love my eyes beheld in her sacred eyes
   I leave unsaid—not only am I afraid                       9

my powers of speech fail, but my memory
   cannot return so far above itself
   unless Another's grace be moved to guide me.              12

This much of what I felt I can report—
   that as I looked at her my will was freed
   of every other wish of any sort,                          15

for the Eternal Bliss that rayed down whole
   into my Beatrice, shone back from her face
   and its reflection there gladdened my soul.               18

And with a smile so radiant that my eyes
   were overcome, she said then: "Turn and listen:
   not in my eyes alone is Paradise."                        21

As, here on earth, the face sometimes reveals
   the wish within, if it is wished so strongly
   that all the soul is gripped by what it feels—             24

so, in the flaming of the holy ray
   to which I turned, I read the inner will,
   and knew that it had something more to say.                27

It spoke thus: "In this fifth limb of the tree
   whose life is from its crown, and bears forever,
   and never sheds a leaf, I would have you see               30

elected spirits who, in the world's use,
　before they came to Heaven, were so renowned
　their great worth would make greater every Muse.　33

Look at the arms of the cross. As the swift flame
　within a flame does, so, within that choir,
　shall flash the splendor of each soul I name."　36

I saw along the cross a streak of light
　as he pronounced the name of Joshua:
　nor did the saying reach me before the sight.　39

And at the name of the great Maccabee
　I saw another, spinning; and the string
　that whirled that top was its own ecstasy.　42

And just as hunters follow their falcons' flights,
　so, at the names of Charlemagne and Roland,
　my rapt attention followed two more lights.　45

Then William of Orange, and then Rinoard
　drew my eyes after them along that cross.
　And then the good duke Godfrey, and Robert
　　　　　　　　　　　　　　　　　　　Guiscard.　48

Then, moving once more through those lights, the light
　that had come down to greet me, let me hear
　its art among the choir of Heaven's height.　51

I turned to my right to learn from Beatrice,
　whether by word or sign, what I should do,
　and I beheld her eyes shine with such bliss,　54

with such serenity, that she surpassed
　the vision of every other accustomed beauty
　in which she had shone, including even the last.　57

And as a man, perceiving day by day
   an increase of delight in doing good,
   begins to sense his soul is gaining way—                    60

so, seeing that Miracle surpass the mark
   of former beauty, I sensed that I was turning,
   together with Heaven, through a greater arc.                63

And such a change as fair-skinned ladies show
   in a short space of time, when from their faces
   they lift the weight of shame that made them
                              glow—   66

such change grew on my eyes when I perceived
   the pure white radiance of the temperate star—
   the sixth sphere—into which I was received.                 69

Within that jovial face of Paradise
   I saw the sparkling of the love that dwelt there
   forming our means of speech before my eyes.                72

As birds arisen from a marshy plain
   almost as if rejoicing in their forage
   form, now a cluster, now a long-drawn skein—               75

so, there, within their sheaths of living light,
   blest beings soared and sang and joined their rays,
   and *D*, then *I*, then *L* formed on my sight.            78

First they sang and moved to their own song;
   then having formed themselves into a letter,
   they stopped their song and flight, though not for
                              long.   81

O holy Pegasean who consecrates
   the power of genius, giving it long life,
   as it, through you, gives life to cities and states—       84

so fill me with your light, that as it shines
   I may show forth their image as I conceive it:
   let your own power appear in these few lines!   87

In five times seven vowels and consonants
   they showed themselves, and I grasped every part
   as if those lights had given it utterance.   90

The first words of that message as it passed
   before me were *DILIGITE IUSTITIAM.*
   *QUI IUDICATIS TERRAM* were the last.   93

Then, in the fifth word, at the final *M*
   they stayed aligned, and silvery Jupiter
   seemed to be washed in a gold glow around them.   96

More lights descended then and took their place
   on top of the *M*, and sang, as I believe,
   a hymn to the Good that draws them to Its grace.   99

Then—just as burning logs, when poked, let fly
   a fountain of innumerable sparks
   (from which fools used to think to prophesy)—   102

more than a thousand of those lights arose,
   some to a greater height, some to a lesser,
   each to the place the Sun that lit it chose.   105

And as each took its place in that still choir
   I saw the head and shoulders of an eagle
   appear in the fixed pattern of that fire.   108

The One who paints there needs no guide's behest.
   He is Himself the guide. From Him derives
   the skill and essential form that builds a nest.   111

The other sparks, at first content to twine
   in the form of golden lilies round the *M*
   now moved a bit, completing the design.   114

O lovely star, how rich a diadem
   shown forth to let me understand our justice
   flows to us from the heaven you begem.        117

Therefore I pray the mind that initiated
   your power and motion, to observe the source
   of the smoke by which your ray is vitiated;    120

that it be moved to anger once again
   against the buyers and sellers in the temple
   whose walls were built of blood and martyr's pain. 123

O soldiery of Heaven to whose array
   my mind returns, pray for all those on earth
   who follow bad example and go astray.          126

In earlier eras wars were carried on
   by swords; now, by denying this man or that
   the bread the Heavenly Father denies to none.   129

But you who scribble only to scratch out,
   remember that Peter and Paul, who died for the
                        vineyard
   you trample, still defend the good you flout.   132

Well may you say: "My heart's wish is so set
   on the image of the saint who lived alone
   and who was forced to give his head in forfeit,  135

as if it were a favor at a ball—
what do I care for the Fisherman or old Paul!"

## Notes

1-3. *that holy mirror*: Cacciaguida. The image is of the blest
soul as a mirror and reflector of God's ray. (Cf. XIV, 40-42.)
*the bitterness*: Of the prophesied exile and of the triumph of
his enemies. *the sweetness*: Of prophesied poetic fame.

4-6. Beatrice tells Dante to put away the bitter part of his thoughts (of revenge). She reminds him that she is close to God whose justice rights all wrongs, and that she will always be there as his protector. Her allegorical function as Divine Revelation is, of course, especially relevant here.

12. *Another's*: God's.

13-18. The vision of God's eternal bliss, rayed directly into Beatrice's eyes, and so reflected to Dante, fills his soul entirely and drives from it all thoughts of seeking revenge for the wrongs done him.

17. *face*: As he often does, Dante uses *aspetto* ("face") to mean "eyes."

25. *the holy ray*: Cacciaguida.

34. *Look at the arms of the cross*: Cacciaguida is speaking from within the base of the cross. He wants Dante to look up to the arms.

38 ff. THE GREAT WARRIORS OF GOD. Joshua, succeeding Moses, led Israel into the promised land. Judas Maccabaeus freed Israel from the Syrian tyranny. Charlemagne, in driving the Moors out of Europe, restored the Empire and freed the Spanish church. Roland (Orlando in Italian) was the nephew of Charlemagne and his greatest knight. (See *Inferno*, XXXI, 17, note.) William of Orange, hero of various medieval French romances, was the ideal of the Christian knight and was said to have died a monk. Rinoardo Rainouart served under William as his chief lieutenant. He was reputed to have been a convert from paganism and to have died in holy orders but he, like William, is largely a legendary figure. Godfrey or Gottfried of Bouillon was the leader of the first crusade and became the first Christian king of Jerusalem. He died in 1100. Robert Guiscard, son of Tancred d'Hauteville, a Norman war leader joined with his brothers in 1046 to war against the Saracens in southern Italy, becoming duke of Puglia and of Calabria. He died in 1085.

39. *nor did the saying reach me before the sight*: I.e., the naming and the flashing of these souls take place in the same instant.

49-63. THE ASCENT TO JUPITER. As usual the transition to the next sphere is rapid. Cacciaguida returns to his place in the right arm of the cross and joins with the choir when it reumes its singing. (Cf. XV, 7-12, and note.) Beatrice becomes till more beautiful and still more radiant and Dante senses that e has entered the next Heaven.

**57. *including even the last*:** The phrasing is unusual but unusually exact. Beatrice grows more beautiful and more radiant with each new ascent. Now, entering the sixth Heaven, her new beauty exceeds not only her accustomed beauty, but even its own last manifestation (see lines 7-12) which Dante lacked power to describe.

**61. *that Miracle*:** Beatrice.

**63. *through a greater arc*:** It is unlikely that such a change of motion would register on merely human senses, but each ascending sphere must, necessarily, revolve through a greater arc than the last, being farther from the center.

**64-69.** Dante has just passed from the redness of Mars to the whiteness of Jupiter, and in about the time it takes a fair-skinned lady to grow pale again when she recovers from a blush of shame, his eyes adjust to the new radiance. Whatever Dante understood of the ability of ladies to recover from a sense of shame, his intent is clear, and the mood of the image is appropriate if the reader will visualize one of those quick flushes of innocence and maiden modesty much admired in the courtly tradition, though rare in ours.

**68. *the temperate star*:** Ptolemy described Jupiter as a temperate mean between hot Mars and cold Saturn. Appropriately, it serves as the Heaven of the wise and just—souls who were the models of proportioned and temperate being.

**70. *jovial*:** The other name of Jupiter is, of course, Jove. Dante is punning, intending both "Jove" and "jovial."

**72. *our means of speech*:** The alphabet.

**70 ff. DANTE'S VISION OF THE WISE AND JUST.** Dante's conception here was unprecedented in his times, but the modern reader can grasp it easily by conceiving the vision as a huge moving electric sign of the sort called "spectaculars." The lights of the sign are the radiances of the spirits themselves. Those lights first spell out a message, one letter at a time. The last word of the message is then transformed into an eagle, which is then ornamented by further recombinations of the lights. In the Canto that follows the eagle will move its beak and speak, and then, taking flight, circle around Dante.

**78-99. THE ALPHABET MESSAGE.** The message formed by the lights, beginning with the letters *D,* and *I,* and *L* running to thirty-five letters, is: *DILIGITE IUSTITIAM QUI IUDICATIS TERRAM*—"Love righteousness, ye that are judges of the earth."

82. *Pegasean*: The Muses drink from the spring called Hippocrene that sprang from the earth where Pegasus struck it with his hoof. The nine Muses together may properly be called Pegaseans. Dante uses the singular form, perhaps to invoke the Muses generally.

88-90. *five times seven*: The thirty-five letters of the spelled-out message. *they*: The souls within their sheaths of light. *as if those lights had given it utterance*: I do not know why hearing a letter spoken should make it more "graspable" than seeing it flash across the sky, but Dante, a primitive art critic at best, was always filled with awe by the sort of visual representation that seemed to make the viewer hear what he was seeing. (Cf. *Purgatorio*, X, 52-60.)

95-96. *silvery Jupiter*: Jupiter was reputed to have a silvery sheen that set it apart from other white stars. The souls, however, are encased in sheaths of golden light.

102. *prophesy*: By asking a question (for example, "How many years shall I live?"), then poking the fire, and counting the sparks to get an answer.

104-105. *greater . . . lesser . . . to the place the Sun that lit it chose*: See once more XIV, 40-42. It is the Sun (God) who decrees the pattern of the eagle, assigning to each soul its place in the pattern according to the amount of grace It rays forth to each.

109-11. The general meaning of this passage is clear enough: God is the creator whose creation is guided by no other, Himself being the guide. The last line, however, is in Dante's densest style. "Essential form" is a Scholastic term equivalent to "form" in the Platonic sense. "Nest," I think, must be taken as a lovely symbol of the way in which God's art fills His creation. Birds though they know nothing about architecture, draw from God the skill (the virtue) that enables them to build intricate and beautiful nests. So, by extension, are all the arts of this world derived from the guidance of the Unguided.

112. *The other sparks*: "Innumerable sparks" shot up from the vision and "more than a thousand of them" rose to form the head and shoulders of the eagle. The other sparks first wove lilies around the *M*; then, moving a little, completed the body of the eagle by filling out the body of the original *M*. If the letter is visualized in the rounded form common in medieval

manuscripts and much like our lower case "m," and if the head nd shoulders of an eagle are drawn in above the "m," it takes ittle imagination to visualize how the "m" could form the eagle's ody. In the figure below, the dotted lines suggest the manner f the change.

113. *lilies*: Could not fail to suggest the French monarchy, s the Eagle could not fail to suggest the Empire. Dante may ery well mean that, were wisdom and justice to rule, France hould adorn the Empire in union with it instead of following its wn divisive course.

115-117. *O lovely star*: Jupiter. Earthly justice is an effect f its influence upon men. It is the ideal of earthly justice the ouls have been expressing in their flashing message and in the ymbolism of the eagle and of the lilies.

122. *the temple*: The Church. Dante, at sight of the Imperial Eagle of justice, is moved to inveigh against papal avarice and orruption. "*M*," as various commentators have pointed out, is he first letter of *Monarchia*. In *De Monarchia*, I, 11, Dante ad argued: "Justice is possible only under a [good] monarchy." f this inference from the *M* is valid (and Dante was, in fact, uch given to such devices) we are once more on the theme of a piritual church within a strong temporal empire as the one hope f Europe.

123. *blood*: If the original text reads "sangue." Some texts ead "*segni*" ("signs," of which the English rendering would be signs/portents/miracles/prophecies").

126. *bad example*: Of papal corruption.

128-129. *now, by denying . . . the bread*: The bread of God
grace, particularly as received through the sacraments. By deny
ing the sacraments through excommunications and interdiction
the papacy wages war against peace and justice, forcing men an
states to buy back the sacraments that should rightfully b
theirs.

130. *you*: Dante uses the singular form *"tu."* He must, there
fore, be referring to a single evil pope. If he is speaking as c
1300 that pope would, of course, be Boniface VIII. *scribb.
only to scratch out*: Instead of preparing bulls that will clari1
God's intent to all time, the evil popes merely scribble excon
munications, interdictions, and denials of justice in order t
cancel them again for a fee.

134. *the image of the saint*: John the Baptist. But in a bitt
irony, Dante portrays the corrupt popes as having their hear
set not on the saint but on his image, for it was stamped on tl
Florentine gold florin. Thus their love of St. John is the love
money. *who lived alone*: In the desert. (See *Luke*, I, 80.)

135-136. *his head in forfeit . . . favor at a ball*: The daught
of Herodias so pleased Herod with her dancing that he offere
her "whatsoever she would ask." She asked for the head
John the Baptist on a charger, and against his own inclinatio
Herod kept his word (*Matthew*, XIV, 1-11. *Mark*, VI, 21-28

137. *the Fisherman*: St. Peter. Used here as a familiar an
contemptuous term. *old Paul*: St. Paul. Again the form of addre
shows lack of respect.

# CANTO XIX

*The Just and Temperate Rulers*
*The Eagle*

*THE EAGLE made up of the many souls of the
Just and Temperate Rulers moves its beak and speaks
as if it were a single entity, announcing that it is the
chosen symbol of DIVINE JUSTICE. Dante is afire to
understand the nature of the Divine Justice and begs
the Eagle to explain it, but he is told that the infinity
of God's excellence must forever exceed his creation,
and that none may fathom His will, whereby it is
presumptuous of any creature to question the Divine
Justice. Man must be content with the guidance of
Scripture and with the sure knowledge that God is
perfect, good, and just.*

*Dante had once pondered the justice of denying
salvation to virtuous pagans. The Eagle tells him it is
not for him to sit in judgment on God's intent. It
affirms that except as he believes in Christ no soul may
ascend to Heaven, yet it adds that the virtuous pagan
shall sit nearer Christ than many another who takes
Christ's name in vain.*

*The Eagle concludes with a DENUNCIATION OF
THE BESTIALIZED KINGS OF CHRISTENDOM in
1300.*

Before me, its great wings outspread, now shone
    the image of the eagle those bright souls
    had given form to in glad unison.           3

Each seemed a little ruby in the sky,
    and the sun's ray struck each in such a way
    the light reflected straight into my eye.        6

What I must now call back from memory
   no voice has ever spoken, nor ink written.
   Nor has its like been known to fantasy.

For I saw and heard the beak move and declare
   in its own voice the pronouns "I" and "mine"
   when "we" and "ours" were what conceived it
                                   there.          12

"For being just and pious in my time,"
   it said, "I am exalted here in glory
   to which, by wish alone, no one may climb;          15

and leave behind me, there upon the earth,
   a memory honored even by evildoers,
   though they shun the good example it sets forth."          18

Just as the glow of many living coals
   issues a single heat, so from that image
   one sound declared the love of many souls.          21

At which I cried: "O everlasting blooms
   of the eternal bliss, who make one seeming
   upon my sense of all your many perfumes—          24

my soul has hungered long: breathe forth at last
   the words that will appease it. There on earth
   there is no food with which to break its fast.          27

I know that if God's justice has constructed
   its holy mirror in some other realm,
   your kingdom's view of it is not obstructed.          30

You know how eagerly I wait to hear;
   you know the what and wherefore of the doubt
   I have hungered to resolve for many a year."          33

Much as a falcon freed of hood and jess
   stretches its head and neck and beats its wings,
   preening itself to show its readiness—                    36

so moved the emblem that was all compounded
   of praises of God's grace; and from it, then,
   a hymn they know who dwell in bliss resounded.    39

Then it began to speak: "The One who wheeled
   the compass round the limits of the world,
   and spread there what is hidden and what revealed, 42

could not so stamp his power and quality
   into his work but what the creating Word
   would still exceed creation infinitely.                   45

And this explains why the first Prideful Power,
   highest of creatures, because he would not wait
   the power of the ripening sun, fell green and sour. 48

And thus we see that every lesser creature
   is much too small a vessel to hold the Good
   that has no end; Itself is Its one measure.           51

Therefore, you understand, our way of seeing,
   which must be only one ray of the Mind
   that permeates all matter and all being,             54

cannot, by its very nature, be so clear
   but what its Author's eye sees far beyond
   the furthest limits that to us appear.                    57

In the eternal justice, consequently,
   the understanding granted to mankind
   is lost as the eye is within the sea:                      60

it can make out the bottom near the shore
   but not on the main deep; and still it is there,
   though at a depth your eye cannot explore.        63

There is no light but from that ever fresh
   and cloudless Halcyon; all else is darkness,
   the shadow and the poison of the flesh.    66

By now, much that was hidden from your view
   by the living Justice of which you used to ask
   so many questions, has been shown to you.    69

For you used to say, 'A man is born in sight
   of Indus' water, and there is none there
   to speak of Christ, and none to read or write.    72

And all he wills and does, we must concede,
   as far as human reason sees, is good;
   and he does not sin either in word or deed.    75

He dies unbaptized and cannot receive
   the saving faith. What justice is it damns him?
   Is it his fault that he does not believe?'    78

—But who are you to take the judgment seat
   and pass on things a thousand miles away,
   who cannot see the ground before your feet?    81

The man who would split hairs with me could find
   no end of grounds for questioning, had he not
   the Scriptures over him to guide his mind.    84

O earthbound animals! minds gross as wood!
   Itself good in Itself, the Primal Will
   does not move from Itself, the Supreme Good!    87

Only what sorts with It is just. It sways
   toward no created good, but of Itself
   creates all Good by sending forth Its rays."    90

As a stork that has fed its young flies round and round
   above the nest, and as the chick it fed
   raises its head to stare at it, still nest-bound—    93

so did that blessed image circle there,
   its great wings moved in flight by many wills,
   and so did I lift up my head and stare.    96

Circling, it sang; then said: "As what I sing
   surpasses your understanding, so God's justice
   surpasses the power of mortal reasoning."    99

Those blazing glories of the Holy Ghost
   stopped, still formed in the sign that spread the honor
   of Rome across the world, to its last coast,    102

grew still, then said: "To this high empery
   none ever rose but through belief in Christ,
   either before or after his agony.    105

But see how many now cry out 'Christ! Christ!'
   who shall be farther from him at the Judgment
   than many who, on earth, did not know Christ.    108

Such Christians shall the Ethiopian scorn
   when the two bands are formed to right and left,
   one blest to all eternity, one forlorn.    111

What shall the Persians say to your kings there
   when the Great Book is opened and they see
   the sum of their depravities laid bare?    114

There shall be seen among the works of Albert,
   that deed the moving pen will soon record
   by which Bohemia shall become a desert.    117

There shall be seen the Seine's grief for the sin
   of that debaser of the currency
   whose death is waiting for him in a pig's skin.    120

There shall be seen the pride whose greed confounds
   the mad Scot and the foolish Englishman
   who cannot stay within their proper bounds.    123

There, the debaucheries and the vain show
  of the Spaniard and the Bohemian who knew
  nothing of valor, and chose not to know.     126

And there, the cripple of Jerusalem:
  a *1* put down to mark the good he did,
  and then, to mark his villainies, an *M*.     129

There, the baseness and the greedy rage
  of the watchdog who patrols the burning island
  on which Anchises closed his long old age;     132

and to make clear how paltry is his case,
  his entry will be signs and abbreviations
  that the record may say much in little space.     135

And there the filthy deeds shall be set down
  of his uncle and his brother, each of whom
  cuckolded a great family and a crown.     138

There shall be marked for all men to behold
  Norway's king and Portugal's; and Rascia's,
  who lost most when he saw Venetian gold.     141

Oh happy Hungary, had she suffered all
  without more griefs ahead! Happy Navarre
  were she to make her peaks a fortress wall!     144

And every Navarrese may well believe
  the omen of Nicosìa and Famagosto
  whose citizens have present cause to grieve     147

the way their beast, too small for the main pack,
keeps to one side but hunts on the same track."

## Notes

10-12. The eagle, though composed of many souls, speaks as
a single entity, so symbolizing the unity of these souls in God.

15. *by wish alone*: No soul may earn such glory by its own merit, but only by the gift of God's grace. (See XIV, 42.)

18. *it*: The memory of those who lived in justice and piety.

25. *breathe forth*: I.e., speak, but phrased in this way in order to continue the figure of flowers breathing forth their perfumes.

26-27. *on earth . . . no food*: Mortal understanding cannot satisfy Dante's hunger to know the nature of God's justice.

28-33. DANTE'S QUESTION ON THE NATURE OF DIVINE JUSTICE. The question is best understood by referring to IX, 61-63. "On high are mirrors (you say 'Thrones') and these reflect God's judgment to us." "On high" as spoken by Cunizza in the sphere of Venus could mean "in Jupiter" or somewhere higher. Whatever the rendering of this point, Dante is asking for nothing less than an explanation of the nature of God's Justice. In reply, he is given many particulars by the way, but the sum of it is that God's Justice is inscrutable and that the question is unanswerable. Not even these enormously elevated souls can know the full answer.

40-45. THE INFINITY OF GOD'S EXCELLENCE. Great as is God's creation, the Word (*Logos*, the creating source) cannot create what it does not Itself infinitely exceed.

46. *the first Prideful Power*: Satan. He was first among all created things, yet (as above) infinitely below his creator. His sin of pride was in wishing to equal God (instead of ripening and growing more perfect in His light) and therefore he fell green and sour.

52. *our*: Some texts read "your," but such a reading would imply that only mortals are inferior to God, whereas the eagle's point is that all parts of His creation (including the angels and the souls of the blest) are infinitely inferior to God. In line 59 the eagle does speak of what would be "your world" (mankind). There it has changed the grounds of the discussion and is explicating the difference between heavenly and mortal understanding—a second infinity of difference that does not invalidate the first.

65. *Halcyon*: God. His revelation is the one light. By comparison, the light of the intellect is a darkness and leads to error (the shadow) and to sin (the poison) of the flesh.

68-69. *of which you used to ask so many questions*: About the nature of divine justice. See lines 25-33.

80. *a thousand miles away*: Is not intended as a map measurement but as a general way of saying "a great distance." From God, as one may understand. From the man by Indus' water. And from both.

82. *with me*: With the eagle, as the heavenly symbol of God's justice. There would be endless grounds for doubts and fine arguments had not Scripture set forth all a man need know about Divine Justice.

91-96. A double long-tail simile: as the stork did, so did the image; as the chick did, so did Dante.

95. *by many wills*: By the conjoined wills of all the gemlike souls that make up the image of the eagle.

97-99. The harmonies and the language of the hymn are beyond Dante's powers of comprehension. He, like a fledgling stork, gapes up at what is beyond him. And so is it with his grasp of Divine Justice.

101. *stopped*: Their circling.

102-105. Note how adroitly this pause serves to mute the effective but no longer needed image of the mother stork circling its chick, and to sound in its place the majesty of the eagle.

105. *before*: By belief in the promised Messiah. *after*: By belief in the risen Christ. It is by allowing a place in Heaven to what may be called the "Messianic Christians" that Dante can seat such souls as Solomon's in Heaven.

106-108. As before Dante rhymes the name of Christ only with itself.

108. *the many who did not know Christ*: So in part to answer Dante's doubts about the virtuous Hindu. All the Virtuous Pagans, to be sure, will be closer to Christ in Limbo than those professing Christians who damned themselves. But since Dante has allowed one pagan (Virgil) to ascend to the Earthly Paradise, it is perhaps his understanding that the Virtuous Pagans will be settled there after the Judgment. Higher, as the eagle has declared in line 104, they cannot go, though in *Purgatorio*, I, 74-75, Cato of Utica is marked for special blessing in the resurrection.

109. *Ethiopian*: Used as a generic term for all pagans.

110. *when the two bands*: At the seat of Judgment when the sheep and the goats are set to Christ's right and left hand.

112. *Persians*: Another generic term for pagans.

115. *Albert*: Albert I, Emperor from 1298 to 1308. He is the "German Albert" of *Purgatorio*, VI, 97 ff. He invaded Bohemia in 1304. As of 1300, therefore, the pen must wait four years before it moves to record his deed.

118-120. *the Seine*: For France, generally. *that debaser of the currency*: Philip the Fair (*v. Purgatorio*, VII, 109, and note; and XX, 85-93, and note). He debased the coinage to finance his wars and brought misery to France. Dante, it is well to remember, punished counterfeiters (*Inferno*, XXX) not out of love of money, but because a sound coinage was an essential principle of social order. *death . . . in a pig's skin*: In 1314, in the course of a royal hunt, a wild boar ran under Philip's horse. Philip was thrown and died soon after of his injuries. Dante certainly relishes such a way of bringing down the mighty and evil.

121-123. *greed*: For more land. *Scot . . . Englishman*: The Scottish and English kings in their endless border wars.

124-126. *the Spaniard*: Probably Ferdinand IV. *the Bohemian*: Probably Wenceslaus IV (*v. Purgatorio*, VII, 102, note). With or without specific identification, Dante's general point is clear.

127-129. *cripple of Jerusalem*: Charles II of Anjou, known as Charles the Lame. (*v.* VIII, 82, note; *Purgatorio*, VII, 124-129, and *Purgatorio*, XX, 79, note.) He was King of Jerusalem only by the act of giving himself that title. In the Book of Judgment his virtues will be marked by the number *1* and his villainies by the letter *M* (a thousand).

131-132. *the watchdog*: Frederick II of Sicily (*v. Purgatorio*, III, 115). *burning island*: Sicily. *on which Anchises*: He died at Drepanum, modern Trapani.

133. *paltry*: So paltry a man could not be allowed much space in the book of the Recording Angel, but his life was so evil that his sins will have to be written down in signs and abbreviations in order to squeeze them all in.

137-138. *his uncle and his brother*: King James of Majorca, brother of James I of Aragon; and James II of Aragon, son of James I. Each disgraced the crown he wore; both disgraced the house of Aragon. *cuckolded*: They disgraced their family and their kingdom from within, as a wife does when she cuckolds her husband.

140. *Norway's king*: In 1300, Hacon VII. *Portugal's*: Dionysus. *Rascia's*: Orosius II. Rascia was part of Serbia. Orosius seems to

have altered the metal content of Venetian money on a substantial scale. *lost most*: His falsifying of the currency would slate him for a meeting with Master Adam in Hell (*v. Inferno*, xxx).

142. *Hungary*: Andrew III, a good king, ruled in 1300. Hungary had endured many ruinous wars. If only her sufferings were all behind her, as of course they are not.

143-144. *Navarre*: The ancient kingdom of what is now southern France and northern Spain. Joanna of Navarre married Philip the Fair of France in 1284 but remained sole ruler of Navarre. After her death in 1304, her son Louis inherited Navarre, and when his father died in 1314, he became Louis X, king of France and Navarre. So Navarre passed under French rule, the bitterness of which they were to learn in full. Hence, they would have been happier had they armed the mountains around them (the Pyrenees) as fortress walls for keeping out the French.

145-149. *Nicosìa and Famagosta*: The two principal cities of Crete. *their beast*: Henry II of the French house of Lusignan was king of Cyprus in 1300, a man given to debaucheries for which the people paid dearly. Every Navarrese would have done well in 1300 to have taken him as an example of French rule and of what Navarre would suffer when it passed under the French crown. *the main pack*: Of the bestialized kings of Christendom. Henry is too small a beast to run in the main pack but he runs along to one side of it on the track of the same bestialities.

# CANTO XX

---

THE SIXTH SPHERE: JUPITER

*The Just and Temperate Rulers*
*The Eagle*

*THE EAGLE PAUSES briefly and the spirits of the blest sing a hymn, not as one symbolic entity, but each in its own voice. The hymn ended, the Eagle resumes speaking in its single voice, and identifies as the chief souls of this sphere those lusters that compose its eye. In order they are: DAVID, TRAJAN, HEZEKIAH, CONSTANTINE, WILLIAM OF SICILY, and RIPHEUS.*

*Dante is astonished to find Trajan and Ripheus in Heaven, both of whom he had thought to be pagans, but the Eagle explains how by the special grace of God Ripheus was converted by a vision of Christ a millennium before His descent into the flesh, and Trajan was returned from Limbo to his mortal body long enough to undergo conversion to Christ and to allow his soul to mount to Heaven.*

*So once again for Dante's doubts about the virtuous Hindu and God's justice, for who can say how many more God has so chosen to his grace? The Eagle concludes with a praise of God's predestined justice, rejoicing even in the limitation of its own knowledge, resting in the assurance that the unknown consequences of God's will cannot fail to be good.*

When the sun, from which the whole world takes its
                                                          light,

    sinks from our hemisphere and the day fades
    from every reach of land, and it is night;      3

the sky, which earlier it alone had lit,
   suddenly changes mode and reappears
   in many lights that take their light from it.      6

I thought of just that change across night's sill
   when that emblem of the world and of its leaders
   had finished speaking through its sacred bill;      9

for all those living lights now shone on me
   more brightly than before, and began singing
   a praise too sweet to hold in memory.      12

O heavenly love in smiling glory wreathed,
   how ardently you sounded from those flutes
   through which none but the holiest impulse
                             breathed.      15

When then those precious gems of purest ray
   with which the lamp of the sixth heaven shone
   let their last angel-harmony fade away,      18

I seemed to hear a great flume take its course
   from stone to stone, and murmur down its mountain
   as if to show the abundance of its source.      21

And as the sound emerging from a lute
   is tempered at its neck; and as the breath
   takes form around the openings of a flute—      24

just so, allowing no delay to follow,
   the murmur of the eagle seemed to climb
   inside its neck, as if the neck were hollow.      27

There it was given voice, and through the bill
   the voice emerged as words my heart awaited.
   And on my heart those words are written still.      30

"Look closely now into that part of me
   that in earth's eagles can endure the Sun,"
   the emblem said, "—the part with which I see.          33

Of all the fires with which I draw my form
   those rays that make the eye shine in my head
   are the chief souls of all this blessed swarm.          36

The soul that makes the pupil luminous
   was the sweet psalmist of the Holy Ghost
   who bore the ark of God from house to house:          39

now, insofar as he himself gave birth
   to his own psalms, he is repaid in bliss,
   and by that bliss he knows what they are worth.          42

Of the five that form my eyebrow's arc, the one
   whose glory shines the closest to my beak
   consoled the widow who had lost her son;          45

now he understands what price men pay
   who do not follow Christ, for though he learns
   the sweet life, he has known the bitter way.          48

The next in line on the circumference
   of the same upper arch of which I speak,
   delayed his own death by true penitence;          51

now he knows that when a worthy prayer
   delays today's event until tomorrow,
   the eternal judgment is not altered there.          54

The third, to give the Shepherd sovereignty,
   (with good intentions though they bore bad fruit)
   removed to Greece, bearing the laws and me;          57

now he knows the evil that began
   in his good action does not harm his soul
   although it has destroyed the world of man.          60

And him you see upon the arc beneath
   was William of that land that mourns the life
   of Charles and Frederick, as it mourns his death;   63

now he knows how heaven's heart inclines
   to love a just king, as he makes apparent
   by the radiance with which his being shines.   66

Who would believe in the erring world down there
   that Ripheus the Trojan would be sixth
   among the sacred lusters of this sphere?   69

Now he knows grace divine to depths of bliss
   the world's poor understanding cannot grasp.
   Even *his* eye cannot plumb that abyss."   72

Like a lark that soars in rapture to the sky,
   first singing, and then silent, satisfied
   by the last sweetness of its soul's own cry—   75

such seemed that seal of the Eternal Bliss
   that stamped it there, the First Will at whose will
   whatever is becomes just what it is.   78

And though my eagerness to know shone clear
   as colors shining through a clearest glass,
   I could not bear to wait in silence there;   81

but from my tongue burst out "How can this be?"
   forced by the weight of my own inner doubt.
   —At which those lights flashed in new revelry.   84

And soon then, not to keep me in suspense,
   the blessed emblem answered me, its eye
   flashing a yet more glorious radiance.   87

"I see that you believe these things are true
   because I say them. Yet, you do not see how.
   Thus, though believed, their truth is hidden
                                  from you.   90

You are like one who knows the name of a thing
    whose quiddity, until it is explained
    by someone else, defies his understanding.                    93

By every living hope and ardent love
    that bends the Eternal Will—by these alone
    the Kingdom of Heaven suffers itself to move.                 96

Not as men bend beneath a conqueror's will.
    It bends because it wishes to be bent.
    Conquered, its own benificence conquers still.               99

You marvel at the first and the fifth gem
    here on my brow, finding this realm of angels
    and gift of Christ made beautiful by them.                   102

They did not leave their bodies, as you believe,
    as pagans but as Christians, in firm faith
    in the pierced feet one grieved and one
                              would grieve.                      105

One rose again from Hell—from whose dead slope
    none may return to Love—into the flesh;
    and that was the reward of living hope;                      108

of living hope, whose power of love made good
    the prayers he raised to God to bring him back
    to life again, that his will might be renewed.               111

And so the glorious soul for whom he prayed,
    back in the flesh from which it soon departed,
    believed in Him who has the power to aid.                    114

Believing, he burst forth with such a fire
    of the true love, that at his second death
    he was worthy of a seat in this glad choir.                  117

The other, by that grace whose blessings rise
   out of so deep a spring that no one ever
   has plumbed its sources with created eyes,                120

gave all his love to justice, there on earth,
   and God, by grace on grace, let him foresee
   a vision of our redemption shining forth.                123

So he believed in Christ, and all his days
   shunning the poisonous stink of pagan creeds,
   he warned the obstinant to change their ways.           126

More than a thousand years before the grace
   of baptism was known, those maids you saw
   at the right wheel, stood for him in its place.          129

Predestination! Oh how deep your source
   is rooted past the reach of every vision
   that cannot plumb the whole of the First Cause!          132

Mortals, be slow to judge! Not even we
   who look on God in Heaven know, as yet,
   how many He will choose for ecstasy.                     135

And sweet it is to lack this knowledge still,
   for in this good is our own good refined,
   willing whatever God Himself may will."                  138

In these words the blest emblem of that sphere
   gave me these gentle curatives of love
   with which my clouded vision was made clear.             141

And as the skillful harpist, string by string,
   makes every cord attend on a good singer,
   adding a greater pleasure to the singing;                144

so, I recall, that as it spoke to me
   these paradisal words, the holy lights
   of Trajan and Ripheus in sweet harmony,                  147

as if they blinked their eyes with one accord,
made their flames pulse in time with every word.

## Notes

1-12. THE DAY AND NIGHT IMAGE AND THE HEAV-
ENLY EAGLE. The metaphor is subtle but its essence simple.
The symbolic eagle (as a unity projected by many blessed wills)
stops speaking through its bill as a single entity and a hymn
rings forth not from the eagle, but from the many lustrous
beings who compose it. Each of these beings is now giving
voice to its joy not through the symbol but from itself.

This change Dante compares to the twin faces of the heavens:
by day there is the one direct light of the Sun (a unity, as with
the Eagle); by night there is the shining of many heavenly
bodies, all of which (according to Dante's astronomy) glow not
from within themselves but by reflecting the light of the Sun
(as these souls glow by reflecting God's ray).

*our hemisphere*: The land mass of the world, all of it north
of the equator, and all contained in an arc of ·180° from India to
Spain. Thus, when the sun is 90° west of Spain it lights
only the waters on the other side of the earth and all the land
mass is dark.

31. *that part*: The eye. The Eagle is once again speaking as a
unified entity. The ancients believed that the eagle could look
straight into the sun. Note that only one eye is mentioned. The
symbolic eagle must be conceived as appearing in heraldic pro-
file, despite the fact that it flew a circle around Dante's head
in the previous canto.

38. *the sweet psalmist*: David. See *Inferno*, IV, 58.

40-42. The first thought here, a simple one, is that the measure
of his present bliss (the reward being proportionate to the act)
lets David know the true worth of his psalms. That thought is
complicated by the parenthetical "insofar, *etc.*" Since the Holy
Ghost moved in David, Dante seems to be saying, some of his
psalms sprang from It, and his present bliss cannot be repayment
to him for an act of the Holy Ghost. As Dante pointed out in
VI, 118-120, part of the delight of each heavenly soul consists
in knowing that his bliss is exactly equal to his merits.

43. *the one*: Trajan. See *Purgatorio*, X, 70-90.

48. *he has known the bitter way*: Trajan had been long in
Limbo. See note to 106 ff., below.

49-54. Hezekiah, offering a true repentance on his death bed,
was allowed to live for fifteen more years (*II Kings*, XX, 1-11;

II *Chron.*, XXXII, 24-26; *Isaiah*, XXXVIII, 1-7). *now he knows*:
To what extent prayer may vary the preordained divine plan
without altering it. These lines are best understood by referring to
*Purgatorio*, VI, 28-51. Few readers will have remembered the
point Dante left open in those lines, but Dante seems never to
forget. To read him is to experience mind in extraordinary
order.

55-60. The Emperor Constantine. With the purest of intentions
(so Dante's version of it) Constantine ceded the Western Empire
to the Church (the Shepherd) and moved his seat of Empire to
Greece, bearing with him Roman law and "me" (the Roman
Eagle). See *Purgatorio*, XXXII, 124-129; *Inferno*, XIX, 109-111,
and notes.

Constantine learns in Heaven that the evil consequences of a
good action (or the good consequences of an evil action) do
not change the nature of the original action—a point made
by Aquinas in his *Summa*.

62. *William*: William II (the Good), king of the Two
Sicilies from 1166 to 1189. He was the last of the house of
Tancred. In Dante's time, the kingdom of Naples passed to
Charles the Lame (XIX, 127) and the Kingdom of Sicily to
Frederick II (XIX, 131). Sicily mourns its present evil as it
mourns the passing of its happiness with the death of William.

65. *as he makes apparent*: The degree of brilliance flashed
forth by each soul is the measure of its relative bliss. William,
by shining more brightly than most there, shows that he is more
blest than most.

68. *Ripheus*: Virgil mentioned him once (*Aeneid*, II, 426 ff.)
as the one most just man among the Trojans and as the one
who most loved the right. No more is known of him, and Dante
is thus free (see below) to invent a pre-Christian conversion for
him. *sixth*: Dante says "fifth" among those who make up the
eyebrow. Beginning with David as the eyeball, such a count
would rank Ripheus sixth among the souls of this sphere; and
rhyme dictating, I have so rendered the passage.

89. *see how*: See how these things can be true.

92. *quiddity*: i.e., "thingness" or "whatness." In Scholastic
terminology: "that which causes a thing to be what it is."

94-99. These paradoxes are, of course, the language of the
mystery: God is unmovable but God is love and as love moves
Him, He yields gladly to it, conquering by His act of love.

102. *and gift of Christ*: Not in Dante's text but necessary
for the line and clearly implicit in what the Eagle is saying.
Trajan and Ripheus, having been pagans, would not have had

the gift of Christ's redemption. It is for this reason that Dante marvels at finding them in Heaven.

103-105. Ripheus and Trajan, as the Eagle will explain, did not "leave their bodies" as pagans but as Christians and firm believers, one (Trajan) in the pierced feet (the Crucifixion) that had already taken place; the other (Ripheus) in the Crucifixion yet to come.

106-117. THE RESURRECTION AND CONVERSION OF TRAJAN. Dante follows a legend that Gregory I (Pope from 590 to 604 and later St. Gregory) prayed so ardently for the salvation of Trajan that God's voice replied "I grant pardon to Trajan." Since God so granted, it was, of course, predestined that he should so grant. Trajan, therefore, could never have been truly damned, for no prayer can help the damned. But since none may go from Hell to Heaven (with the exception of those souls Christ took with him in the Harrowing of Hell), it was necessary to restore Trajan to the flesh long enough to permit his conversion to Christ.

108. *living hope* : Of Gregory.

120. *created eyes*: Nothing God has created can plumb the mystery of its creator. Compare lines 130-132 below.

121-129. THE CONVERSION OF RIPHEUS. Unhampered by any historical record, Dante creates a legend of Ripheus as a Christian before the fact. Granted a vision of Christ to come, he believed utterly and was saved. In place of baptism (over a thousand years before baptism came into being) the three maids who stood at the right wheel of the Chariot of the Church in the Pageant of the Terrestrial Paradise (i.e., the Three Theological Virtues) stood as his godmothers in some equivalent ritual. (*V. Purgatorio*, XXIX, 121 ff.)

132. *that cannot plumb*: As, certainly, no human vision can. As even the chosen souls of Heaven cannot.

135. *how many He will choose*: Had Dante cared to, he could have made a rather accurate guess as to God's intention when he reached the Empyrean. In XXX, 128-132, he tells us that few seats are left open in Paradise (Judgment Day will take place when the last throne of Heaven is filled). And in XXXII, 25-27, he has St. Bernard point out the empty thrones, the number of which Dante might reasonably have guessed, though had he done so he would have found himself prophesying the end of the world within fairly tight limits, a prophecy Dante wisely chose not to utter. Poetry is, among other things, the art of knowing what to leave out.

# CANTO XXI

---

THE SEVENTH SPHERE: SATURN
                    *The Contemplative: Peter Damiano*

*BEATRICE AND DANTE ENTER the Sphere of
Saturn. BEATRICE DOES NOT SMILE in her new
bliss to announce their arrival, for her radiance would
then be such that Dante's mortal senses would be consumed, as Semele was consumed by the Godhead of
Jupiter. Rather, Beatrice announces that they are there
and commands Dante to look into the crystalline substance of that Heaven for the vision he will see of the
SOULS OF THE CONTEMPLATIVE.*

*Dante turns and beholds a vision of a GOLDEN
LADDER on which countless Splendors arise and
descend wheeling like birds in flight. That host of the
blessed descends only as far as a given rung, but one
radiance among them draws closer to Dante and indicates by its radiance that it is eager to bring him joy.
It is the soul of PETER DAMIANO, a Doctor of the
Church, renowned for a severely ascetic life even in high
church office. Peter Damiano explains to Dante that
THE MYSTERY OF PREDESTINATION is beyond the
reach of all but God, and that men should not presume
to grasp it. He concludes with a DENUNCIATION OF
PAPAL CORRUPTION, and at his words, all the souls
of Saturn fly down to form a ring around him and
thunder forth HEAVEN'S RIGHTEOUS INDIGNA-
TION at evildoers. So loud is their cry that Dante cannot
make out their words, his senses reeling at that thunder-
clap of sound.*

My eyes were fixed once more on my lady's face;
   and with my eyes, my soul, from which all thought,
   except of her, had fled without a trace.        3

She did not smile. "Were I to smile," she said,
   "You would be turned to ash, as Semele was
   when she saw Jupiter in his full Godhead;        6

because my beauty, which, as it goes higher
   from step to step of the eternal palace,
   burns, as you know, with ever brighter fire;        9

and if it is not tempered in its brightening,
   its radiance would consume your mortal powers
   as a bough is shattered by a bolt of lightning.    12

We have soared to the Seventh Splendor, which is now
   beneath the Lion's blazing breast, and rays
   its influence, joined with his, to the world below.    15

Now make your eyes the mirror of the vision
   this mirror will reveal to you, and fix
   your mind behind your eyes in strict attention."    18

Could any man conceive what blessed pasture
   my eyes found in her face when I turned away,
   at her command, to find another nurture—    21

then would he know with what a rush of bliss
   I obeyed my heavenly escort, balancing
   one side and the other, that joy against this.    24

Within the crystal that bears round the world
   the name of its great king in that golden age
   when evil's flag had not yet been unfurled,    27

like polished gold ablaze in full sunlight,
   I saw a ladder rise so far above me
   it soared beyond the reaches of my sight.    30

And I saw so many splendors make their way
  down its bright rungs, I thought that every lamp
  in all of heaven was pouring forth its ray.          33

As grackles flock together at first light,
  obeying a natural impulse to move as one
  to warm their night-chilled feathers in glad flight;  36

after which, some go off and do not come back,
  others return to the points from which they came,
  and others stay with the flock in its wheeling track; 39

—just such an impulse seemed to work among
  those sparkling essences, for they flocked together
  the instant they had reached a certain rung.         42

One that came nearest where we stood below
  then made itself so bright I said to myself:
  "I well know with what love for me you glow!"        45

But she from whom I await the how and when
  of my speech and silence, was still; and despite my
                                                yearning
  I knew it was well to ask no questions then.         48

She saw in the vision of Him who sees all things
  what silence held my eager tongue in check,
  and said to me: "Give your soul's impulse wings!"    51

"O blessed being hidden in the ray
  of your own bliss," I said in reverence,
  "I am not worthy, but for her sake, I pray,          54

who gives me leave to question, let me know
  why you, of all this sacred company,
  have placed yourself so near me, here below;         57

and tell me why, when every lower sphere
   sounds the sweet symphony of Paradise
   in adoration, there is no music here."          60

"Your sight is mortal. Is not your hearing, too?"
   he said. "Our song is still for the same reason
   Beatrice holds back her smile—for love of you.   63

Only that I might make your spirit gladder
   by what I say and by the light that robes me,
   have I come so far down the sacred ladder.       66

Nor was it greater love that spurred me: here
   as much—and more—love burns in every soul,
   as the flaming of these radiances makes clear.    69

But the high love that makes us prompt to serve
   the Judge who rules the world, decrees the fate
   of every soul among us, as you observe."          72

"O sacred lamp," I said, "I understand
   that in this court glad love follows the will
   of Eternal Providence, needing no command;       75

but the further point I cannot grasp is this:
   why, among all these blisses with whom you dwell,
   were you alone predestined to this office?"       78

Before I finished speaking, that lamp of grace
   like a millstone at full speed, making an axle
   of its own center, began to spin in place.        81

And then the Love within the lamp replied:
   "I feel the ray of God's light focused on me.
   It strikes down through the ray in which I hide.  84

Its power, joined to my own, so elevates
   my soul above itself, that I behold
   the Primal Source from which its emanates.        87

My bliss flames only as that ray shines down.
  As much of glory as I am given to see
  my flame gives back in glory of its own.          90

But in all Heaven, the soul granted most light,
  the Seraph that has God in closest view,
  could not explain what you have asked to know.    93

The truth of this is hidden so far down
  in the abyss of the Eternal Law,
  it is cut off from all created vision.            96

Report what I have said when you are back
  in the mortal world, that no man may presume
  to move his feet down so profound a track.        99

On earth the mind is smoke; here, it is fire.
  How can it do there what it cannot do
  even when taken into heaven's choir?"             102

I left that question, his own words having thus
  prescribed me from it; and, so limited,
  was content to ask him humbly who he was.         105

"Not far from your own birthplace, row on row
  between Italy's two shores, peaks rise so high
  that on them thunder sounds from far below.       108

A humpback ridge called Catria rises there.
  Beneath it stands a holy hermitage
  once given entirely to meditation and prayer."    111

So, for the third time now, that soul of grace
  began to speak, continuing: "I became
  so rooted in God's service in that place,         114

I lived on lenten olive-food alone
  and bore both heat and cold indifferently,
  rejoicing ever more in contemplation.             117

Once that cloister sent here, sphere on sphere,
   harvests of souls. Now all its works are vain
   as, soon now, righteous punishment shall make
                       clear.   120

I was Peter Damiano there, and became
   Peter the Sinner by the Adriatic
   in the abbey sacred to Our Lady's name.   123

Little was left me of my mortal course
   when I was chosen and summoned to wear the hat
   that seems forever to pass from bad to worse.   126

Cephas, and the great ark of the Holy Ghost
   once came among mankind barefoot and gaunt,
   eating by chance, with charity as their host.   129

But now your pastors are so bloated and vain
   they go propped on either side, with a man before
   and another coming behind to bear the train.   132

They cover even their mounts with the cloaks they wear
   so that two beasts move under a single hide.
   O Heavenly Patience, how long will you forebear!"   135

As he spoke these words, I saw more ardors yearning
   downward in circling flight, from rung to rung;
   and grow more radiant with every turning.   138

Round him they came to rest, and all burst forth
   in unison of love: a cry so loud
   the like of it has not been heard on earth.   141

Nor could I understand it, for the peal
   of that ominous thunder made my senses reel.

## Notes

5. *as Semele was*: Semele loved Jupiter (Zeus) and Juno
(Hera) tricked the girl into begging Jupiter to show himself to

her in the full splendor of his godhead (as the other gods saw him). Semele was consumed to ash by that radiance. (See Ovid, *Metamorphoses*, III, 253 ff., and *Inferno*, XXX. 1-2, note.)

13-15. *the Seventh Splendor*: The Seventh Heaven (Saturn). Once again the arrival is instantaneous. For the reasons given, Beatrice does not manifest the new bliss by smiling, but simply announces that they have arrived. *the Lion*: The Constellation Leo. Dante describes Saturn as being in conjunction with Leo, as in fact it was in parts of March and April of 1300. Thus the influence of Leo is mixed with that of Saturn.

17. *this mirror*: The Sphere of Saturn. All the spheres are, in one sense, crystalline reflectors of God's light. In another sense, of course, they let the light through undiminished, but such differences are of the mystery. Dante uses the same figure for the sun in *Purgatorio*, IV, 62.

19-24. A graciously turned devotion. The thought is complex yet sweetly balanced. Sense: "Could the reader begin to imagine how sweet it was to feast my eyes (like lambs in blessed pasture) on the beatitude of Beatrice's face, then he might understand how sweet it was to obey even her command to turn away from such bliss to find another."

25-27. *the crystal*: The Sphere of Saturn. It bears around the world the name of Saturn, who was the world's king in the Golden Age of man before sin had appeared among mankind.

28-42. THE VISION OF THE HEAVENLY LADDER. "And he dreamed, and beheld a ladder set up on earth, and the top of it reached to heaven: and behold the angels of God ascending and descending on it." So *Genesis*, XXVIII, 12, describes Jacob's ladder. Here, however, Dante adapts it to his own purposes, placing it within the crystal of the Sphere of Saturn, describing it as being made of blazing gold (to signify the worth of the contemplative soul? as the height of the ladder signifies that soul's ascent to the top of heaven?).

The normal course of the contemplative soul would, of course, be to ascend rather than to descend the ladder. Love, however, remains a first principle, and to welcome Dante and Beatrice in purest love, these souls descend joyously, though forever rising again, to return to their natural height of bliss.

42-45. *a certain rung*: Dante offers no further specifications. The rung seems simply to fix a point below which these souls (whose natural impulse is to rise) choose not to descend at first, though one spirit does draw closer (as, later, all do). This first spirit indicates, by the increase of his radiance, the love it feels for Dante, and its readiness to offer him any service, though protesting that its love is no greater than that of any other soul of this host.

43. *And one*: St. Peter Damiano (1007-1072), as he will later identify himself. He was never officially canonized though he was venerated in Ravenna. He was, however, officially pronounced a Doctor of the Church. His many writings enjoin strict monastic rules and mortification of the flesh.

Born in Ravenna, he became a Benedictine and entered the Camadolese house at Fonte Avellana in 1035, became prior about 1043, and Cardinal-Bishop of Ostia in 1057 or 1058, accepting his elevation, as all reports agree, against his own inclination, and continuing in every high office a life of monastic severity.

46-51. Beatrice's allegorical role as Divine Revelation is especially relevant here. Looking into the vision of all-seeing God, she sees Dante's yearning and gives him permission to speak to the waiting soul.

52-60. DANTE'S QUESTIONS. With Beatrice's permission, Dante asks the spirit, first, why it was chosen to come closer than the others, and, second, why there is no heavenly harmony to be heard in this Sphere, since all the Spheres below ring with joyous singing. The second question, being the more important, is answered first (lines 61-63), and then the first (lines 64-72).

67-69. The reply may, perhaps, best be taken as an example of heavenly modesty. At the same time, however, it is partly a statement of fact: all souls in heaven are glorious with love (as the radiances about the poet make clear), and since Peter Damiano is not the foremost soul in Heaven, there are those whose souls will shine more brightly than does his.

70-72. These lines are, in effect, Dante's way of introducing the theme of predestination, which will be discussed later. If the language is difficult, the difficulty lies not in the language itself but in the fact that the concept is unusual and necessarily abstruse. Peter Damiano explains that he descended farther than the other souls because he was predestined to by the will of God. In so saying, he makes clear that every action of all these souls, as each goes up and down the ladder, is similarly predestined. Every heavenly soul, in the grace of love that is granted to it, is a glad servant of the Divine will that assigns the fate of each.

And here, certainly, is the extension of what Virgil foresaw dimly in *Purgatorio*, XXVII, 140-143, in telling Dante he was free to follow his own inner impulse. "Here," Virgil says, "your will is upright, free, and whole." At the Paradisal level, however, glorified by revelation, Dante makes it clear that it is not a

matter of the individual will but of joyous identification with
the service for which God has predestined each soul. (*Cf.* III,
85: "In His will is our peace." See also XX, 130 ff.)

74. *this court*: The court of Heaven.

75. *Eternal Providence*: It may be well, in this discussion
of predestination, to remind some readers that "providence" derives from Latin *pro*, before, and *videre*, to see. Note also that
the heavenly souls need not be commanded to follow God's
foreseeing and predestined will: this glad love suffices to move
them in concord with God.

79-81. *Before I finished speaking*: Before the last three words
of line 78. It is at the sound of the word "predestination" that
the soul of Peter Damiano begins to spin for joy. Dante does
not specifically say that it went on spinning as it talked, but he
does describe the soul as beginning to spin, and he does not
say that it stopped. The spinning seems an aptly Dantean way
to indicate great joy. The soul, moreover, goes into a trance
in which it has a direct vision of God; and the spinning might
well serve as an established symbol of the trancelike state (cf.
"whirling dervish"). There is also the thematic precedent of the
grackles in whirling flight, whereby the act of spinning becomes a
motif of this canto. Allegorically, too, it may be said that the
contemplative soul revolves around its own center (which is, of
course, love).

For all these reasons, I think the soul of Peter Damiano should
be visualized as spinning on through the rest of the canto,
whirled round and round in a glorious vision of God.

82-90. PETER DAMIANO'S VISION OF GOD. Speaking in a
trance of bliss, spinning for joy in the rapture of its vision, yet
moved by heavenly Love to share its joy with Dante, the soul
explains that it is experiencing a vision of God, who focuses His
ray into the ray in which the soul hides. (Dante says "in
which I embowel myself," i.e., embody myself, and I have been
unable to render this felicity.) As has been explained in XIV,
40-42, this is God's grant of grace, and the soul shines brighter
to the extent that grace enables it to reflect God's ray.

96. *created vision*: The vision of which any created thing
is capable. Only God's uncreated vision can plumb the mystery
of predestination. And if the truth is beyond the highest soul
in Heaven—as Peter Damiano goes on to say—how can the feeble
mind of man think to reach to it? For this reason, he charges
Dante, upon his return to the world, to warn men away from
presuming to know the unknowable (for such a presumption
would involve the sin of pride).

99. *to move his feet*: As a hunter does.

104-105. *so limited, was content*: The question of the soul's identity is not a trivial one. In due observance of fit proportion, however, it has to be recognized as a lesser matter than the abysmal mystery of predestination.

109. *Catria*: Lies between Gubbio and Pergola. Below it (the "holy hermitage") stands the monastery of Santa Croce di Fonte Avellana of the Camaldolese rule (established at Camaldoli about 1012 by St. Romualdo). This rule minimized the community organization of the monastery but established a particularly severe rule for the individual monks.

115-116. *lenten olive-food*: Olive oil being common in Italy, and butter and lard (like all animal products) being expensive, and therefore luxurious, lenten food (*"cibi di liquor di'ulivi"*) was prepared in nothing but olive oil. Here we should probably understand a diet of simple crusts dipped in olive oil. Even at that, Peter Damiano seems to be suggesting that he ate high on the ecclesiastical hog: Rohrbacher's "Ecclesiastical History" (cited by Scartazzini) gives the diet of the order as plain bread and water for four days of each week, with a few greens added on other days, and with such feasting regularly interrupted by days of fasting. *both heat and cold*: The rule required the monks to go barefoot.

120. *as . . . righteous punishment shall make clear*: As everyone in Heaven seems to do, Peter mourns for the good old days when Fonte Avellana sent whole harvests of monks to heaven (and particularly, one may infer, to Saturn, which is the kingdom of the contemplative). Now, however, the saintly rule has been corrupted, and since God's justice will not long tolerate such a state of affairs, that corruption shall be made manifest by the punishment God shall, soon now, send down upon it.

121-123. This tercet has been a scholar's battleground and reputations have fought and died over the question of its proper punctuation and of its relevance to the historical record, such as it is. Civilian readers need only know that Peter went by both names, adopting the second as an act of piety (he had adopted the first in gratitude to his brother, who had made possible his education), and that he went to Ravenna ("by the Adriatic") as a papal emissary. He lived there for two years in the monastery of Santa Maria Pomposa.

124. *little was left me of my mortal course*: Peter became a cardinal in 1057 or 1058. He died in 1072.

125-126. *the hat*: Of a cardinal. In passing from one wearer to another, it seems forever to go from a bad man to a worse—another lament for the corruption of the times.

127. *Cephas*: The name Christ gave to Simon, who became Peter. The word means "rock" in Hebrew, as *"pietra"* does in Italian, "Pietro" being the masculine form of the word used as a man's name. Cf. "founded on a rock." *the great ark of the Holy Ghost*: St. Paul.

130. *pastors*: Can only mean "popes" here—those who fill the offices once held by the pastors Peter and Paul. The parish priests of Dante's time may have eaten better than did Peter Damiano, but they did not move about without a great retinue, a warder out in front to clear the way, servants and officials on either side to press back the throng, and a trainbearer following to carry the trailing skirts of their opulent robes.

136-138. *yearning . . . and grew more radiant*: So moved by their renewed joy in the justice of Peter Damiano's denunciation; for their love of what is good and their righteous indignation at what is evil, are a conjoined impulse in them. They proceed to cry out like thunder against the evils Peter Damiano has condemned, their cry so loud that Dante's senses reel at the thunderous sound and are unable to make out the words of the cry. Heaven has no other voice in which to speak of evil. Such, on the Paradisal level, is righteous indignation. Cf. *Inferno*, VIII, 43 and note.

# CANTO XXII

THE SEVENTH SPHERE: SATURN
>*The Contemplative*: St. Benedict

ASCENT TO THE SPHERE OF THE FIXED STARS

THE EIGHTH SPHERE: THE FIXED STARS
>Dante Looks Back at the
>Universe Below

*DANTE'S SENSES STILL REELING*, he turns to
Beatrice, who reassures him, and prophesies that he
will live to see *GOD'S VENGEANCE DESCEND ON
THE CORRUPTORS OF THE CHURCH*. She then
calls his attention to the other souls of this sphere.
Looking up, Dante sees *A HUNDRED RADIANT
GLOBES*, one of which draws near and identifies itself
as the heavenly splendor that had been *ST. BENEDICT*.

Benedict explains that the Golden Ladder, like the
contemplative life, soars to the summit of God's glory,
and he laments that so few of his Benedictine monks
remain eager to put the world behind them and begin
the ascent, for they are lost in the degeneracy of bad
days. Yet God has worked greater wonders than would
be required to restore the purity of the church.

So saying, Benedict is gathered into his heavenly choir
of radiances, and the whole company ascends to the
top of the sky and out of sight.

Beatrice then makes a sign and Dante feels himself
making the *ASCENT TO THE EIGHTH SPHERE,
THE SPHERE OF THE FIXED STARS*. But before
the souls of that Sphere are revealed to him, Beatrice
bids him look back to see how far she has raised him.
Dante looks down through the Seven Spheres in their
glory, seeing all the heavens at a glance, and the earth
as an insignificant speck far below. Then turning from
it as from a puny thing, he turns his eyes back to the
eyes of Beatrice.

My sense reeled, and as a child in doubt
  runs always to the one it trusts the most,
  I turned to my guide, still shaken by that shout;        3

and she, like a mother, ever prompt to calm
  her pale and breathless son with kindly words,
  the sound of which is his accustomed balm,             6

said: "Do you not know you are in the skies
  of Heaven itself? that all is holy here?
  that all things spring from love in Paradise?           9

Their one cry shakes your senses: you can now see
  what would have happened to you had they sung,
  or had I smiled in my new ecstasy.                    12

Had you understood the prayer within their cry
  you would know now what vengeance they
                                    called down,
  though you shall witness it before you die.           15

The sword of Heaven is not too soon dyed red,
  nor yet too late—except as its vengeance seems
  to those who wait for it in hope or dread.            18

But look now to the others. Turn as I say
  and you shall see among this company
  many great souls of the Eternal Ray."                21

I did as she commanded. Before my eyes
  a hundred shining globes entwined their beams,
  soul adding grace to soul in Paradise.                24

I stood there between longing and diffidence
  and fought my longing back, afraid to speak
  for fear my questioning might give offense.           27

And the largest and most glowing globe among
  the wreath of pearls came forward of its own
                             prompting
  to grant the wish I had not given tongue.                        30

These words came from within it: "Could you see,
  as I do, with what love our spirits burn
  to give you joy, your tongue would have been free.   33

To cause you no delay on the high track
  to the great goal, I shall address myself
  to none but the single question you hold back.        36

The summit of that mountain on whose side
  Cassino lies, once served an ill-inclined
  and misted people in their pagan pride.                39

And I am he who first bore to that slope
  the holy name of Him who came on earth
  to bring mankind the truth that is our hope.          42

Such grace shone down on me that men gave heed
  through all that countryside and were won over
  from the seductions of that impious creed.            45

These other souls were all contemplatives,
  fired by that warmth of soul that summons up
  the holy flowers and fruits of blessèd lives.          48

Here is Romualdus, and Maccarius, too.
  Here are my brothers who kept within the cloister
  and, never straying, kept hearts sound and true."     51

And I to him: "The love you have made clear
  in speaking as you have, and the good intent
  I see in all the glories of this sphere,               54

have opened all my confidence: it grows
   and spreads wide on your warmth, rejoicing in it
   as does, in the Sun's heat, a full-blown rose.          57

I therefore beg you, Father: can I rise
   to such a height of grace that I may see
   your unveiled image with my mortal eyes?"             60

And he then: "Brother, this shall be made known
   in the last sphere. Your wish will be answered there
   where every other is, including my own.                63

There, every wish is perfect, ripe, and whole.
   For there, and there alone, is every part
   where it has always been; for it has no pole,          66

not being in space. It is to that very height
   the golden ladder mounts; and thus you see
   why it outsoars the last reach of your sight.           69

The patriarch Jacob saw it, saw it mount
   to lean on that very sill, that time he dreamed it
   covered with angels beyond all mortal count.            72

To climb it now, however, none makes haste
   to lift his feet from earth. My rule lives on
   only to fill the parchments it lays waste.              75

The walls that were retreats in their good hour
   are dens for beasts now; what were holy cowls
   are gunny sacks stuffed full of evil flour.             78

But even compound usury strikes less
   against God's will and pleasure, than does that fruit
   whose poison fills the hearts of monks with madness. 81

For all the goods of the Church, tithes and donations,
   are for the poor of God, not to make fat
   the families of monks—and worse relations.             84

The flesh of mortals is so weak down there
   that a good beginning is not reason enough
   to think the seedling tree will live to bear.    87

Peter began with neither silver nor gold;
   I, with prayer and fasting. And Brother Francis
   in humble poverty gathered souls to his fold.    90

And if you look at the origins of each one,
   then look again at what it has become,
   you will see that what was white has changed
                        to dun.    93

Yet Jordan flowing backward, and the sea
   parting as God willed, were more wondrous sights
   than God's help to His stricken church would be."   96

So did he speak; then faded from my eye
   into his company, which closed about him,
   and then, like a whirlwind, spun away on high.    99

And my sweet lady with a simple sign
   raised me along that ladder after them,
   conquering my nature with her power divine.    102

There never was known down here, where everything
   rises or falls as natural law determines,
   a speed to equal the motion of my wing.    105

Reader, so may I hope once more to stand
   in that holy Triumph, for which I weep my sins
   and beat my breast—you could not draw your hand   108

out of a tongue of flame and thrust it back
   sooner than I sighted and had entered
   the sign that follows Taurus on Heaven's track.    111

O glorious constellation! O lamp imbued
   with great powers, to whose influence I ascribe
   all my genius, however it may be viewed!     114

When I drew my first breath of Tuscan air
   the Sun, the father of all mortal life,
   was rising in your rays and setting there.     117

And then when I was granted Heaven's grace
   to enter the great wheel that gives you motion,
   I was led upward through your zone of space.     120

To you devoutly now my prayer is sped:
   make my soul worthy of the call it hears
   to the great passage that still lies ahead!     123

"You are so near the final health of man
   you will do well to go clear-eyed and keen
   into that good," my Beatrice began.     126

"Therefore, before you enter further here
   look down and see how vast a universe
   I have put beneath your feet, bright sphere
                       on sphere.     129

Thus may you come in the fullness of delight
   to the Triumphant Court that comes in joy
   through the round ether to your mortal sight."     132

My eyes went back through the seven spheres below,
   and I saw this globe, so small, so lost in space,
   I had to smile at such a sorry show.     135

Who thinks it the least pebble in the skies
   I most approve. Only the mind that turns
   to other things may truly be called wise.     138

I saw Latona's daughter glowing there
  without that shadow that had once misled me
  to think her matter was part dense, part rare.   141

My eyes looked on your son, Hyperion,
  nor did they falter. And wheeling close around him,
  I saw the motion of Maia and Dione.   144

Next I saw how Jupiter mediates
  between his father and son, and I understood
  why the motion of one and the other vacillates.   147

And all the seven, in a single view,
  showed me their masses, their velocities,
  and the distances between each in its purlieu.   150

And turning there with the eternal Twins,
  I saw the dusty little threshing ground
  that makes us ravenous for our mad sins,   153

saw it from mountain crest to lowest shore.
Then I turned my eyes to Beauty's eyes once more.

## Notes

13-15. *the prayer within their cry:* Dante heard the sound of
the cry, but not the prayer within it (what the words said). We
may now understand that these souls called on God to show
His wrath at the corruption of the Church, and perhaps of the
papacy in particular. What retribution Dante will witness before
he dies is not specified. History suggests the capture of Boniface VIII at Alagna by the mercenaries of Philip the Fair under
William de Nogaret as one possible vengeance (*v. Purgatorio*,
XX, 85-93 and note). Or it may suggest Philip's maneuver in
1304 whereby Clement V was elected Pope and the papacy removed to Avignon (*v. Purgatorio*, XXXII, 158 and note). But
neither event can be taken as a large-scale visitation of God's
wrath, and neither, certainly, ended papal corruption. Beatrice's
prophecy is best taken, I believe, as simply one more way of
denouncing the corrupt. Dante would, of course, have welcomed

such a visitation of God's wrath, but he clearly has no specific event in mind.

16-18. Beatrice is making the point that God's vengeance is always taken at the proper and inevitable moment, never too soon, and never too late, though to the wicked (who wait for it with dread) it seems always to come too soon, and to the pious (who wait for it with hope for the downfall of evil) it seems always to come too late.

19. *the others*: Dante's attention has been fixed on St. Peter Damiano. Now Beatrice directs his attention to the other great spirits of this sphere.

28-29. *the largest and most glowing globe*: Contains the spirit of St. Benedict (480-543). There is some historic uncertainty about his life, the recorded facts having been subject to pious increment. He was born at Nursia in Umbria and went to Rome for his education. There, appalled by the wickedness of the Romans, he left the world about the year 500 and lived in a cave on Mount Subiaco, his rigid ascetism and holiness drawing disciples to him, though he seems never to have been ordained. About 525 he moved with his followers to Monte Cassino and there, after destroying a temple to Apollo, founded the great central monastery of the Benedictine order on the rule he had already established for his followers on Subiaco. He died at Monte Cassino on March 21, his feast day, and was buried in the same grave with his sister, Ste. Scholastica.

33. *your tongue would have been free*: To ask the questions Dante held back from speaking.

34-36. St. Benedict's exact point in this passage will be clear if one recalls that many of the heavenly spirits have answered not only the questions Dante had spoken or framed in his mind, but others, too, though he had not yet thought to think them. To speed Dante on his way, St. Benedict will answer only the one question Dante has clearly in mind.

38. *once served*: By having upon its peak a temple of Apollo. Especially in the outlying districts, paganism survived well into the Middle Ages. St. Benedict is saying that he was the first to bring Christianity to the mountain people on and around Cassino.

45. *that impious creed*: The cult of Apollo.

49. *Romualdus*: St. Romualdo (956-1027), founder of the Camaldolese Order (*v.* note to XXI, 109). *Maccarius*: Probably St. Maccarius of Alexandria (died 404) a disciple of St. Anthony.

He lived in the desert between the Nile and the Red Sea and was reputed to have been the leader of 5000 eremites. Dante may have had in mind Maccarius the Egyptian (circa 301-391) also a disciple of St. Anthony. Or Dante may have thought of the two as one person.

55-57. A literal rendering of these lines might read: ["These things] have caused my confidence to dilate just as the sun does a rose, which, when opened, becomes as great as it has the power to become."

60. *unveiled image*: The image in which the soul would appear were Dante's eyes not blinded by the radiance that veils it.

61. *Brother*: Dante has addressed him as "Father" out of respect, but all the souls in Heaven are brothers and sisters of the one Father, and above honorary titles.

62. *in the last sphere:* In the Empyrean. There (v. XXXII, 35) St. Benedict does appear to Dante among the glories of the mystic rose.

63. *including my own*: My own wish to content you in your wish. St. Benedict does not imply that every wish finds fulfillment in the presence of God, but rather that "this good" and "every other" do.

64-69. Only the mystery of revelation will make clear, and only to the elected soul, these mysteries of God's love. In one sense, we may gather from the vocabulary of exaltation, all good is from God, and since no part of good has ever left Him, every part of every good wish, in being returned to God's presence, is back where it always has been. For God is also ubiquitous, His presence limited by no boundary, since it is not a dimension of space.

It is to the crown of that sublimity that exists beyond dimension that the Golden Ladder mounts, outsoaring the reach of any soul's (physical or spiritual) sight.

70-72. The vision of Jacob's ladder is described in *Genesis*, XXVIII, 12 ff.

73-75. Another sounding of the theme of latter-day degeneracy, St. Benedict's rule for the contemplative was designed to raise the soul toward Heaven (as if climbing the ladder). Now, however, none of his monks are in any hurry to forego the pleasures of the earth, and so the Benedictine rule lives on as a waste of the parchments on which it is copied, since none observe it.

78-84. Once the clerics sought God in prayer, meditation, and acts of charity. Then all the possessions of the church were held in trust for the poor, to be distributed to them at need. Now, however, the fruit of avarice has poisoned the hearts of clerics, and the wealth that should be used to help God's poor is used by the monks themselves to swell the purse and position of their families, or for worse relations (the latter probably signifying that corrupt monks kept mistresses and bad companions in luxurious establishments).

86-87. Dante says, literally: "A good beginning is not enough [to certify the interval] from the birth of the oak to the harvest of acorns."

91. *each one*: Of the three folds founded by the three great saints.

94-96. *Jordan . . . the sea parting*: Most commentators read these lines as a statement of hope: "The same will that caused the Jordan to flow backward and the Red Sea to divide, could will the lesser miracle of restoring purity to the church." Others read it in the opposite sense: "It would be more wondrous to see Jordan flow backward and the sea divide than to see the church restored to purity." Especially in view of the fact that Beatrice has promised Dante that he would live to see God's vengeance on the corruptors of the Church, the more hopeful interpretation seems to be the more likely.

98. *his company*: The other souls of the Contemplative. Their choir closes about him (an allegory of the unity of the souls of Heaven?) and instantly ascends to the top of the sky.

100-111. ASCENT FROM SATURN TO THE SPHERE OF THE FIXED STARS. Once again the ascent is instantaneous. Beatrice, by a simple sign, raises Dante to the next sphere, her power overcoming his nature. On one level his "nature" is his mortal weight, which is here uplifted despite the forces of gravity. On another, it is the human soul, gross and imperfect in itself, yet able by the power of Divine Revelation to soar toward God.

103. *down here*: On earth, and within the operations of earth's natural laws, from which Dante has escaped.

105. *my wing*: To signify "my flight." But note that Dante says "wing" rather than "wings." He may have intended an allegorical point. The soul, while still earthbound, may seek to soar with reason as one wing and with faith as the other. In Heaven, however, the ascent is accomplished by the single wing of faith, that power of the soul that brings it to the transcendent recognition of God.

108. *beat my breast*: In penitence.

108-109. *draw your hand . . . and thrust it back*: The sequence of this action is deliberately reversed in another hysteron-proteron. See note to II, 23-24.

111. *the sign that follows Taurus*: Gemini. *Heaven's track*: The Zodiac.

112-123. INVOCATION OF GEMINI. Dante's invocation is spoken not in the *persona* of the pilgrim en route, but in that of the poet at his desk, looking back to his great journey.

Gemini, Dante lets us know, is the zodiacal sign under which he was born (lines 115-117) and whose influence determined his poetic genius (lines 112-114). In 1265 the Sun entered the sign of Gemini on May 18 and passed from it on June 17. (The exact date of Dante's birth is not known, but these dates set firm limits for it.) It is allegorically felicitous certainly, that Dante, in ascending to (being born into), the Sphere of the Fixed Stars, should pass through his natal constellation.

124. *the final health of man*: God.

134. *this globe*: The Earth.

139. *Latona's daughter*: The Moon (as Diana, sister of Apollo, the Sun, both children of Latona).

140-141. *without that shadow*: See II, 46 ff. Dante is looking now at the face of the moon we call the dark side and which is never visible from Earth. The sun that lights it, moreover, must be between it and Dante, probably to one side, though it would be nothing now for his Heaven-heightened vision to see through the sun. As the next tercet indicates, Dante was at least able to look directly into the sun.

142. *your son, Hyperion*: The Sun as the son of Hyperion, himself the son of Uranus and Terra.

144. *Maia and Dione*: Here stand for Mercury and Venus. Maia was one of the seven sisters of the Pleiades and the mother of Mercury. Dione was the mother of Venus. I do not know why Dante takes the mothers for the children here.

145-147. *Jupiter . . . his father and son*: Jupiter was the son of Saturn and the father of Mars. The temperate planet, Jupiter, lies between the excessively hot planet Mars and the excessively cold planet Saturn. Such are the terms of Dante's astrology. Dante does not explain how this theory of a temperate mean between fire and ice allows him to understand the eccentricities of the orbits of Mars and Saturn—perhaps he conceives Jupiter as a moderating force that attracts the planets on its either side. Whatever the theory, the observable fact is that these planets, as seen from Earth, do wander all over the star chart; their orbits swing sometimes close to the sun and sometimes away, and they rise sometimes before it and sometimes after it. But Dante's reference here is all the more confusing in that all the planets wander in this way.

150. *purlieu*: Dante uses the word *"riparo"* (the place to which one repairs in the same sense that astrologers speak of "the house" of Mars or of some other planet. Hence Dante must mean the orbit of each considered as the place that is particularly its own.

151. *the eternal Twins*: Gemini.

152. *the dusty little threshing ground*: The Earth, so described as an insignificant and busy flat patch of dust as compared to the glory and serenity of the Heavens.

153. *Beauty's eyes*: The eyes of Beatrice, which are the eyes of Heaven.

# CANTO XXIII

---

THE EIGHTH SPHERE: THE FIXED STARS

> *The Triumph of Christ*
> *The Virgin Mary*
> *The Apostles*
> *The Angel Gabriel*
> *St. Peter*

*BEATRICE STARES expectantly toward that part of the sky where the Sun is at its highest point, and Dante, moved by the joy of her expectation, follows her look. Almost at once there descends from the highest Heaven the radiant substance of the VISION OF CHRIST TRIUMPHANT as it rays forth on the garden of all those souls who have been redeemed through Christ. The splendor too much for his senses, DANTE SWOONS. He is recalled to himself by Beatrice and discovers that, newly strengthened as he has been by the vision of Christ, he is able to look upon her smile of bliss.*

*Beatrice urges him to look at the Garden of Christ's Triumph, upon the Rose of the VIRGIN MARY and the Lilies of the APOSTLES. Christ, taking mercy on Dante's feeble powers, has withdrawn from direct view and now rays down from above.*

*Dante fixes his eyes on the brightest splendor (the Virgin Mary) and sees a crown of flame descend to summon her back to the Empyrean. It is the ANGEL GABRIEL. So summoned, Mary ascends to where her son is, and the flames of the souls yearn higher toward her. There, among the souls that remain below, Dante identifies ST. PETER.*

As a bird in its sweet canopy of green
  covers the nest of its beloved young
  through all the night when nothing can be seen;        3

but eager for the loved, lit face of things,
  and to go hunting for its fledglings' food
  in toil so glad that, laboring, she sings;        6

anticipates the day on an open bough
  and in a fire of love awaits the sun,
  her eyes fixed eagerly on the pre-dawn glow—        9

just so my lady waited—erect, intense—
  all her attention toward that part of heaven
  beneath which the sun's daily pace relents:        12

and I, observing her blissful expectation,
  became like one who yearns for more than he has,
  feeding his hope with sweet anticipation.        15

But the interval between *when* and *when* was slight—
  the *when* of my waiting, I say, and the *when* of seeing
  the sky begin to swell with a new light.        18

And Beatrice said: "Before you now appears
  the militia of Christ's triumph, and all the fruit
  harvested from the turning of the spheres."        21

I saw her face before me, so imbued
  with holy fire, her eyes so bright with bliss
  that I pass on, leaving them unconstrued.        24

As Trivia in the full moon's sweet serene
  smiles on high among the eternal nymphs
  whose light paints every part of Heaven's scene;        27

I saw, above a thousand thousand lights,
  one Sun that lit them all, as our own Sun
  lights all the bodies we see in Heaven's heights;        30

and through that living light I saw revealed
  the Radiant Substance, blazing forth so bright
  my vision dazzled and my senses reeled.          33

Oh my Beatrice, sweet and loving guide!
  "What blinds you," she said to me, "is the very power
  nothing withstands, and from which none may hide. 36

This is the intellect and the sceptered might
  that opened the golden road from Earth to Heaven,
  for which mankind had yearned in its long night." 39

Fire sometimes spreads so wide that it shoots forth
  from a cloud that can no longer hold it in,
  and against its nature, hurtles down to earth.          42

That feast of bliss had swollen my mind so
  that it broke its bounds and leapt out of itself.
  And what it then became, it does not know.          45

"Open your eyes and turn them full on me!
  You have seen things whose power has made you able
  to bear the bright smile of my ecstasy!"          48

As one whose senses have been stricken blind
  by a forgotten vision comes to himself
  and racks his wits to call it back to mind—          51

such was I at that summons, my spirit moved
  to a thankfulness that shall live on forever
  within the book where what is past is proved.          54

If there should sound now all the tongues of song
  Polyhymnia with her eight sisters nourished,
  giving their sweetest milk to make them strong,          57

they could not help me, singing thus, to show
  a thousandth part of my lady's sacred smile,
  nor with what glory it made her features glow.          60

Just so, that Heaven may be figured forth,
　　my consecrated poem must make a leap,
　　as a traveler leaps a crevice there on earth.　　63

My theme is massive, mortal shoulders frail
　　for such a weight. What thoughtful man will blame me
　　for trembling under it for fear I fail?　　66

The seas my ardent prow is plowing here
　　are no place for small craft, nor for a helmsman
　　who will draw back from toil or cringe in fear.　　69

"Why are you so enamored of my face
　　you do not turn your eyes to see the garden
　　that flowers there in the radiance of Christ's grace?　　72

The Rose in which the Word became incarnate
　　is there. There are the lilies by whose odor
　　men found the road that evermore runs straight."　　75

Thus Beatrice. And I, prompt to her guidance
　　in fullest eagerness, raised my feeble lids
　　once more to battle with that radiance.　　78

At times when the sun, through broken clouds, has rayed
　　one perfect beam, I have seen a field of flowers
　　blazing in glory, my own eyes still in shade:　　81

just so, I saw a host of hosts made bright
　　by rays of splendor striking from above,
　　but could not see the source of that pure light.　　84

O Majesty that seals them in such glory!
　　you raised yourself on high, withdrawing there
　　in order that my feeble eyes might see!　　87

The name of that Sweet Flower to which I pray
　　morning and night, seized all my soul and moved it
　　to fix my eyes upon the brightest ray;　　90

and when both my eyes had been allowed to know
   the luster and magnitude of that chosen star
   that triumphs there as it triumphed here below,   93

from Heaven's height a torch of glory came,
   shaped like a ring or wreath, and spinning round her,
   it wound and crowned her in its living flame.   96

The sweetest strain that ever swelled aloud
   to draw the soul into itself down here,
   would be as thunder from a shattered cloud,   99

compared to the melody that then aspired
   from the bright lyre that crowned the purest gem
   by which the brightest heaven is ensapphired.   102

"I am the Angelic Love that wheels around
   the lofty ecstasy breathed from the womb
   in which the hostel of Our Wish was found;   105

so shall I wheel, Lady of Heaven, till
   you follow your great Son to the highest sphere
   and, by your presence, make it holier still."   108

Thus the encircling melody of that flame
   revealed itself; and all the other lamps
   within that garden rang out Mary's name.   111

The royal mantle whose folds are spread abroad
   round all the spheres, and that most burns
                       and quickens
   being nearest to the breath and ways of God,   114

turned its inner shore at such a height
   above the point at which I then was standing
   that I could not yet bring it into sight.   117

I could not, therefore, with my mortal eyes
   follow the flight of that crowned flame that soared
   to join her son in the highest Paradise.    120

And as a newly suckled infant yearns
   after its mother with its upraised arms,
   expressing so the love with which it burns;    123

each of the splendors of that company
   extended its flame on high in such a way
   as made its love of Mary plain to me.    126

Then they remained there, still within my sight,
   singing *"Regina coeli"* in tones so sweet
   the memory still fills me with delight.    129

Oh what treasures cram and overflow
   those richest coffers of the eternal grace
   who sowed such good seed in the world below!    132

Here is true life and relish of the treasure
   their tears laid up in the Babylonian exile,
   in which Christ left man gold beyond all measure.    135

Here sits in triumph under the lofty Son
   of God and the Virgin Mary in His triumph,
   and in the company of everyone    138

crowned from the New or the Old Consistory,
the soul that holds the great keys to such glory.

## Notes

1-15. THE EAGERNESS OF BEATRICE. Beatrice is awaiting the vision of the Triumph of Christ. Dante does not know
what expected delight has filled her with such bliss, but seeing
her so tranced in expectation, he, too, begins to yearn for what
has not yet been revealed.

The poet expresses this feeling of intense and joyous anticipation in a memorable long-tail simile of a mother bird that has
spent the night covering its young, held there by love and by
the night that keeps her from the joyous labors of hunting their
food. Before the light of day, the mother bird is already out
of the leaf-canopy, poised on an open bough to await the new
dawn, and to begin her love's labors at the first possible instant.

Beatrice is compared to that mother bird. (Thematically, this
expectation of a great new rebirth of the light must certainly be
related to the fact that Dante is in Gemini, his zodiacal birth
sign.) Dante, as if he were her fledgling, is fired by the con-
tagion of Beatrice's blissful expectation.

This memorable figure marks the transition to the upper Heav-
en, for Dante and Beatrice are now beyond the planetary
spheres, in the sphere of the Fixed Stars, and beyond them lies
only the Empyrean itself, which is the total presence of God.

12. *the sun's daily pace relents*: At meridian the Sun seems to
slow its pace. Beatrice is looking toward that part of Heaven
where the Sun (Divine Illumination) is at its noon height. It is
all but inevitable that the vision of the Triumph of Christ
should come from that portion of the sky.

16. *when*: Dante uses "when" (*quando*) as it is used in
Scholastic terminology, meaning "time of" or "duration."

20-21. *all the fruit harvested from the turning of the spheres*:
The first-created angels of Heaven did, of course, share in
Christ's triumph, but they were not part of its harvest, which consisted of the redemption of the souls of men. Once the soul had
entered into that triumph (mounted to Heaven), it would manifest
itself in one of the spheres, though it was in essence in the choir
of the Empyrean. Thus the militia of Christ must contain all the
souls of glory whose manifestations populate the spheres of
Heaven (including now the Sphere of the Fixed Stars).

In another sense "harvested from the turning of the spheres"
intends the shaping influences of the spheres upon the souls
of men, disposing them to the good that gains their triumph.
And, of course, the phrase also intends "harvested from time"
(i.e., distinct from the angels, who were never temporal).

24. *unconstrued*: In Scholastic terminology "to construe"
meant "to express the true essense of a thing."

25-26. *Trivia*: Diana, the Moon, in her manifestation as a
nymph. *eternal nymphs*: The stars. See *Purgatorio*, XXXI, 106.

30. *lights all the bodies*: Lights all stars (which are supposed,
as the moon does, to send forth only the reflection of the sun's
light).

32. *the Radiant Substance*: Of Christ.

33. *my vision dazzled*: Only a moment ago (XXII, 142-143) Dante had looked straight into the Sun without discomfort. At the vision of the radiance of Christ, however, Dante's senses reel, and in a moment he will swoon. The art of juxtaposing details in a way that constantly gives scale to an all-containing system of values is one of the marvels of Dante's genius.

35. *the very power*: Of Christ.

40. *fire*: Lightning.

42. *against its nature*: The nature of fire is to ascend toward the Sphere of Fire (*v.* I, 115, and *Purgatorio*, XXXII, 109 ff.). Contrary to its nature (which is to rise to God), Dante's spirit swoons and falls.

43. *That feast of bliss*: The vision of the Triumph of Christ.

46-48. See XXI, 4 ff. and 62 ff. There Beatrice had to hold back her smile of ecstasy because it would have destroyed Dante, whose sense could not have contained it. Now, allegorically, having sustained the vision of the Triumph of Christ and looked upon His Radiant Substance, Dante's eyes have been prepared for the full glory of Beatrice (Divine Revelation).

56-57. *Polyhymnia*: The Muse of sacred songs. (Her name means "many-hymned.") She and her eight sisters were the fountainhead of all song and all poetry. *their sweetest milk*: The Muses gave suck to the poets, thereby transmitting to them the powers of song. How these virgin sisters maintained their milk supply is one more item to be filed among the sacred mysteries.

61. *Just so*: Just as it is impossible to describe to mortal sensibilities the glory of the smile of Beatrice (an allegory of revelation), so must the poem that would describe Heaven leap over such matters as human understanding cannot fathom.

67-69. Cf. the opening lines of Canto II.

73-75. *The Rose*: The Virgin Mary. *the Word*: Logos. *the lilies*: Primarily, perhaps, the Apostles, but also the total of all souls that share in the Triumph of Christ, their example forever showing the straight way to others. *whose odor*: Cf. the common pious phrase, "odor of sanctity."

77. *lids*: Rather than eyes. Dante has just swooned at the radiance of Christ. Now, obedient to the command of Beatrice,

he turns to look again, but with his eyes lidded, his mortal senses bracing themselves to bear the ineffable radiance (cf., too, his admonition in line 69. Only the spirit that will risk all may dare the glories of Heaven).

79-87. The figure is based on the common phenomenon of seeing a ray of sun light a field of flowers while one is standing in the shadow of covering cloud. So the rays of Christ's glory strike down to illuminate the souls of the redeemed, Christ, of his infinite mercy, having withdrawn from Dante's sight, for it could not have borne the full glory of His shining. Lines 85-87 may certainly be pondered as a possible allegory of the resurrection of Christ.

85. *seals:* The seal here would be the ray; the flowers, the wax that takes the impress of the light and shines forth as marked by the light.

88 ff. THE VISION OF THE VIRGIN MARY. Beatrice (line 73) has told Dante that Mary was among the radiances he saw before him. When Dante finally manages to fix his eyes on the splendor before him (the radiance of Christ having withdrawn mercifully) he makes out the brightest star in that host of splendors. As he watches, a crown of flame descends from the Empyrean and encircles her. This new radiance is God's messenger, Gabriel, the Angel of the Annunciation. *Sweet Flower, brightest ray:* The Virgin Mary. *had been allowed to know:* As always in Paradise, it is not Dante's will that discerns the vision (though he wills it utterly) but the souls that reveal themselves to him.

101-102. *gem . . . ensapphired:* The original is *zaffiro . . . s'inzaffira.* Dante must have chosen the sapphire as the gem of purest blue, the color of Heaven. *purest gem:* The Virgin Mary. *the bright lyre:* The Angel Gabriel. *the brightest heaven:* The Sphere of the Fixed Stars.

105. *Our Wish:* Christ. The womb of Mary was the hostel in which the Word found lodging in mortal flesh.

107. *the highest sphere:* The Empyrean.

110. *revealed itself:* Dante says literally, "impressed its seal," the equivalent of writing its signature, i.e., "identified itself."

112-114. *the royal mantle:* The Primum Mobile. *most burns:* With ardent joy. *and quickens:* Being the outer sphere whose revolutions control the turning of all those it encloses, it turns faster than any of the others.

115. *its inner shore*: The spheres, of course, have depth. Could Dante's vision have reached to see the Primum Mobile it would have seen only its inner surface, here called a shore.

120. *to join her son*: As Gabriel had prayed her to do.

128. *Regina coeli*: Queen of Heaven.

133-135. Both the text and the interpretation of the original are disputed. I have settled for what seems to be the most direct rendering, taking "the Babylonian exile" to signify the soul's time on earth. Heaven, then, would be the longed-for Jerusalem. In their exile, in steadfast faith and holy tears, these souls laid up the heavenly treasure they now enjoy, as Christ left it to all men.

139. *Old and New Consistory*: The Old and the New Testament.

140. *the soul that holds the keys*: St. Peter.

# CANTO XXIV

*The Triumph of Christ*
*St. Peter*
*The Examination of Faith*

*CHRIST AND MARY having ascended to the Empyrean, St. Peter remains as the chief soul of the Garden of Christ's Triumph. Beatrice addresses the souls in Dante's behalf, and they, in their joy, form into a dazzling VERTICAL WHEEL OF SPINNING RADIANCES.*

*Beatrice then begs St. Peter to conduct an EXAMINATION OF DANTE'S FAITH. St. Peter thereupon questions Dante on the NATURE OF FAITH, THE POSSESSION OF FAITH, THE SOURCES OF FAITH, THE PROOF OF THE TRUTH OF FAITH, MAN'S MEANS OF KNOWING THAT THE MIRACLES OF FAITH ACTUALLY TOOK PLACE, and finally on THE CONTENT OF CHRISTIAN FAITH.*

*Dante answers eagerly, as would a willing candidate being examined by his learned master. The examination concluded, St. Peter shows his pleasure by dancing three times around Dante.*

"O spirits of that chosen company
    that feeds on the Lamb of God, the flesh of which
    satisfies hunger to all eternity—          3

if by God's grace this man is given a foretaste
    of what falls from your table, before death
    takes him from time and lays his body waste,     6

consider the boundless thirst with which he burns;
  bedew him from your plenty. You drink forever
  the waters of that spring for which he yearns!"  9

So spoke Beatrice, and those blissful souls,
  flaming as bright as comets, formed themselves
  into a sphere revolving on fixed poles.  12

As the wheels within a clockwork synchronize
  so that the innermost, when looked at closely
  seems to be standing, while the outermost flies;  15

just so those rings of dancers whirled to show
  and let me understand their state of bliss,
  all joining in the round, some fast, some slow.  18

From one I saw, the loveliest of them all,
  there grew a radiance of such blessedness
  that it outshone the hosts of the celestial.  21

Three times it danced round Beatrice to a strain
  so heavenly that I have not the power
  so much as to imagine it again.  24

Therefore my pen leaps and I do not write;
  not words nor fantasy can paint the truth:
  the folds of heaven's draperies are too bright.  27

"O sacred sister whose prayer is so devout,
  the ardor of your love enters my bliss
  within that lovely sphere and calls me out."  30

—When it had come to rest, that Fire of Love
  directed its breath to my lady and spoke these words
  exactly as I have set them down above.  33

And she: "Eternal Light of the great priest
  to whom Our Lord brought down and gave the keys
  to the sublimities of this joyous feast;  36

at your own pleasure, whatever it may be,
  test this man on the greater and lesser points
  of the faith in which you once walked on the sea.   39

If love and hope and faith are truly his
  you will discover it, for your eyes are turned
  where you can see the image of all that is.          42

But since this realm is peopled from the seed
  of the true faith, he will the better praise it,
  could he discuss with you the perfect creed."        45

As a bachelor arms himself for disquisition
  in silence till the master sets the terms
  for defending, not deciding, the proposition;        48

so did I arm myself for the expression
  of every proof, preparing while she spoke
  for such an examiner, and such profession.           51

"Speak, good Christian, manifest your worth:
  what is faith?" —At which I raised my eyes
  to the light from which these words had been
                                    breathed forth:    54

then turned to look at Beatrice, and she
  urged me with her eyes to let the waters
  of the spring that welled within my soul pour free.  57

"May the Grace that grants the grace of this confession
  to the captain of the first rank," I began,
  "grant that my thoughts may find worthy
                                    expression!"        60

Continuing: "Father, as it was set down
  by the pen of your dear brother, who, with you,
  set Rome on the road that leads to glory's crown,    63

faith is the *substance* of what we hope to see
    and the *argument* for what we have not seen.
    This is its *quiddity*, as it seems to me."    66

Next I heard: "This is, in fact, the essence.
    But do you understand why he classifies it
    first with *substances*, then with *argument*?"    69

And I in answer: "The profundities
    that here reveal themselves so liberally
    are so concealed, down there, from mortal eyes    72

they exist in belief alone. On belief the structure
    of high hope rises. It is *substant*, therefore,
    or 'standing under' by its very nature.    75

Starting with this belief, it is evident,
    we must reason without further visible proofs.
    And so it partakes, by nature, of *argument*."    78

I heard: "If all that mortal man may know
    through mortal teaching were as firmly grasped,
    sophists would find no listeners there below."    81

Such was the breath from that Love's Ecstasy,
    continuing then: "You have assayed this coinage,
    its weight and metal content, accurately;    84

now tell me if you have it in your possession."
    And I then: "Yes. I have. So bright, so round,
    usage has worn down none of its impression."    87

After these words the breath once more resounded
    from the light that shone before me: "This dear gem
    on which all good and power of good are founded—    90

whence comes it to you?" And I, "The shower of gold
    of the Holy Ghost, which pours down endlessly
    over the sacred Scrolls, both New and Old,    93

reasons it to such logical certainty
   that, by comparison, all other reasoning
   can only seem confused and dull to me." 96

And I heard: "These propositions, the Old and New
   that move you to this conclusion, for what reason
   do you accept them as divinely true?" 99

And I: "The proof that shows the truth to me
   is in the works that followed. Never has nature
   heated and forged such iron in its smithy." 102

And I was answered: "Tell me how you know
   there were such works. What seeks to prove itself—
   it only and nothing more—swears it was so." 105

"If the whole world became Christian without the aid
   of the miraculous, that is a miracle
   a hundred times greater than the rest," I said, 108

"for poor and hungry, by faith alone upborne,
   you entered the field and sowed there the good plant
   that was a vine once, and is now a thorn." 111

This said, that high and holy choir let ring
   *"Te Deum laudamus!"* sounding through the spheres
   such melody as the souls of heaven sing. 114

And that Baron, who, examining my belief
   from branch to branch, had drawn me out already
   to where we were approaching the last leaf, 117

began again: "The grace whose loving good
   had pledged itself to your mind, has moved
                                    your mouth,
   up to this point, to open as it should. 120

I approve what has emerged thus far, but now
   it is time you should explain *what* you believe,
   and from what source it comes to you, and how."   123

"O holy Father, spirit that now can see
   what faith once held so firmly that you were prompter
   than younger feet to the tomb in Galilee,"   126

my answer ran, "you wish me to expound
   the *form* of my own promptness to believe,
   and you ask what reasons for it I have found.   129

And I reply: I believe in one God, loved,
   desired by all creation, sole, eternal,
   who moves the turning Heavens, Himself
                   unmoved,   132

And for this faith I have the evidences
   not only of physics and of metaphysics,
   but of the truth that rains down on my senses   135

through Moses, the prophets, the psalms, through
                   the Evangel,
   and through you and what you wrote when the
                   Ardent Spirit
   made you the foster father of God's People.   138

And I believe in three Persons; this Trinity,
   an essence Triune and Single, in whose being
   *is* and *are* conjoin to eternity.   141

That this profound and sacred nature is real
   the teachings of the evangels, in many places,
   have stamped on the wax of my mind like a
                   living seal.   144

This is the beginning, the spark shot free
   that gnaws and widens into living flame,
   and, like a star in Heaven, shines in me."   147

As a master who is pleased by what he hears
    embraces his servant as soon as he has spoken,
    rejoicing in the happy news he bears;           150

so, that glorious apostolic blaze
    at whose command I had spoken heard me out,
    and blessing me in a glad chant of praise,      153

danced three times round me there in the eighth
                              great rim,
such pleasure had my speaking given him.

## Notes

1-9. PRAYER OF BEATRICE TO THE TRIUMPHANT
HOSTS. Now that Christ and Mary have returned to highest
heaven, the triumphant spirits are gathered around St. Peter (an
allegory of Peter's role as Christ's vicar following the Resurrection). As usual, Beatrice asks the spirits to grant Dante's still
unspoken wish. The tone of her prayer is clear enough, but its
ellipses and metaphoric shifts require some agility of the reader:

What Dante is burning for is, of course, the revelation on
which these spirits feed, forever replete (the Feast of the
Lamb of God). God's grace has given him a foretaste of that
feast while he is yet in the flesh: not, so to speak, a seat at
Heaven's table but some of the scraps from it.

In recognition of the immensity and worthiness of Dante's wish,
therefore, Beatrice asks these spirits to bless his thirst to know
("bedew him from your plenty"). Dew as a blessing and a
refreshment is a well-established metaphor. Beatrice carries it
a step further (relating it to the scraps of Heaven's table) by
pointing out that the elect drink forever (their thirst forever
sated) the waters of that Font (the Presence of God) for which
the man thirsts (who would be gratified by so much as a drop
from the waters of that illimitable spring).

10-18. It is a little difficult to visualize the dance of the
triumphant souls. Dante says they formed into a sphere with fixed
poles and compares them to clockwork. But Dante often uses
"sphere" and "wheel" interchangeably. It is reasonable, therefore, to visualize the souls as forming into a great wheel of substantial depth (perhaps another millstone) that revolves around
a fixed axis ("fixed poles"). The image of clockwork suggests

(and the action of the next two cantos verifies) that the wheel is above Dante and broadside to him.

Within that vertical wheel the souls dance in circles to express the joy they feel in being able to give joy to Dante and Beatrice. So rapidly do they spin their circles that they appear only as wheels of light. Like clockwork—i.e., many motions contained within one master motion—the individual wheels spin at various rates. Since the speed with which each soul circles indicates the degree of bliss it feels, and knowing Dante's inclination to set things forth in exact gradations, it seems well to think of each wheel as being produced by the circling of a single soul rather than by a group of souls dancing in a ring.

19. *one . . . the loveliest of them all*: The radiance of St. Peter.

22. *three times*: It would be all but impossible for Dante to use the number three without intending the Trinity.

23-24. *my imagination fails*: Dante is not only unable to express, but he cannot even reimagine the blessed beauty of Peter's song.

25. *my pen leaps*: Cf. XXIII, 62.

27. *the folds of Heaven's draperies are too bright*: To indicate the folds of a drapery, a painter must shadow the recesses of the cloth while highlighting the raised surfaces. But the inner radiance of heavenly things is such that the folds shine as bright as the surfaces, or, perhaps, Dante means to say more brightly.

Or in another, or in a complementary sense: A painter can depict the folds of draperies only when subtleties of color are available to him, and human speech and human imagination are too gross to portray the subtleties of Heaven.

31. *that Fire of Love*: St. Peter. Note that he has already descended from the great wheel, so prompt are the souls of Heaven to give joy.

39. See *Matthew*, XIV, 28 ff.

44. *he will the better praise it*: To men, on his return to Earth.

46. *bachelor*: As in "bachelor of arts," i.e., a candidate for a learned degree.

48. *for defending, not deciding*: The candidate marshals and evaluates the evidence which he submits to the master. Only the master decides. The relation is essentially that of lawyer and judge.

51. *such an examiner*: St. Peter. *and such a profession*: Of the Christian faith.

52-147. THE EXAMINATION OF FAITH. It may seem a spectacular action for Dante to be examined on his catechism by St. Peter himself (in the next two cantos he is further examined by St. James as the Apostle of Hope and by St. John as the Apostle of Love), yet, properly understood, the conception is a sublime one. For in a final sense every man of the faith must answer to nothing less than the Apostolic Creed, making himself worthy to be examined by the true source. As, allegorically, all values must be derived from the supreme test of values.

The examination is divided into six parts:

52-81. WHAT IS FAITH? The anonymous *Epistle to the Hebrews* (which Dante attributes to St. Paul) provides the source of the first answer (XI, 1) "Now faith is the substance of things hoped for, the evidence of things not seen."

*substance*: In Scholastic terminology "what exists in itself." But Aquinas had set forth that "No quality is a substance; but faith is a quality." Faith, therefore, could not be a substance. Dante circumvents this difficulty, perhaps more ingeniously than persuasively, by rendering the *"substantia"* of *Hebrews* as "that which stands under" (*sub* and *stare*).

*argument*: The means whereby the intellect reaches toward the inherent truth of things. It is necessary but limited, as reason is limited.

*quiddity*: See XX, 92. The companion term "quality" signifies the likeness of a thing to something else, "quiddity" signifying the way in which a thing is like itself.

59. *captain of the first rank*: St. Peter. Dante calls him *"l'alto primipilo,"* literally, "the chief fighter in the first rank" according to the classifications of the Roman army. Such is St. Peter's rank in the militia of Christ.

62. *of your dear brother*: St. Paul.

79-81. *through mortal teaching*: As distinct from Heavenly revelation. Could all men grasp that much as firmly as Dante has done, the fine spun arguments of the sophists would find no audience on earth, for none would pay attention to them.

82-87. THE POSSESSION OF FAITH. *Such was the breath of that love's ecstasy*: Below this height of Heaven Dante had been content with such phrases as "so spoke that radiance." But the conversations of high Heaven will not answer to the terms that describe human discourse. Dante is conversing not with a man but with a breath that issues from a radiance. *this coinage*: The golden coinage of faith by which man purchases Heaven. *weight*: Faith as argument. *content*: Faith as substance.

Peter then asks if Dante has faith: "Have you this coinage in your purse?" (I could find no rhyme for "purse" and had to settle for "in your possession.") Dante affirms that he does indeed have it, so bright (clear) and so round (not worn down by usage nor clipped or shaved by subterfuge) that he is left in no doubt of the mint impression (i.e., there is no uncertainty about his faith).

89-96. THE SOURCES OF FAITH. Dante affirms that his faith comes to him from the word of God as set forth in the Testaments ("the Sacred Scrolls, both New and Old"). *this dear gem*: Faith.

97-102. THE PROOF OF THE TRUTH OF FAITH. Dante affirms that he knows the divine truth of Scripture by the proof of the works (the miracles) that followed from them. *these propositions*: The Testaments. A metaphoric extension of the preceding terminology of logic. *works that followed*: Miracles. Nothing in nature (here conceived as a smithy) could bring such works into being.

103-114. HOW DO WE KNOW THE MIRACLES DE-SCRIBED IN THE OLD AND NEW TESTAMENTS ACTUAL-LY OCCURRED? Scripture, says St. Peter, seeks to prove itself as the word of God by asserting the existence of miracles. But if one has not actually observed a miracle, he has only Scripture's own word for it. How then can he be sure of the truth of miracles?

With the sort of ingenuity that characterizes Scholastic argument at times, Dante delivers his final and (to him) most telling argument: had the miracles reported by Scripture not taken place, one would have to assert an even greater miracle to explain how Christianity had spread through "the whole world" without divine intercession. St. Augustine had used the same argument as proof of the truth of Scripture.

At Dante's words the redeemed souls break into a hymn of praise.

*what seeks to prove itself*: Scripture. *field*:     Battlefield. As God's Captain of the first rank Peter entered the field of pagan Rome and sowed there the good seed of faith. *that was a vine . . . now a thorn*: Another denunciation of papal corruption. Peter had planted the Lord's vineyard (the Church) but corruption has left only a barren thicket choked by thorns.

115-147. IN WHAT DOES A CHRISTIAN HAVE FAITH?
That Baron" (St. Peter) asks in *what* Dante believes and
rom what source he derives it and how he derives it. Dante
ffirms his belief in a single triune and everlasting God, and
leclares that he is persuaded to believe by physical, metaphysical,
nd scriptural proofs.

124-125. *now can see what faith once held so firmly*: The
Triumph of Christ, a matter of faith during his mortal life,
a fact forever before his eyes in Heaven.

125-126. *you were prompter than younger feet*: See *John,
XX*, 3-10. St. John was the first to approach the tomb of
Christ, but Peter was the first to enter it and the first to believe
n the resurrection. The greater promptness indicates the greater
eal, and thus the greater triumph of the heavenly soul.

128. *form*: In Scholastic terminology, the same as the Platonic
Form, the idea of the thing, which is independent of particular
nstances, as, for example, the "form" of Justice would exist
noumenally, if only in God's mind, even if no single instance
of Justice could be found on earth. Contingency is that which
comes into being as an instance of form, the form itself being
eternal.

130-132. THE ATTRIBUTES OF GOD. *loved, desired*: See I,
77. *sole*: Not plural as believed by the pagans and by various
heretical sects. *eternal*: Without beginning or end, contrary to
the heresy that ascribed a beginning to God and, hence, duration. *moves . . . . Himself unmoved*: against the heresy that God
was moved (affected) by things, Dante asserts his unchange-
ability, for God is perfect and any change (motion) in Him
would have to be away from perfection.

136-138. *Moses, the prophets, the psalms*: I.e., the Old Testament. *the Evangel and through you*: The New Testament, com-
monly divided into the Evangelical and Apostolic books. *you*:
The Italian is the plural form *"voi."* The reference, therefore, is
to all the apostles. *people*: In mercy's heavenly name, the reader
is requested to avert his eyes as he passes this rhyme.

143. *the teachings of the evangels in many places*: Among
various New Testament passages that assert the Unity of the
Trinity, see *Matthew XXVIII*, 19, and *John V*, 19ff.

154. *danced three times round me*: Dante implies no proud
boast in being so honored by St. Peter. Peter would rejoice in the
same way over any soul that has shone Dante's zeal and faith.

# CANTO XXV

*DANTE, blessed by St. John himself as a reward for
his labors and his hope, declares that if his poem may
serve to soften his sentence of exile from Florence, he
will return to his baptismal font at San Giovanni and
there place on his own head the poet's laurel wreath.
Such is one of the great hopes of his poem, and on
that note ST. JAMES, the Apostle of Hope, shows himself.*

*Beatrice begs James to conduct the EXAMINATION
OF HOPE and she herself, in answer to the first question, testifies to Dante's POSSESSION OF HOPE. Dante
then replies on THE NATURE OF HOPE, on the CON-
TENT OF HIS HOPE, and on the SOURCES OF HOPE.*

*The examination triumphantly concluded, a cry in
praise of the grace of hope rings through Paradise
and thereupon ST. JOHN THE APOSTLE appears.
Dante stares into John's radiance hoping to see the lineaments of his mortal body. The voice of John, the
Apostle of Love (caritas) calls to him that what he
seeks is not there, and when Dante looks away he discovers he has been BLINDED BY THE RADIANCE
OF LOVE.*

If ever it comes to pass that the sacred song,
    to which both heaven and earth so set their hand
    that I grew lean with laboring years long,

wins over the cruelty that exiles me
　　from the sweet sheepfold where I slept, a lamb,
　　and to the raiding wolves an enemy;　　　　　　6

with a changed voice and with my fleece full grown
　　I shall return to my baptismal font,
　　a poet, and there assume the laurel crown;　　　9

for there I entered the faith that lets us grow
　　into God's recognition; and for that faith
　　Peter, as I have said, circled my brow.　　　　12

Thereafter another radiance came forth
　　from the same sphere out of whose joy had come
　　the first flower of Christ's vicarage on earth.　　15

And my lady, filled with ecstasy and aglow,
　　cried to me: "Look! Look there! It is the baron
　　for whom men throng to Galicia there below!"　　18

At times, on earth, I have seen a mating dove
　　alight by another, and each turn to each,
　　circling and murmuring to express their love;　　21

exactly so, within the eighth great sphere,
　　one glorious great lord greeted the other,
　　praising the diet that regales them there.　　　24

Those glories, having greeted and been greeted,
　　turned and stood before me, still and silent,
　　so bright I turned my eyes away defeated.　　　27

And Beatrice said, smiling her blessedness:
　　"Illustrious being in whose chronicle
　　is written our celestial court's largesse,　　　30

let hope, I pray, be sounded at this height.
　　How often you personified that grace
　　when Jesus gave His chosen three more light!　　33

"Lift up your head, look up and do not fear,
    for all that rises from the mortal world
    must ripen in our rays from sphere to sphere."     3(

So spoke the second flame to comfort me;
    and I raised my eyes to the mountains that before
    had borne them down by their weight of majesty.     3(

"Since of His grace Our Lord and Emperor calls
    and bids you come while still in mortal flesh
    among His counts in His most secret halls;     4(

that you, the truth of this great court made clear,
    may make the stronger, in yourself and others,
    the hope that makes men love the good down there,     4(

say what it is, what power helped you to climb,
    and how you bear its flowering in your mind."
    —So spoke the second flame a second time.     4

And that devout sweet spirit that had led
    the feathers of my wings in that high flight
    anticipated my reply, and said:     5(

"Church Militant, as is written in the Sun
    whose ray lights all our hosts, does not possess
    a single child richer in hope—not one.     5(

It was for that he was allowed to come
    from Egypt to behold Jerusalem
    before his warring years had reached their sum.     5(

The other two points—raised not that you may know
    but that he may report how great a pleasure
    hope is to you, when he returns below—     6(

I leave to him. They will not be difficult.
    Nor will the truth seem boastful. Let him answer
    and may God's grace appear in the result."     6(

As a pupil who is eager to reply
  to his professor, knowing his subject well,
  and quick to show his excellence—such was I.        66

"Hope," I said, "is the certain expectation
  of future glory. It is the blessed fruit
  of grace divine and the good a man has done.        69

From many stars this light descends to me,
  but it was first distilled into my heart
  by the ultimate singer of Ultimate Majesty.        72

'Let them hope in Thee,' sang the God-praising poet,
  'whoso doth know Thy name!' And who can feel
  a faith as firm as mine is and not know it?        75

And your epistle sent down once again
  a fresh dew on his dew, till I was full
  and overflowed to others your sweet rain."        78

While I was speaking thus a luminescence
  trembled within the bosom of that flame,
  sudden and bright as lightning's incandescence.        81

"Love that still burns in me," I heard it breathe,
  "for that grace that followed even to the palm,
  and till I left the field for happy death,        84

moves me to speak further: you know the true
  and lasting joy she brings: gladden me, therefore,
  by telling me what Hope holds forth to you."        87

And I: "From scripture, new and old, descends
  the symbol, and the symbol points me to it.
  All those whom God has chosen as His friends—        90

as Isaiah testifies—they shall be dressed
  in double raiment in their native land;
  and that land is this sweet life with the blest.        93

And your brother, where he writes so ardently
  of the white robes, sets forth this revelation
  in great detail for all of us to see."                    96

As soon as I had spoken there rang clear
  from overhead, "Let them hope in Thee, O Lord!"
  and the response rang back from all that sphere.          99

At once within that choir there blazed a ray
  so bright that if the Crab had such a star
  one month of winter would be a single day.                102

And as a joyous maid will rise and go
  to join the dance, in honor of the bride
  and not for any reasons of vain show,                     105

so did that radiant splendor, there above,
  go to the two who danced a joyous reel
  in fit expression of their burning love.                  108

It joined them in the words and melody;
  and like a bride, immovable and silent,
  my lady kept her eyes fixed on their glory.               111

"This is he who lies upon the breast
  of Our Pelican; and this is He elected
  from off the cross to make the great behest."             114

So spoke my lady, nor, her pose unbroken,
  did she once let her rapt attention stray,
  either before or after she had spoken.                    117

As one who stares, squinting against the light,
  to see the Sun enter a partial eclipse,
  and in the act of looking loses his sight—                120

so did I stare at the last flame from that sphere
  until a voice said, "Why do you blind yourself
  trying to see what has no true place here?                123

My body is earth in earth where it shall be
  one with the rest until our numbers grow
  to fill the quota of eternity.                              126

Only the Two Lamps that are most aglow
  rose to their blessed cloister doubly clad.
  Explain this to your world when you go below."             129

And when these words were said the flaming wreath
  broke off the dancing and the sweet accord
  in which it had combined its three-part breath,            132

as oars that have been striking through the sea
  pause all together when a whistle sounds
  to signal rest or some emergency.                          135

Ah, what a surge of feeling swept my mind
  when I turned away an instant from such splendor
  to look at Beatrice, only to find                          138

I could not see her with my dazzled eyes,
  though I stood near her and in Paradise!

## Notes

1-12. DANTE'S HOPE. Dante has just been examined on his
Faith, the first of the Christian Graces. Now he will be examined
on Hope, the second. As a first sounding of the theme of Hope,
perhaps to demonstrate that hope is ever green within him, he
declares his dream of returning to Florence and of being crowned
with a laurel wreath (baptized as a poet) at the font of "his
beautiful San Giovanni" at which he was baptized into the faith,
for the possession of which St. Peter so honored him at the end
of the last canto.

3. *that I grew lean*: With the labor of writing his great poem.

5-6. *the sweet sheepfold*: Florence. *the wolves*: The leaders
of Florentine politics.

7. *with a changed voice*: He will return not as a singer of love

songs, as he began, but as the master singer of God's universal scheme. And not as a baby but as a man. *and with my fleece full grown*: Continues the lamb image of line 5.

13. *Thereafter*: After St. Peter had three times circled Dante's brow.

14. *the same sphere:* Not from the Sphere of the Fixed Stars, the Eighth Heaven, in which Dante, Beatrice, and these souls are, but from the sphere of light the souls had formed for joy when Beatrice uttered her prayer (XXIV, 12).

17-18. *the baron . . . Galicia*: The second of the barons of Christ is St. James. His tomb is in Santiago di Compostela in Galicia, Spain, and was a shrine to which many pilgrimages were made in the Middle Ages.

23. *one glorious great lord*: St. Peter. *the other*: St. James.

24. *the diet that regales them there*: The love of others, *caritas*.

29-33. *in whose chronicle . . . largesse*: i.e., "whose writings tell of the generosity and benevolence of the court of Heaven." See *Epistle of James*, I, 5, 17. Dante seems to have confused two St. Jameses into one. The *Espistle of James* is generally attributed to the James called "the Lord's brother" in *Gal.*, I, 19 (see also *Acts*, XV, 13), not to James the Apostle whose shrine is in Compostela. *let hope be sounded at this height*: St. James was particularly associated with the grace of hope. In Heaven, however, there is nothing to hope for, all having been achieved. *his chosen three*: Matthew (XVII, 1 ff.), Mark (IX, 1), and Luke (VIII, 51, and IX, 28) all cite the special trust Jesus placed in Peter, James, and John ("gave his chosen three more light"). Medieval commentators on Scripture cited them as the three pillars of the church and had them representing the Christian Graces, Peter representing Faith; James, Hope; and John, Charity (*caritas*).

34-36. *do not fear*: Dante is afraid the splendor will blind him. St. James, as a first example of hope, perhaps, reassures him: these rays do not destroy but strengthen, preparing Dante's developing soul for the vision of God. "Sphere to sphere" is a rhyme-forced addition, not in the text but implicit.

37. *second flame*: St. James.

38. *mountains*: Peter and James. So called to indicate their stature among the blessed. (See *Psalms*, LXXXVI, 1, CXX, 1, and *Matthew*, V, 14.)

48. *So spoke*: This, of course, is Dante's way of saying that St. James had spoken lines 34-36, that Dante had obeyed him

(lines 37-39), and that St. James had then continued (lines 40-47).

49. *that devout sweet spirit*: Beatrice.

49-63. THE EXAMINATION OF HOPE. In lines 46-47, St. James has put three questions to Dante, the last of which asks if Dante possesses the Grace of Hope. Before Dante can speak, Beatrice answers for him that no man in the church possesses more, for how else could he have ascended to Heaven itself? Were Dante to speak the greatness of his hope, however, his words might seem immodest. It is for this reason that she (Divine Revelation) speaks for him.

The other two questions are "What is Hope?" and "What are its sources?" On these points she will let Dante speak, not that James (who already knows) needs his reply, but to let Dante say it out in order that he may return to Earth with a full accounting in terms mortal reason can grasp.

52. *the Sun*: God. Dante's hope is known to God and, therefore, to all the blessed.

56-57. *Egypt*: The mortal life, earthly bondage. *Jerusalem*: Heaven, deliverance. *warring years*: Dante's mortal years in the church militant.

58. *not that you may know*: Since he knows already, informed by the ray of God.

59-60. *how great a pleasure hope is to you*: As the special patron of the grace he himself no longer needs.

67-69. THE NATURE OF HOPE. These lines are Dante's answer to "say what it is" (line 45).

70-78. THE SOURCES OF HOPE. Dante offers no physical or metaphysical proofs. Hope arises in man as a direct revelation, its light coming "from many stars" (many sacred writings), the first of them, for him, being the Psalms and the second St. James' own epistle. *ultimate singer of Ultimate Majesty . . . the God-praising poet*: David. *"Let them hope in thee . . ."* *Psalms*, IX, 11.

83-84. *that grace*: Hope. *the palm*: Martyrdom. *left the field*: Abandoned the warfare of the church militant for the bliss of the church triumphant, i.e., heaven.

86. *her*: Hope.

88-96. THE PROMISE (OR OBJECT) OF HOPE. The one hope that matters is, of course, the hope of Heaven. *the symbol*:

Of the blessings to which hope leads. *it*: Hope. Sense: The scriptures show the good that awaits those who hope in God, and the good so symbolized points me to hope.

91-92. *Isaiah testifies*: See *Isaiah*, LXI, 7. *double raiment*: The glory in which Dante sees the souls clad plus the glory of the resurrected flesh after the Day of Judgment.

94-96. *your brother*: St. John. *where he writes . . . white robes*: Apocal., VII.

97-102. Dante has affirmed the promise of hope offered by the revelations of Scripture, particularly of Isaiah in the Old Testament and of John in the New. As soon as he has spoken, the words of the Ninth Psalm ring out from far above and all the whirling spheres chorus the response. Then, from among them, there grows a splendor that outshines all others there. It is the soul of St. John, the apostle of love, and brightest of the chosen three as Love (*caritas*) is the greatest of the Christian Graces.

100. *a ray*: St. John.

101-102. *so bright*: That if the Crab (the constellation which is the zodiacal sign for December and January) contained a star as bright, that winter month would be one long day, the light of such a star replacing the light of the sun during the night hours.

113. *Our Pelican*: One of the medieval epithets for Christ. The pelican was believed to nourish its young by striking its breast until it bled and then giving them its blood. Another legend ran that the pelican performed in this way when it found its young dead, reviving them with its blood.

113-114. *chosen from off the cross*: Chosen by Christ while He was on the cross to remain behind and be a son to Mary (*John*, XIX, 26-27).

118-135. THE LEGEND OF ST. JOHN. *John*, XXI, 20-23, provided the basis for the medieval legend that St. John had been translated to heaven body and soul. Here, Dante sets out to correct that misinterpretation of scripture.

He starts with a long-tail simile of a man who has heard there will be a partial eclipse of the sun and who, therefore, allows himself to look directly at it and becomes blind in trying to see what he cannot bear. The eclipse here would, of course, be the darkening of the soul's radiance when the physical body moves in front of it.

As Dante is staring, the voice of St. John asks why he is

blinding himself in the useless effort to see what is not there (see *I Corinthians*, XV, 50). St. John's mortal body, as he tells Dante, is in the earth. Only Jesus and Mary ascended to heaven in their physical bodies. (Some readers will recall that Enoch and Elijah were translated to heaven in their physical bodies, but Dante is obviously following the legend that they were borne only as high as the Terrestrial Paradise.)

125. *one with the rest*: One among all other mortal bodies left in the earth and indistinguishable from them until the resurrection.

125-126. *until our number . . . quota of eternity*: Clearly, Dante believes that God has ordained salvation for some exact number of souls and that the Judgment will follow when the last elected soul has been gathered to Heaven.

127-128. *the Two Lamps that are most aglow*: Christ and Mary. *doubly clad*: In body and soul.

130-135. In the usual order of his long-tail similes, Dante puts the likeness first and then compares to it the thing that is like it. Here he reverses that usual order, first describing the action, and then comparing it.

136. DANTE SUFFERS TEMPORARY BLINDNESS. Turning from the splendors before him to speak to Beatrice, Dante discovers that he cannot see her! I take St. John's remarks at the beginning of the next canto as the key to this allegory on the progress of the soul. God is beyond our mortal senses. The true vision can come, therefore, only when the senses are enlarged, having been shattered in the blaze of revelation and replaced by a new perception. As St. John says in line 12 of the next canto, Beatrice (Divine Revelation) has the power to heal. Not only will she remove Dante's blindness but he will see the better for it.

# CANTO XXVI

---

THE EIGHTH SPHERE: THE FIXED STARS
*Examination of Love (Caritas)*
*Adam*

JOHN ASSURES DANTE that Beatrice will restore
his sight. Dante expresses his willingness to await her
will since he knows her to be Love. John, thereupon,
begins the EXAMINATION OF LOVE, asking Dante
to explain how he came into the POSSESSION OF
LOVE, and what drove him to seek it. He then asks
Dante to describe the INTENSITY OF LOVE and to
discuss the SOURCES OF LOVE.

Dante concludes with a praise of God as the source
of Love. At his words all Heaven responds with a paean,
and immediately DANTE'S VISION IS RESTORED.

There appears before him a fourth great splendor
which Beatrice identifies as the soul of ADAM. Dante
begs Adam to speak, and learns from him the DATE
OF ADAM'S CREATION, HOW LONG ADAM RE-
MAINED IN EDEN, THE CAUSE OF GOD'S
WRATH, and WHAT LANGUAGE ADAM SPOKE IN
HIS TIME ON EARTH.

While I stood thus confounded, my light shed,
 out of the dazzling flame that had consumed it
 I heard a breath that called to me, and said:    3

"Until your eyes once more regain their sense
 of the light you lost in me, it will be well
 for discourse to provide a recompense.    6

Speak, therefore, starting with the thing that most
 summons your soul to it, and be assured
 your sight is only dazzled and not lost;    9

for she who guides you through this holy land
   has, in a single turning of her eyes,
   the power that lay in Ananias' hand." 12

"As she wills, late or soon, let remedy
   come to my eyes," I said, "the gates through which
   she brought the fire that ever burns in me. 15

The Good that is this cloister's happiness
   is the Alpha and Omega of the scripture
   love reads to me with light and heavy stress." 18

The same voice that had soothed my fear away
   when I found suddenly that I could not see
   called me back to the question. I heard it say: 21

"Surely a finer sieve must sift this through.
   You must explain what made you draw your bow
   at this exalted target—what and who." 24

And I: "By the arguments of philosophy
   and by authority that descends from here
   such Love has clearly stamped its seal upon me. 27

For the Good, to the extent imperfect sense
   grasps its goodness, kindles love; the brighter
   the more we understand its excellence. 30

To the Essence then in which lies such perfection
   that every good thing not immediate to It
   is nothing more than Its own ray's reflection— 33

to It, above all else, the mind must move
   once it has seen the truth that is the proof
   and argument that so compels man's love. 36

That truth he first made evident to me
   whose proofs set forth the First Cause and First Love
   of every sempiternal entity. 39

It was proved by the True Maker's voice sent forth
  to Moses when It said, meaning Itself,
  'I shall cause you to see a vision of all worth.'     42

And proved by you in the high proclamation
  that cries to earth the secrets of this heaven
  more clearly than any other revelation."     45

And I heard: "As human reason and Holy Writ
  in harmony have urged you, keep for God
  the first, most sovereign passion of your spirit.     48

But tell me if you feel yet other ties
  bind you to Him. Say with how many teeth
  this love consumes you." So in Paradise     51

Christ's Eagle spoke his sacred purpose whole,
  concealing nothing; rather, urging me
  to make a full profession of my soul.     54

I therefore: "All those teeth with power enough
  to turn the heart of any man to God
  have joined in my heart, turning it to Love.     57

The existence of the world, and my own, too;
  the death He took on Himself that I might live;
  and what all believers hope for as I do—     60

these and the living knowledge mentioned before
  have saved me from the ocean of false love
  and placed me by the true, safe on the shore.     63

The leaves that green the Eternal Garden's grove
  I love to the degree that each receives
  the dew and ray of His all flowering love."     66

The instant I fell still, my love professed,
  all Heaven rang with "Holy! Holy! Holy!"
  my lady joining with the other blest.     69

As bright light shatters sleep, the man being bid
  to waken by the visual spirit running
  to meet the radiance piercing lid by lid,                    72

and the man so roused does not know what he sees,
  his wits confounded by the sudden waking,
  till he once more regains his faculties;                     75

so from my eyes, my lady's eyes, whose ray
  was visible from a thousand miles and more,
  drove every last impediment away;                            78

in consequence of which I found my sight
  was clearer than before, and half astonished,
  I questioned her about a fourth great light                  81

near us, and she: "In that ray's Paradise
  the first soul from the hand of the First Power
  turns ever to its maker its glad eyes."                      84

As a bough that bends its crown to the wind's course,
  and then, after the blow, rises again
  uplifted by its own internal force;                          87

so did I as she spoke, all tremulous;
  then calmed again, assured by a desire
  to speak that burned in me, beginning thus:                  90

"O first and only fruit earth ever saw
  spring forth full ripe; O primal sire, to whom
  all brides are equally daughters and daughters-in-
                                              law;             93

speak, I beg, devoutly as I may.
  You know my wish. To hear you speak the sooner
  I leave unsaid what there is no need to say."                96

An animal, were it covered with a shawl
  and moved beneath it, would reveal its motion
  by the way in which the cloth would rise and fall; 99

in the same way, that first soul let me see
  through the motion of its covering, with what joy
  it moved in Heaven to bring joy to me.    102

Then breathed forth: "Without any need to hear
  what you would say, I know your wish more surely
  than you know what you take to be most clear.   105

I see it in the True Mirror, Itself the perfect
  reflector of all things in Its creation,
  which nothing in creation can reflect.    108

You wish to know how many years it is
  since God created me in the high garden
  where she prepared you for these stairs to bliss;   111

and how long my eyes enjoyed the good they prized;
  and the true reason for the great rejection;
  and the tongue I spoke, which I myself devised.   114

Know, my son, that eating from the tree
  was not itself the cause of such long exile,
  but only the violation of God's decree.    117

Longing to join this company, my shade
  counted four thousand three hundred and two suns
  where your lady summoned Virgil to your aid.    120

And circling all its signs, I saw it go
  nine hundred and thirty times around its track
  during the time I was a man below.    123

The tongue I spoke had vanished utterly
  long before Nimrod's people turned their hands
  to the work beyond their capability,    126

or nothing of the mind is beyond change:
    man's inclination answers to the stars
    and ranges as the starry courses range.       129

That man should speak is nature's own behest;
    but that you speak in this way or in that
    nature lets you decide as you think best.       132

Till I went down to the agony of Hell
    the Supreme Good whose rays send down the joy
    that wraps me here was known on earth as *EL*;       135

and then was known as *JAH*; and it must be so,
    for the usage of mankind is like a leaf
    that falls from the branch to let another grow.       138

On the peak that rises highest, my total stay,
    in innocence and later in disgrace,
    was from the first bright hour of my first day,       141

to the hour after the sixth, at which the sun
    changed quadrant, being then at meridian."

## Notes

12. *the power . . . Ananias' hand*: Ananias cured the blindness
of St. Paul by the laying on of hands. *Acts*, IX, 10 ff.

16-18. The gist of this passage is that the love of Beatrice
(Revelation) is identical with the love of God. Beyond that gist,
almost every commentator has his own interpretation. "The
Good" is clearly God, the joy of heaven's cloister, and the
Alpha and Omega of all scripture. But is scripture to be taken
as specifically Holy Scripture, as all that Christian Love has
been able to read of God's intent, or as both together? And is
"light and heavy stress" to be taken poetically to signify "both
accented and unaccented feet" (i.e., reading every last
syllable), or to signify "both the more and the less important
messages," or (again) some combination of the two?

19-66. THE EXAMINATION ON LOVE. In lines 4-9 St. John had called on Dante to discourse on love (the love of God, Christian love, *caritas*) assuring him in lines 10-12 that Beatrice (Divine Revelation) would restore his sight. Dante replies that he will await her pleasure since it was through his eyes that she first brought him the fire of love with which he burns. He then adds the generalized and elusive comment of lines 16-18. Now St. John calls Dante to a more searching examination and a more detailed answer. So to the first question of the examination proper: by whose hand (by what means) was the bow of his intention aimed at such a target as love?

26. *from here*: Heaven. The authority from Heaven is Scripture.

26-63. THE SOURCES OF LOVE. Dante answers that the knowledge of God's goodness inevitably leads to love and that the sources of that knowledge are, jointly, human reason and divine revelation. St. John, however, presses Dante to speak of the intensity of love and of his other promptings to it. So pressed, Dante cites the existence of the world as the creation of Divine Love, his own existence, the death Jesus took upon Himself, and the hope that is common to all faith.

37. *That truth*: That God is the Supreme Good and Supreme Love. *he*: Possibly Plato. "The Symposium" identifies love as the first of all the eternal essences. But more likely Aristotle who argued a single God of Love as the first principle of creation, the "unmoved mover" of "The Metaphysics" which is "the object of desire."

40-42. See *Exodus*, XXXIII, 19.

43-45. "I am Alpha and Omega, the beginning and the ending, saith the Lord which is, and which was, and which is to come, the Almighty" (*Revelation*, I, 8).

50-57. *teeth*: Urgings, promptings. It is not by accident that the Apostle of Love uses such a figure and that Dante repeats it. A softer figure would detract from the ardor necessary to the love of God, about which there can be nothing bland.

52. *Christ's Eagle*: St. John.

61. *the living knowledge mentioned before*: That God is the Supreme Good.

63. *by the true*: By the sea of true love. Cf. *Inferno*, I, 91 ff.

64-66. The Eternal Gardener is, of course, God; His grove, the world; its leaves, mankind. Heretofore Dante has discussed only Love of God. Here he adds Love of Others. Men are worthy of love to the extent each is loved by God. (Cf. *Inferno*, XX, 26-30, where Virgil scolds Dante for the impiety of pitying those whom God has justly damned.)

70-72. In simplest gloss: "As a bright light wakes a sleeping man." But how does the light reach the man's consciousness when he is asleep? Dante follows medieval authorities, Albertus Magnus among them, who posited a "visual spirit," an essence of man's nervous system which rises to respond to the light penetrating the layers of the eyelid and eye. Albertus Magnus theorized that this visual spirit rose from the vapors of certain delicate foods.

78. *drove every last impediment away*: The power of Beatrice's thousand-mile ray having penetrated the lids (of blindness) that covered Dante's eyes after the dazzling vision of St. John, rouses Dante's visual spirit and he is able to see again, more clearly than before. The figure will seem strange to present-day physiologists but the moral is clear: only as one loses his mortal senses can he endure the enlargement of revelation.

83. *the first soul*: Adam.

91. *only*: Eve might be thought to be such a fruit but Dante must have thought of her as part of Adam. *Genesis*, II, 22-24 would have given him ample scriptural authority for such a view.

97-102. Not Dante's most felicitous figure. It hardly honors the First Father to be compared to an animal under a cloth, the cloth representing his enshrouding radiance. Adam, moreover, is *in* not *under* the radiance. Yet the figure does convey a sense of how things are perceived in Heaven.

109-114. Dante's first wish is to know the date of Adam's creation. (*the exalted garden*: The Terrestrial Paradise. *she*: Beatrice.) His second is to know how long Adam remained there. His third, to know the exact cause of God's wrath. His fourth, to know what language Adam invented for himself.

Adam answers not in the order in which he finds these questions in Dante's mind, but in the order of their importance (a fine subtlety in portraying the heavenly souls) beginning with Original Sin.

118-120. *this company*: Of elected souls. *suns*: Annual, not daily. Were daily suns intended the time would amount to less than twelve years. And any possible ambiguity is resolved in line 121 where Adam speaks of the sun turning through all the signs of the zodiac. *where your lady summoned Virgil*: Limbo.

121-123. *all its signs*: Of the Zodiac. *nine hundred and thirty*: Adam's age at death is so given in *Genesis*, V, 5. *below*: on earth.

124-132. In *De vulgari eloquentia*, I, 6, Dante had claimed that Adam's original language was used by all of mankind up to the time Nimrod and his people were stricken at the Tower of Babel; and that it was still spoken thereafter by the Hebrews. As a mortal theorist, Dante was speculating there, as he is here. As the master builder of his own great metaphor, however, this touch in which revelation cancels the earlier error of human reason, is a superb detail. *answer to the stars*: To the influence of the stars. What we call the stars do not vary notably in their courses, but the moon and the planets (stars to Dante) wander all over the face of the heavens causing ever shifting conjunctions.

133-138. *EL . . . JAH*: Dante has Adam speak these syllables as *"J"* and *"EL,"* the *"J"* being a form of *"Y."* In that order *"Y"* or *"YEH"* or *"JAH"* followed by *"EL"* may suggest some primitive form of JAHVEH or JAHVEL. Such an interpretation is conjectural, however, and I have transposed the two syllables for rhyme purposes.

139-143. Adam declares that his whole sojourn in the Terrestrial Paradise was six hours (and perhaps part of the seventh). His time was from the dawn on the day of his creation, to the hour that follows the sixth. The total circuit of the sun is 360°, which divides into four quadrants of 90° or six hours. Assuming the time of Adam's creation to be at the vernal equinox, when day and night are each twelve hours long, the first hour of light would be from six to seven A.M., the end of the sixth would be at noon, and the hour after the sixth would be from noon to one P.M. Adam says "from the first hour . . . to the hour after the sixth." He does not say how far into that hour he remained, but it would be native to Dante's mind and style to intend Adam's expulsion to fall exactly at high noon. Half an allegorical day is about as long as any man can stay innocent.

# CANTO XXVII

---

*Denunciation of Papal*
*Corruption*

ASCENT TO THE PRIMUM MOBILE

*ST. PETER GROWS RED with righteous indignation
and utters a DENUNCIATION OF PAPAL CORRUP-
TION. All Heaven darkens at the thought of such evil.
Peter's charge, of course, is that the papacy has become
acquisitive, political, and therefore bloody. Having so
catalogued the crimes of the bad popes, Peter specifically charges Dante to repeat among mankind the wrath
that was spoken in Heaven.*

*The triumphant court soars away and Dante is left
with Beatrice who tells him to look down. Dante finds
he is standing above a point midway between Jerusalem
and Spain, and having seen earth (and all its vaunted
pomps) as an insignificant mote in space, Dante once
more turns his thoughts upward as Beatrice leads him
in the ASCENT TO THE PRIMUM MOBILE, dis-
coursing en route on the NATURE OF TIME (which
has its source in the Primum Mobile). The TIME OF
EARTH'S CORRUPTION, Beatrice tells Dante, is drawing to a close.*

"Glory to the Father, the Son, and the Holy Ghost"—
    a strain so sweet that I grew drunk with it
    rang from the full choir of the heavenly host.     3

I seemed to see the universe alight
    with a single smile; and thus my drunkenness
    came on me through my hearing and my sight.     6

O joy! O blessedness no tongue can speak!
  O life conjoint of perfect love and peace!
  O sure wealth that has nothing more to seek!          9

The four great torches were still burning there,
  and the one that had descended to me first
  began to outshine all else in that sphere.          12

As Jupiter might appear if it and Mars
  were birds and could exchange their glowing plumes—
  such it became among the other stars.          15

The Providence that assigns to Heaven's band
  the offices and services of each,
  had imposed silence there on every hand          18

when I heard: "You need not wonder that I change hue,
  for as I utter what I have to say
  you shall see all these beings change theirs, too.          21

The usurper of the throne given to me,
  to me, to me, there on the earth that now
  before the Son of God stands vacant, he          24

has made a sewer of my sepulcher, a flow
  of blood and stink at which the treacherous one
  who fell from here may chuckle there below."          27

With the same color I have seen clouds turn
  when opposite the rising or setting sun,
  I saw the sweet face of all heaven burn.          30

And as a modest lady whose pure bearing
  is self-secure, may blush at another's failings,
  though they be only mentioned in her hearing;          33

so Beatrice changed complexion at a breath,
  and such eclipse came over heaven then
  as when Supreme Might suffered mankind's death.  36

Then he continued speaking as before,
   his voice so changed, so charged with indignation
   that his appearance could not darken more:   39

"The bride of Christ was not suckled of old
   on blood of mine, of Linus, and of Cletus
   to be reared as an instrument for grabbing gold.   42

It was to win this life of blessedness
   Sixtus, and Pius, and Calixtus, and Urban
   let flow the blood and tears of their distress.   45

We never meant that men of Christian life
   should sit part on the right, part on the left
   of our successors, steeled for bloody strife.   48

Nor that the keys consigned into my hand
   should fly as emblems from a flag unfurled
   against the baptized in a Christian land.   51

Nor that my head should, in a later age,
   seal privilege sold to liars. The very thought
   has often made me burn with holy rage!   54

From here in every pasture, fold, and hill
   we see wolves dressed as shepherds. O hand of God,
   mankind's defender, why do you yet lie still?   57

Gascons and Cahorsines are crouched to drink
   our very blood. Oh excellent beginning,
   to what foulest conclusion will you sink?   60

Yet the high Providence that stood with Rome
   and Scipio for the glory of the world
   will once again, and soon, be seen to come.   63

You, son, who must yet bear around earth's track
   your mortal weight, open your mouth down there:
   do not hold back what I have not held back!"   66

Just as the frozen vaporings sift down
  out of our earthly atmosphere when the horn
  of heaven's Goat is burnished by the Sun;          69

Just so, up there, I saw the ether glow
  with a rising snow of the triumphant vapors
  who had remained a while with us below.          72

My eyes followed their traces toward the height,
  followed until the airy medium
  closed its vast distance on my upward sight;          75

at which my lady, seeing me absolved
  from service to the height, said: "Now look down
  and see how far the heavens have revolved."          78

I looked down once again. Since the last time,
  I had been borne, I saw, a length of arc
  equal to half the span of the first clime;          81

so that I saw past Cadiz the mad route
  Ulysses took; and almost to the shore
  from which Europa rode the godly brute.          84

And yet more of this little threshing floor
  would have been visible but, below my foot,
  the sun was ahead of me by a sign and more.          87

My mind, which ever found its Paradise
  in thinking of my lady, now more than ever
  burned with desire to look into her eyes.          90

If nature or art ever contrived a lure
  to catch the eye and thus possess the mind,
  whether in living flesh or portraiture,          90

all charms united could not move a pace
  toward the divine delight with which I glowed
  when I looked once more on her smiling face.          96

In one look then I felt my spirit given
   a power that plucked it out of Leda's nest
   and sent it soaring to the swiftest heaven. 99

From its upper and lower limits to its center
   it is so uniform, I cannot say
   what point my lady chose for me to enter. 102

But she, knowing what yearning burned in me,
   began thus—with so rapturous a smile
   God seemed to shine forth from her ecstasy: 105

"The order of the universe, whose nature
   holds firm the center and spins all else around it,
   takes from this heaven its first point of departure. 108

This heaven does not exist in any place
   but in God's mind, where burns the love that turns it
   and the power that rains to it from all of space. 111

Light and Love contain it in one band
   as it does all the rest; and such containment
   only the Cunctitenant can understand. 114

Its own motion unfactored, all things derive
   their motions from this heaven as precisely
   as ten is factored into two and five. 117

So may you understand how time's taproot
   is hidden in this sphere's urn, while in the others
   we see its spreading foliage and its fruit. 120

O Greed that has drawn down all Adam's blood
   so deep into its dark that none has strength
   to raise his eyes above its evil flood! 123

The will of man comes well to its first flower,
   but then the rain that sets in endlessly
   blights the good fruit and leaves it green and sour. 126

Faith and innocence are found nowhere
    except in little children; and both have fled
    before their cheeks have sprouted a first hair.    129

Still young enough to lisp, one fasts and prays;
    then, his tongue freed, devours all sorts of food
    even in Lent, even on fasting days.    132

Another will love his mother and behave
    while yet a lisper, who, with his freed speech
    will be impatient to see her in her grave.    135

So the fair daughter of Him who leaves us night
    and brings us morning, changes her complexion,
    and her white skin turns black in Heaven's sight.    138

Consider, if you marvel at what I say,
    how there is none to govern on the earth,
    whereby the human family goes astray.    141

But before January falls in spring
    because of that odd day in each hundred years
    that all neglect down there, these spheres shall ring    144

so loud with portents of a season's turn
    that the long awaited storm will sweep the fleet,
    blowing the bows around to dead astern    147

and set the true course straight. Then all shall see
first blossom turn to good fruit on the tree."

## Notes

10-11. *the four great torches*: Peter, James, John, and Adam.
*the one that had descended to me first*: Peter.

13-15. Jupiter (white) and Mars (red) are conceived here
as two firebirds who partially exchange their glowing plumage.
The point is that the aura of St. Peter, without losing its

essential white brilliance, begins to glow with a redder (more martial) light. The change indicates a change of mood: a fiercer St. Peter is about to denounce the corruption of the Papacy by his evil successors.

17. *offices*: Empowering appointments. Cf. "office of the mass." *services*: the times each is called upon to perform his offices. Since all is preordained by God, each slightest action is from God's will.

21. *change theirs*: Change their hues.

22. *the usurper*: Boniface VIII.

25. *my sepulcher*: Rome as the seat of papal authority. According to tradition, Peter was buried there.

26. *the treacherous one*: Satan.

35-36. "Now from the sixth hour there was darkness over all the land until the ninth hour." *Matthew*, XXVII, 45. See also *Mark*, XV, 33, and *Luke*, XXIII, 44-45. The apostles report the eclipse as darkness and Dante treats it as a reddening. It seems unlikely it was so dark a red as to suggest night shadow. Perhaps Dante saw that flush of righteous indignation as showing like night on earth, but blush-red as seen from heaven's height.

37-39. The quality of the reaction invites a speculation: men work themselves into moods and are carried away by them at times, but heavenly beings express instant recognition and total justice; they register instantly, therefore, the exactly right reaction to things.

41-44. All these here named were early bishops of Rome, Peter's first successor being traditionally believed to be Linus, and his successor, Cletus (Anacletus). The others followed at various intervals: Sixtus 117-circa 127, Pius 142-circa 149, Calixtus 217-222, and Urban 222-230. Not all were martyred, as line 45 would seem to suggest, but all suffered in the flesh and in the spirit for the sins of mankind.

47-48. *part on the right, part on the left*: To indicate any warring parties of Christians, the bloody divisions of Dante's time being first the Guelfs and the Ghibellines, and then the Black and the White Guelfs, those divisions often incited or abetted by the corrupt Popes for purposes of their own politics.

49-51. *keys*: The papal keys, emblems of the Pope's authority were used on the banner of the Vatican States, which had often been carried into battle against Christians—a bloody perversion, in Dante's view, of the papal mission.

52-53. *my head . . . a seal*: The papal seal, stamped on
many documents whose intent was venial, bore the purported
likeness of St. Peter.

58. *Gascons and Cahorsines*: Clement V was from Gascony;
John XXII from Cahors. Both filled the Papal Court with greedy
favorites from their native lands. And both, of course, were
guilty of the further sin of being French in Italy.

61-63. God's foreseeing provision, as Dante would have understood it, must have helped Scipio overthrow Hannibal, else
Rome would not have remained the glory of the world and
could not have become the proper seat of holy church.

64-66. This charge, laid upon him by St. Peter himself, is,
of course, Dante's ultimate license to denounce papal corruption.
Effectively enough, the very charge is itself the ultimate
denunciation.

67-75. All the souls who remained below when Mary ascended
now rise to the Empyrean like a reverse snowfall. The figure
Dante chooses for their ascent is not his most felicitous in that
the snow image cannot suggest either the radiance of the souls
nor the necessary speed of their ascent. *when the horn of
heaven's Goat is burnished by the Sun*: The sun is in Capricorn
(heaven's Goat) at about mid-January, hence at the time when
"frozen vaporings" come down as snow.

79 ff. The last (and first) time Dante looked down was as
he entered the Sphere of the Fixed Stars (XXII, 127 ff.). Now,
as he is about to leave this Sphere, he looks down again and
sees he has revolved through 90°. He has, therefore, been in this
heaven six hours, one quarter of a daily turn. 90° is the
amount of arc equal to half the span of the first clime.
Geographers of Dante's time divided the northern hemisphere
into seven habitable "climes" or "climates" running parallel to
the equator. The southern hemisphere, of course, was taken to
be water, the Mount of Purgatory excepted, and the northern
landmass was taken to spread 180° from Spain to India.

The earthly point above which Dante is passing is about midway between Jerusalem and Spain. He can see the eastern shore
of the Mediterranean and westward beyond Spain into the
Atlantic. It would be allegorically pleasant to be able to say
he was over Rome at this moment before ascending into the
last sphere, and Dante may well have had that thought in
mind, but nothing in the text permits more than a guess.

82-84. *past Cadiz*: The Atlantic. *the mad route Ulysses took*:
See *Inferno*, XXVI, 90 ff. *the shore from which Europa*:

Phœnicia on the eastern coast of the Mediterranean. Zeus appeared to Europa there as a bull and, taking her on his back, bore her to Crete. "Godly brute" is rhyme-forced: Dante says, literally, "the shore on which Europa became a sweet burden."

85-87. *threshing floor*: The Earth. (See XXII, 127 ff.) *more . . . would have been visible*: Dante's view is cut off by darkness because the Sun is ahead of him in Aries. He is in Gemini. The sign of Taurus lies between. A zodiacal sign covers 30°. The sun, therefore, is something more than two hours ahead of him and perhaps as much as four (if it is in the middle of Aries and he in the middle of Gemini). Part of the world below Dante must, therefore, lie in shadow.

98. *Leda's nest*: Gemini, the sign of the twins, Castor and Pollux. Zeus appeared to Leda as a swan and, according to the most common legend, she bore him Castor and Pollux. "Nest" is a *jeu d'esprit* derived from Zeus's traveling costume when he called on Leda.

100-102. ENTRANCE INTO THE PRIMUM MOBILE. Dante knew he entered the Eighth Sphere at the point of heaven marked by Gemini (XXII, 152). The Ninth Sphere, however, is so uniform that he can make out no point of reference. Beatrice, of course, knows his confusion and hastens to explain to him the nature of the Ninth Sphere.

103. *what yearning*: To understand the nature of the new sphere.

106-108. The firmly held center is the Earth. In the nature of the Ptolemaic universe, whose originating motion is the Primum Mobile, all else is made to revolve around that center.

114. *the Cunctitenant*: God, the all-containing. He contains the Primum Mobile as it contains all else.

115-117. Ten is precisely determined as the product of the factors two and five. The Primum Mobile, itself unfactorable (i.e., defined and limited by nothing), imparts the factors that determine every other motion, setting the speed, regularity, and deviation of every other heavenly motion.

118-120. Time is measured by the motion of the heavenly bodies, but the source of time, like the root of a tree, is hidden in the urn (flowerpot) of the Primum Mobile, while the heavenly bodies show forth in the other spheres as the foliage and fruit of the hidden cause. *So may you understand*: By what I say.

131. *his tongue freed*: When he has grown out of his childish lisp.

132. I have translated what I take to be Dante's intent rather than his words. Dante says simply "in whatever moon," meaning both "in whatever month" (including Lent) and "at whatever time of the month" (including Fridays and other stated days of fasting).

136-138. Few of Dante's tercets are open to so many interpretations. I follow Scartazzini-Vandelli in reading the passage as a denunciation of the corruption of the church, the fair daughter of the Sun (it being always, in Dante, a symbol of God). The Sun, arriving, brings morning and, departing, leaves night. The fair daughter, once immaculately white (the color of innocence) and still apparently so in mortal manifestation shows black (corrupt and evil) in the sight of Heaven.

140. *none to govern*: The Church being corrupt and the Emperor having abandoned Italy.

143. *that odd day in each hundred years*: The calendar as reformed under Julius Caesar fixed the year at 365 days and 6 hours, introducing an error of about 13 minutes, approximately one hundredth of a day. In each century, therefore, the calendar would move the months a day forward into the advancing season. In a millennium, January would have moved ten days nearer the spring. In 1582, the Gregorian calendar (developed under Pope Gregory XIII) substantially corrected this error.

# CANTO XXVIII

THE NINTH SPHERE: THE PRIMUM MOBILE

*The Angel Hierarchy*

DANTE TURNS *from Beatrice and beholds a vision
of* GOD AS A NON-DIMENSIONAL POINT OF
LIGHT *ringed by* NINE GLOWING SPHERES *representing the* ANGEL HIERARCHY.

Dante is puzzled because the vision seems to reverse
the order of the Universe, the highest rank of the
angels being at the center and represented by the
smallest sphere. Beatrice explains the mystery to Dante's
satisfaction, if not to the reader's, and goes on to
catalogue the ORDERS OF THE ANGELS.

When she whose powers imparadise my mind
    had so denounced and laid bare the whole truth
    of the present state of miserable mankind;       3

just as a man before a glass can see
    a torch that burns behind him, and know it is there
    before he has seen or thought of it directly;      6

and turns to see if what the glass has shown
    is really there; and finds, as closely matched
    as words to music, the fact to its reflection;      9

just so, as I recall, did I first stare
    into the heaven of those precious eyes
    in which, to trap me, Love had set his snare;      12

then turned, and turning felt my senses reel
    as my own were struck by what shines in that heaven
    when we look closely at its turning wheel.      15

I saw a Point that radiated light
  of such intensity that the eye it strikes
  must close or ever after lose its sight.                18

The star that seems the smallest, seen from here,
  would seem a moon, were it placed next to this,
  as often we see star by star appear.                   21

And at about the distance that a halo
  surrounds a heavenly radiance that paints it
  on the densest mist that will yet let it show;         24

so close around the Point, a ring of fire
  spun faster than the fastest of the spheres
  circles creation in its endless gyre.                  27

Another surrounded this, and was surrounded
  by a third, the third by a fourth, the fourth
  by a fifth, and by a sixth the fifth, in turn,
                              was bounded.   30

The seventh followed, already spread so wide
  that were Juno's messenger to be made complete
  she could not stretch her arc from side to side.       33

And so the eighth and the ninth, and each ring spun
  with an ever slower motion as its number
  placed it the further out from the first one,          36

which gave forth the most brilliant incandescence
  because, I think, being nearest the Scintilla,
  it drew the fullest share of the true essence.         39

I was on tenterhooks, as my lady saw.
  To ease my mind she said: "From that one Point
  are hung the heavens and all nature's law.             42

Look at the closest ring: I would have you know
   it spins so fast by virtue of Love's fire,
   the ray of which pierces it through and through." 45

And I to here: "Were the ordering we find
   in the universe like that of these bright wheels,
   what I have seen would satisfy my mind. 48

But in the sensible universe one can see
   the motions of the spheres become more godlike
   the nearer they are to the periphery. 51

If there is food for my soul's appetite
   in this most glorious and angelic temple
   whose only boundaries are love and light, 54

you must explain why it has been so planned
   that the form and the exemplum are at odds;
   for by myself I cannot understand." 57

"It is small wonder such a knot defies
   your fingers, for since none has ever tried it,
   the coils have set together like a vise." 60

So spoke my lady, going on to say:
   "If you would understand, grasp what I tell you,
   and around it give your mind's best powers full play. 63

The physical spheres are graduated in size
   according to the power that infuses each
   and fixes it to its station in the skies. 66

The greater good intends a greater grace.
   A greater body can hold more of good
   if all its parts are perfect, as in this case. 69

This sphere, then, that spins with it as it goes
   all of the universe, must correspond
   to the angel sphere that most loves and most knows. 72

If you will measure not by what appears
   but by the power inherent in these beings
   that manifest themselves to you as spheres,     75

you will observe a marvelous correspondence
   of greater power to larger, and lesser to smaller,
   between each Heaven and its Intelligence."     78

As the airy hemisphere serenes and glows,
   cloudless and blue into its furthest reach,
   when from his gentler cheek Boreas blows,     81

purging and dissolving with that breeze
   the turbulent vapors, so that heaven smiles
   with the beauty of its every diocese;     84

so was it in my mind, once I was given
   my lady's clear reply; and I saw the truth
   shining before me like a star in heaven.     87

And at her last word every angel sphere
   began to sparkle as iron, when it is melted
   in a crucible, is seen to do down here.     90

And every spark spun with its spinning ring:
   and they were numberless as the sum of grain
   on the last square of the chessboard of the king.     93

From choir to choir their hymn of praise rang free
   to the Fixed Point that holds them in fixed place,
   as ever was, as evermore shall be.     96

And she who felt uncertainty bedim
   my dazzled mind explained: "The first two circles
   have shown you the Seraphim and Cherubim.     99

Being led, they chase the reins in their eagerness
   to resemble the Point the more, and they can the more
   the more they look upon Its blessedness.     102

he beings in the next bright wheel you see
  are titled Thrones of the Eternal Aspect;
  and they complete the first great trinity.                    105

nd know that all these raptures are fulfilled
  to the degree that each can penetrate
  the Truth in which all questioning is stilled.                 108

Hence one may see that the most blest condition
  is based on the act of seeing, not of love,
  love being the act that follows recognition.                   111

hey see as they are worthy. They are made
  to their degrees by grace and their own good will.
  And so their ranks proceed from grade to grade.    114

he second trinity that blossoms here
  in this eternal springtime of delight
  whose leaves nocturnal Aries does not sear,                    117

arble 'Hosannah!' everlastingly,
  and their three melodies sound the three degrees
  of blessedness that form this trinity.                         120

hese are the divinities therein found:
  Dominations first, then Virtues, then, in order,
  the ranks of Powers within the widest round.                   123

n the next two dances of this exhaltation
  whirl Principalities first, then the Archangels.
  The last contains the Angelic jubilation.                      126

All fix their eyes on high and as their sight
  ascends their power descends to all below.
  So are all drawn, as all draw, to God's height.                129

Dionysius gave himself to contemplation
  of these same orders with such holy zeal
  that he named and ranked them just as I
                        have done.    132

Gregory, later, differed with his conclusions.
  But hardly had he wakened in this heaven
  than he was moved to laugh at his own delusions.

And if a truth so hidden was made clear
  by one still in the weight of mortal dust,
  you need not wonder: one who saw it here          138

returned and told him this: this and much more
of the bright truth these circles hold in store."

## Notes

1-21. The figure is based on *Psalms*, XIX, 1: "The heavens
are telling the glory of God and the firmament proclaims his
handiwork." Wherever we look in the Primum Mobile, Dante
tells us in lines 13-15, we see the glory of God.

He proceeds to describe this glory as a vision of God and
the Hierarchies of the Angels. (What David saw dimly from
Earth, Dante sees in detail at heaven's height.)

But first the image is approached by seeing it reflected in
the heaven of Beatrice's eyes (revelation) to which Dante's
soul is ever drawn by love. From the revelation of Love (a
heaven in itself), Dante turns to the glory itself, to find the
fact in exact accord with the reflection.

It is an elaborate and sublimely conceived figure, and will
certainly do as an example of Dante's fully let out paradisal
style, of the high range of his rhetoric as opposed to some of
the deliberate coarsening of style he found necessary in treating
the Inferno.

6. *directly*: Not reflected.

14. *my own*: His own eyes. *that heaven*: The Primum Mobile.

16. *a Point*: The term is used in its strict mathematical sense
to symbolize God as an immaterial and non-spatial essence.

19. *from here*: From Earth.

26. *the fastest of the spheres*: The Primum Mobile.

32. *Juno's messenger*: Iris, the rainbow. As Juno's messenger,
the rainbow is conceived as descending from heaven to earth;
at most, therefore, as a quarter of a circle. Were the rainbow

to be extended to a full 180° across the sky, the distance it could span at its greatest spread could not equal the circumference of the seventh ring.

21-36. THE HIERARCHY OF ANGELS. They surround God as the heavenly spheres surround the Earth, but their motions, contrary to those of the heavenly spheres, are greater as they lie closer to the center. Opposition (paradox) is a natural part of the language of mysticism. These spheres seem at first to be a sort of counter-universe. But note that the principle of both "universes" remains the same, for in either system, the spheres have greater motion and greater "virtue" as their placement draws nearer to God. In lines 52-57 below, Dante begs Beatrice to explain the mystery of this seeming paradox and in 58-78 Beatrice resolves Dante's uncertainties, going on then (97-129) to set forth the nine orders of the angelic beings grouped in three trinities: First Trinity: Seraphim, Cherubim, Thrones; Second Trinity: Dominations, Virtues, Powers; Third Trinity: Principalities, Archangels, Angels.

36. *the first one*: The first ring. Not to be confused with The Point.

37. *which*: The first ring.

38. *the Scintilla*: God. The Point.

50. *more godlike*: Possessed of greater powers as indicated by greater speed and greater brilliance.

56. *the form*: Platonic form, the essential, unchanging noumenal concept of which any exemplum is an instance.

59. *since none has tried it*: Small wonder. Since Dante is the first to have reached this height of Heaven and to have returned from it, Dante is the first to state the problem.

58-60. BEATRICE'S REPLY. The gist of Beatrice's reply is that Dante is to observe a marvelous correspondence between each of the physical spheres and its assigned Angel Intelligence. Yet the juxtaposition of these two, so to speak, mirror images, speaks a masterful conception. God conceived as the center of the Angel Hierarchy and God conceived as the circumference of the physical universe, are not two but one, twin manifestations of one creative force; and the interplay of these two images is powerfully relevant to Dante's belief that physical and spiritual law co-exist and interplay as twin manifestations of one will. God is the radiating center of all spiritual energy and He is simultaneously the all-containing bound and limit of physical creation.

Yet, aside from the magnificence of Dante's conception here, there remain problems of interpretation in Beatrice's reply. If the largest physical sphere corresponds to the smallest angelic sphere, what then of the assertion that a larger body contains more good than a smaller one, if both are perfect? Dante, even as a pilgrim awaiting instruction, must have grasped that the greater power results from closer proximity to God: the whole journey of the *Comedy* is scaled to that proximity. It is odd that Beatrice, having mentioned so much else, does not mention proximity to God as the essence of the mystery.

In accepting the beauty of Beatrice's revelation, Dante certainly implies that we must ponder these points. Perhaps the central clue is in lines 73-75: Dante does not see the Angel Hierarchy as it is but as it manifests itself to him in the form of nine spheres. Seen from all lower levels, these spheres are contained in God and surrounded by Him, for God is Allness. Seen in this nonphysical manifestation at the height of Heaven, the spheres surround Him, for God is nondimensional essence.

65. *the power*: The "virtue" of each, its power to influence the course of what lies below it. The power, of course, descends to each as a ray from God, more powerfully to the nearer spheres, but in each the amount of power is infused through all parts of the sphere equally.

70. *this sphere*: The Primum Mobile, the source of all motion in the physical universe. As the most powerful of the spheres and as the one closest to God, it corresponds to the inner ring of the Angel Hierarchy, the Seraphim.

78. *Intelligence*: The Angel Intelligence of each sphere.

82. *Boreas*: The North Wind. When he blows straight out of his mouth the wind is from the north, which in Italy is from the Alps. Italians call that wind *"il tramontano,"* and think of it as the stormy source of bitter winter cold. When Boreas blows from his left cheek, the resultant northeaster (*"il grecale"*) is thought of as a source of storms and of cloudy skies. But when he blows from the right (the gentler) cheek, Italians experience *"il maestrale,"* the sky-clearing wind from the northwest.

84. *every angel sphere*: The rings of the Angel Hierarchy. They react to the perfection of Beatrice's answer with a sparkling shower of joy.

91. *is worked:* Dante says only "iron that boils." But molten iron does not shoot sparks in the quantity Dante suggests unless it is hammered or poured. *spun with its spinning ring*: On earth,

sparks tend to fly away from their sources. Here they stay in place, keeping pace with the rotation of the heavenly ring. The sparks may be taken as the individual angel intelligences within each ring; the added brightness of each, as evidence of the increase of its joy.

92-93. *the chessboard of the king*: The legend is still common and variously told. In one form, the inventor of chess offered the game to the king, who was so pleased with it that he ordered the inventor to name his own reward. The inventor asked that a single grain of wheat be placed on the first square of the board, two on the second, four on the third, and so on until the 64th increment was reached. The king, no mathematician, agreed gladly. It must have been at about the twelfth square (1,080,576 grains, if my figuring is sound) that the king began to learn the power of mathematics and that the number of grains would mount by the 64th square to something more than 18,000,000,000,000,000,000.

99. *have shown you*: As ever in Heaven, Dante does not see through the power of his own senses; rather, visions are manifested to him out of *caritas*. These symbolic visions cannot be taken as the thing itself, for the mystery of heavenly being is beyond Dante; as, in one sense, it is beyond all but God. Dante is offered symbolic representations at a level he can begin to grasp with the aid of Beatrice (Revelation).

100-102. *Being led, they chase the reins*: The figure should become clear if one thinks of the opposite condition of drawing back from the reins. The Angel Intelligences are all eagerness to pursue what leads them ever faster. *to resemble the Point, etc.*: To make themselves more godlike. Pride, the first of sins, it must be noted, springs from man's desire to be himself God. The Angel Intelligences yearn toward God in love (as it is man's charge to make himself over in God's image), not in rebellion, as Satan was moved.

102-105. Dante, ever a symbolic numerologist, divides the nine ranks into three trinities. Each rank, likely, expresses an aspect of God. The first two ranks of the first trinity may well be taken as being entirely beyond human understanding. Of the Thrones he has already spoken in IX, 61-62: "On high are mirrors (you say 'Thrones') and these reflect God's judgment to us." Thus the Thrones would seem to be God's aspect as Supreme Justice.

106. *all these raptures*: All the angelic beings of all the nine ranks, not simply those of the first trinity.

108. *the Truth in which all questioning is stilled:* God.

116-117. *springtime . . . nocturnal Aries:* In spring the sun is in Aries and its stars are not visible in the day sky. In autumn the sun has moved to the opposite sign (Libra) and the stars of Aries are visible at night. Thus nocturnal Aries may be said to be the sign under which the plants that blossomed in spring turn to seared leaves.

118. *warble:* The idea of "warbling" Hosannah may seem odd and yet it is native to the language Dante has invented for his *Paradiso.* The angel beings sing their praises with an ecstasy akin to the nisus of birds. The word Dante uses is *"sverna"* (*svernare*—literally, "to unwinter," and by extension, "to sound the glad spring song of birds").

121-123. *therein:* Within the second trinity. *the widest round:* The third of the second trinity.

124. *dances:* Ranks, orders. Called dances to denote exhaltation.

130. *Dionysius:* St. Dionysius the Areopagite. A Greek mystic of the first century A.D. His conversion by St. Paul is recorded in *Acts*, XVII, 34. To him was attributed the thesis *De coelesti hierarchia,* from which Dante draws the details for his Angel Hierarchy.

133. *Gregory:* St. Gregory (*circa* 540-604), called "the Great." Pope from 590. Among many other writings he revised Dionysius' treatise on the angel hierarchies. As Beatrice tells it, he had hardly awakened in heaven before he saw how wrong he had been, whereupon he was moved to laugh at his own delusions. His error, to be sure, was a harmless mistake; not a heresy, nor in any way sinful.

138. *one who saw it here:* St. Paul (*II Corinthians*, XII, 2 ff.) tells of his ascent to the third heaven "whether in the body or out of the body I do not know." Dante's presumption here is that Paul told Dionysius what he had seen in heaven, and thus the accuracy of Dionysius' description (through if he were merely reporting what he had been told by Paul, he need hardly have given himself to such zealous contemplation as Beatrice ascribes to him in 130-132).

140. *hold in store:* A rhyme-forced addition. Dante says simply "of the truth of those circles." Since that truth is the revelation that awaits the pious soul, I hope I may argue that "hold in store" is implicit.

# CANTO XXIX

*The Angel Hierarchy*

*BEATRICE, gazing on God, sees Dante's unspoken questions and explains to him GOD'S INTENT IN WILLING THE CREATION, THE ETERNITY OF GOD, and the SIMULTANEITY OF CREATION.*

*She proceeds then to explain the TIME FROM THE CREATION TO THE REVOLT OF THE ANGELS, HOW THE LOVING ANGELS BEGAN THEIR BLISSFUL ART, and that GRACE IS RECEIVED ACCORDING TO THE ARDOR OF LOVE.*

*She then DENOUNCES FOOLISH TEACHINGS, and concludes by pointing out THE INFINITY AND THE DISTINCTION OF THE ANGELS.*

When Latona's twins, one setting in the sign
    of Aries and the other rising in Libra,
    are belted by the same horizon's line;        3

as long then as the zenith's fulcrum bears
    their perfect balance, till one and other leave
    their common belt and change their hemispheres,        6

so long did Beatrice, smiling her delight,
    stay silent, her eyes fixed on the Fixed Point
    whose power had overcome me at first sight.        9

Then she began: "I do not ask, I say
    what you most wish to hear, for I have seen it
    where time and space are focused in one ray.        12

Not to increase Its good—no mil nor dram
   can add to true perfection, but that reflections
   of his reflection might declare 'I am'—          15

in His eternity, beyond time, above
   all other comprehension, as it pleased Him,
   new loves were born of the Eternal Love.          18

Nor did He lie asleep before the Word
   sounded above these waters; 'before' and 'after'
   did not exist until His voice was heard.          21

Pure essence, and pure matter, and the two
   joined into one were shot forth without flaw,
   like three bright arrows from a three-string bow.          24

And as in glass, in amber, or in crystal
   a ray shines so that nothing intervenes
   between its coming and being, which is total;          27

so the threefold effect rayed from its Sire
   into created being, without beginning
   and without interval, instantly entire.          30

Order was the co-created fact
   of every essence; and at the peak of all,
   these angel loves created as pure act.          33

Pure potential held the lowest ground;
   between, potential-and-act were tied together
   so tight they nevermore shall be unbound.          36

Hieronymus wrote to you of the long span
   of centuries in which such beings existed
   before the other world was made for man;          39

but the Scribes of the Holy Ghost clearly declare
   the true account in many passages,
   as you will see if you will read with care.          42

It can, in part, be grasped by intellection,
    which cannot grant such powers could long exist
    apart from the functioning of their perfection.    45

This much will answer where, and when, and how
    the angels were created; and so are quenched
    the first three flames of your desire to know.    48

Nor could you count to ten and ten before
    some of those angels fell from Heaven to roil
    the bedrock of the elemental core.    51

The rest remained here and around their Cause
    began the art you see, moved by such bliss
    that their glad revolutions never pause.    54

It was accursèd pride for which they fell,
    the pride of that dark principal you saw
    crushed by the world's whole weight in deepest
                           Hell.    57

These you see here were humble, undemanding,
    and prompt in their acknowledgment of the Good
    that made them capable of such understanding;    60

whereby their vision was exalted higher
    by illuminating grace and their own merit,
    in which their wills are changeless and entire.    63

Now hear this and, beyond all doubt, believe it:
    the good of grace is in exact proportion
    to the ardor of love that opens to receive it.    66

And now, if you have heeded what I said,
    you should be able to observe this college
    and gather much more without further aid.    69

But since your earthly schoolmen argue still
   that the angelic nature is composed
   of understanding, memory, and will,    72

I will say this much more to help you see
   the truth that is confounded there below
   by the equivocations of sophistry:    75

these beings, since their first bliss in the sight
   of God's face, in which all things are revealed,
   have never turned their eyes from their delight.    78

No angel's eye, it follows, can be caught
   by a new object; hence, they have no need
   of memory, as does divided thought.    81

So men, awake but dreaming, dare to claim,
   believing it or not, they speak the truth—
   though the hypocrite's is the greater sin and shame.    84

You mortals do not walk a single way
   in your philosophies, but let the thought
   of being acclaimed as wise lead you astray.    87

Yet heaven bears even this with less offense
   than it must feel when it sees Holy Writ
   neglected, or perverted of all sense.    90

They do not count what blood and agony
   planted it in the world, nor Heaven's pleasure
   in those who search it in humility.    93

Each man, to show off, strains at some absurd
   invented truth; and it is these the preachers
   make sermons of; and the Gospel is not heard.    96

One says the moon reversed its course to throw
   a shadow on the sun during Christ's passion
   so that its light might not shine down below;    99

others say that the sun itself withdrew
 and, therefore, that the Indian and the Spaniard
 shared the eclipse in common with the Jew.  102

These fables pour from pulpits in such torrents,
 spewing to right and left, that in a year
 they outnumber the Lapi and Bindi in all Florence. 105

Therefore the ignorant sheep turn home at night
 from having fed on wind. Nor does the fact
 that the pastor sees no harm done set things right. 108

Christ did not say to His first congregation:
 'Go and preach twaddle to the waiting world.'
 He gave them, rather, holy truth's foundation.  111

That, and that only, was the truth revealed
 by those who fought and died to plant the faith.
 They made the Gospel both their sword and shield. 114

Now preachers make the congregation roar
 with quips and quirks, and so it laugh enough,
 their hoods swell, and they ask for nothing more. 117

But in their tippets there nests such a bird
 that the people, could they see it, would soon know
 what faith to place in pardons thus conferred.  120

Because of these such folly fills the earth
 that, asking neither proof nor testimonials,
 men chase whatever promise is held forth.  123

On such St. Anthony's pig feeds on, unstinted,
 and others yet more swinish feast and guzzle
 and pay their way with money never minted.  126

But we have strayed. Therefore before we climb
 turn your attention back to the straight path
 that we may fit our journey to our time.  129

So many beings are ranked within this nature
    that the number of their hosts cannot be said
    nor even imagined by a mortal creature.     132

Read well what Daniel saw at heaven's height.
    You will soon see that when he speaks of 'thousands'
    every finite number is lost from sight.     135

To all, the Primal Light sends down Its ray.
    And every splendor into which it enters
    receives that radiance in its own way.     138

Therefore, since the act of loving grows
    from the act of recognition, the bliss of love
    blazes in some of these, and in some it glows.     141

Consider then how lofty and how wide
    is the excellence of the Eternal Worth
    which in so many mirrors can divide     144

its power and majesty forevermore,
Itself remaining One, as It was before."

## Notes

1-9. Latona (or Leto) was, according to early legend, the
wife of Zeus before he married Hera. Later legend has her as
his mistress. In any case she bore him Apollo (the Sun) and
Diana, or Artemis (the Moon).

At the vernal equinox the sun sets in Aries as the moon rises
in the opposite sign of Libra. For a moment, with the zenith
as the fulcrum of these sky-wide scales, they are perfectly
balanced and wear the line of the horizon as a common belt.
Then, each changing hemisphere—one dropping below the horizon, the other rising above it—the balance is broken.

The language of astronomy, legend, and the zodiac is not as
immediate to us as it was to Dante and the figure may seem
strained, yet it does describe Beatrice's brief pause with tonal
embellishments sweetly appropriate to the Paradisal elevation.
Gist of this passage: "Beatrice looked up a moment in silence."

12. *where time and space focus into one ray*: God, ubiquitous and eternal.

13-15. A much disputed passage. (Where I have used "reflected" Dante used *"splendore,"* but Dante always used the verb *"splendare"* or the noun *"splendore"* to mean reflected rather than direct light.) God, being perfect, cannot add to His own good, already having all. It was not for self-increase that He created other beings, but that His ray of love, reflected to His created beings, might permit those reflections to say "I am," *i.e.,* to share in the joy of existence.

18. *new loves*: The angels.

19-21. The question would be: "Where was God and what did He do before the Creation?" The answer: "He was Himself, sufficient, perfect, and eternal." *Before* and *after* are conditions of time, and God, as stated in line 16, is beyond time.

21-24. THE SIMULTANEITY OF CREATION. All created things came into being in the same instant, projected perfectly from God's perfect will.

There were, in fact, three-string crossbows in Dante's time. The figure, therefore, has precedent, but the numerological significances of trinity are always apt and may be read into the figure at will.

*Pure essence*: Immaterial intelligences. The angels. *pure matter*: The physical materials of the universe and the lower animals. *the two joined into one*: Creatures composed of both soul and physical matter. Mankind.

31-36. The Creation is an act of love imposed upon formless chaos. It was, therefore, inherently orderly. All the essences of that instant creation emerged in fixed ranks within the order of creation. The angels rank highest because (see XXVIII, 127-129) they have the power to influence what lies below them, having been created as pure act. At the bottom rank stands man, the material intelligence that exists as pure potential, as the receiver of divine influences he cannot influence. In between, the heavens were created as both act and potential, subject to influences from above, and able to influence what lies below.

37. *Hieronymus*: St. Hieronymus, also known as St. Jerome (c. 342-420), was one of the first great biblical scholars. *wrote to you*: "To you," of course, is the equivalent of "to mankind." In one of his epistles he asserted the precreation of the angels, a doctrine opposed to the one Beatrice is expounding.

40. *the Scribes of the Holy Ghost*: The writers of scripture. All of them were said to have been "entered" (*i.e.*, inspired by) the Holy Ghost.

42-45. Dante must not be understood to imply that the angels, whose pure act or function is to move toward God, would cease to exist if they were denied the exercise of their perfection. Rather, they are eternal, which is to say they cannot cease to exist; and, as even man's intellect may understand, for such perfect action and existence to be expended on nothing would be chaos and a denial of the orderliness of creation. Since that order cannot be denied, the angels cannot be denied their perfect function.

51. *the elemental core*: Earth. Its elements are earth, air, fire, and water. Earth is, of course, the bedrock of the material universe; its core, Hell; and Hell's core, Satan. Beatrice informs Dante that Satan and his rebellious crew plunged to Earth (roiling the elemental core in the splash that raised the Mount of Pugatory, and roiling it since by their very existence) within a twenty-count of the Creation. The inherent orderliness of creation—a force for setting things instantly in their right ranking—could not tolerate the presence of perverted angels in Heaven for more than an instant.

At the end of Canto XXVI, Adam told Dante that his stay in the Terrestrial Paradise was less than seven hours. Beatrice has already asserted the simultaneity of the Creation. Since Satan was in the Garden and tempting Eve for some time before the Fall, he could not, in any case, have remained long in Heaven.

53. *this art*: Of circling around God, their cause. The art of the angels is to receive God's ray from above and to spread its influence below.

56. *that dark Principal*: Satan.

61-66. Dante intends a distinction here between illuminating grace and consuming grace. He is following Aquinas (*Summa theologica* I, 62, 4). Illuminating grace is God's gift to the soul, which may then, through zealous love, earn the consuming grace of the direct vision of God. The power of illuminating grace is, in fact, directly measurable by the ardor of love with which the soul receives it.

67-69. Beatrice tells Dante he is now prepared to look about this heaven and to observe its nature without further help from her. Characteristically, however (was Dante indulging a gentle and tender humor on the narrative level?), she talks on to the end of the canto.

81. *divided thought*: Human intelligence, lacking absolute content and concentration, must categorize, dividing its attention, which is to say, putting some things out of mind at times to be summoned back later by memory. The intelligence of angels, on the contrary, is eternally aware of all knowledge and memory and, therefore, irrelevant to it.

83. *believing it or not:* None has the truth, but some are only deluded, whereas others, ambitious for reputation and gifts, preach as truth what they do not themselves believe. These latter, as hypocrites and falsifiers, are clearly more sinful than those who are merely misled.

97-102. An eclipse of the sun by the moon would throw only a limited cone of shadow, whereas were the sun itself to withdraw, the whole earth (from Spain to India) would be dark. Recent commentators have disputed the text of this passage. As I have done throughout, I follow the reading established by Scartazzini-Vandelli.

104. *spewed to right and left*: In the manner of demagogic oratory.

105. *the Lapi and Bindi*: Lapo and Bindo were, and are, common Florentine surnames. An equivalent reading in American terms might be: "they outnumber the Joneses and Smiths in the phonebook."

111. *holy truth's foundation*: "For no other foundation can one lay than that which is laid, which is Jesus Christ." *I Corinthians* III, 11.

117. *their hoods swell*: With pride in their clownish performances. "Hoods" here for "heads."

118. *in their tippets*: The tippet is the long hanging point of a monk's hood or sleeves. Mendicant friars stuffed their tippets with all sorts of dubious religious articles and trade goods to be sold to pious simpletons along with unauthorized indulgences. Thus did they do the devil's work, and so the bird that nests in their tippets is the devil himself.

122. *testimonials*: Documents bearing papal or episcopal seals as authority to sell indulgences. Genuine documents of this sort did exist, but false documents seemed to work equally well upon the gullible.

124-126. St. Anthony the Eremite (251-356) was usually depicted with a pig (representing the devil) rooting at his feet.

In Florence, pigs belonging to the various monastery herds were called St. Anthony's pigs and enjoyed the status of sacred cows, rooting in gardens, and even in houses, with no interference from the superstitious and pious folk. On such credulity, St. Anthony's pigs (these swinish mountebank monks) feed, and with them others yet (concubines, cronies, relatives) who eat and drink their fill, paying with fantastic and worthless promises (money never minted).

127-129. To digress from a subject is, metaphorically, to wander from the straight path. The straight path of this sphere is toward the study of the angelic nature. Having strayed from it, Beatrice and Dante must now hurry if they are to complete their set course in the time remaining to them before they ascend to the Empyrean.

130. *this nature*: The angelic nature.

# CANTO XXX

*THE GREAT THEME is drawing to a close. Here
1 the Empyrean, Beatrice is at last at home, her
eauty made perfect, and Dante utters a lofty PRAISE
OF BEATRICE.*

*Beatrice promises Dante a VISION OF BOTH HOSTS
OF PARADISE. He is blinded by a new radiance,
ears a voice announce that he shall be given new
owers, and immediately he sees a VISION OF A
RIVER OF LIGHT. As in the Terrestrial Paradise, he
s commanded to drink. No sooner is his face sub-
merged in the water than the vision grows circular
nd re-forms as a VISION OF THE MYSTIC ROSE.*

When, as may be, the sun's noon heat is shed
   six thousand miles away, while, where we are,
   earth's shadow makes an almost level bed;      3

when, at our zenith, the sky begins to show
   such changes that a star or two begins
   to fade from the eyes of watchers here below;    6

nd as the sun's most radiant serving maid
   comes nearer yet, and heaven puts out its lamps
   one by one, till the loveliest, too, must fade—    9

just so that Triumph that forever races
   around the blinding ray of the fixed Point
   that seems embraced by what Itself embraces,    12

faded from sight, degree by slow degree;
   at which I turned my eyes from the lost vision
   to Beatrice, as love commanded me.    15

If all that I have said of her below
   were gathered now into a single paean,
   that would be scant praise of her beauty now.    18

The beauty I saw there transcends all measure
   of mortal minds. I think only her Maker
   can wholly comprehend so great a treasure.    21

Here I concede defeat. No poet known,
   comic or tragic, challenged by his theme
   to show his power, was ever more outdone.    24

As feeblest eyes, struck by the sun, go blind,
   so the remembrance of my lady's smile
   strikes every recognition from my mind.    27

From the first day I looked upon her face
   in this life, to this present sight of her,
   my song has followed her to sing her praise.    30

But here I must no longer even try
   to walk behind her beauty. Every artist,
   his utmost done, must put his brushes by.    33

So do I leave her to a clarion
   of greater note than mine, which starts to draw
   its long and arduous theme to a conclusion.    36

She, like a guide who has his goal in sight
   began to speak again: "We have ascended
   from the greatest sphere to the heaven of
                               pure light.    39

Light of the intellect, which is love unending;
  love of the true good, which is wholly bliss;
  bliss beyond bliss, all other joys transcending;   42

here shall you see both hosts of Paradise,
  one of them in the aspect you shall see
  when you return the day all bodies rise."   45

As a flash of lightning striking on our sight
  destroys our visual spirits, so that the eye
  cannot make out even a brighter light;   48

just so, an aureole burst all about me,
  swathing me so completely in its veil
  that I was closed in light and could not see.   51

"The Love that keeps this Heaven ever the same
  greets all who enter with such salutation,
  and thus prepares the candle for His flame."   54

No sooner had these few words penetrated
  my hearing than I felt my powers increase
  beyond themselves; transcendant and elated,   57

my eyes were lit with such new-given sight
  that they were fit to look without distress
  on any radiance, however bright.   60

I saw a light that was a river flowing
  light within light between enameled banks
  painted with blossoms of miraculous spring;   63

and from the river as it glowed and rolled
  live sparks shot forth to settle on the flowers.
  They seemed like rubies set in bands of gold;   66

and then, as if the fragrance overthrew
  their senses, they dove back into the river;
  and as one dove in there, out another flew.   69

"The flame of high desire that makes you yearn
    for greater knowledge of these things you see
    pleases me more the more I see it burn. 72

But only this same water satisfies
    such thirst as yours. You must bend down and drink."
    —So spoke the sun and pole-star of my eyes. 75

And added: "The river and the jewels you see
    dart in and out of it, and the smiling flowers
    are dim foretastes of their reality. 78

Not that these fruits are in their natures tart
    and unformed, but that you still lack the vision
    of such high things. The defect is on your part." 81

No babe in arms that ever wakened hungry
    from having slept too long could turn its face
    to its dear mother's milk more eagerly 84

than I bent down to drink in Paradise
    of the sweet stream that flows its grace to us,
    so to make better mirrors of our eyes. 87

No sooner were my eyes' eaves sweetly drowned
    in that bright stream to drink, than it appeared
    to widen and change form till it was round. 90

I have seen masqueraders here below
    shed the disguises that had hidden them
    and show their true appearances. Just so, 93

the sparks and spring flowers changed before my eyes
    into a greater festival, and I saw
    the vision of both courts of Paradise. 96

O splendor of God eternal through which I saw
    the supreme triumph of the one true kingdom,
    grant me the power to speak forth what I saw! 99

There in Heaven, a lamp shines in whose light
   the Creator is made visible to His creature,
   whose one peace lies in having Him in sight.   102

That lamp forms an enormous circle, such
   that its circumference, fitted to the Sun
   as a bright belt, would be too large by much.   105

It is made up entirely of the reflection
   of rays that strike the top of the first-moved sphere,
   imparting to it all its power and motion.   108

And as a slope shines in the looking glass
   of a lake below it, as if to see itself
   in its time of brightest flower and greenest grass;   111

so, tier on tier, mounting within that light,
   there glowed, reflected in more than a thousand
                          circles,
   all those who had won return to Heaven's height.   114

And if so vast a nimbus can be bound
   within its lowest tier, what then must be
   the measure of this rose at its topmost round?   117

Nor were my eyes confounded by that sea
   and altitude of space, but took in all,
   both number and quality, of that ecstasy.   120

There, far and near cause neither loss nor gain,
   for where God rules directly, without agents,
   the laws that govern nature do not pertain.   123

Into the gold of the rose that blooms eternal,
   rank on rank, in incenses of praise
   it sends up to the Sun forever vernal—   126

I, yearning to speak and silent—Beatrice drew me,
   and said: "Now see how many are in the convent
   of the white robes. Behold our far-flung city.       129

And see the benches—every one a throne—
   how every rank of them is filled so full
   that few are wanted before all is done.       132

That great throne with the crown already set
   above it draws your eyes. To it shall come—
   before your own call to this nuptial banquet—       135

the soul, already annointed, of Henry the Great,
   who will come to Italy to bring law and order
   before the time is ripe to set things straight.       138

Tranced in blind greed, your ever deepening curse,
   you have become as mindless as an infant
   who screams with hunger, yet pushes away
                            his nurse.       141

The prefect of the holy court will be
   a man who will profess his cause in public
   while working to defeat it secretly.       144

But after that God will not long permit
   his simony, he shall be stuffed away
   where Simon Magus, headfirst in the pit,       147

pays for his guilt. There, paying for his own,
   he shall force the guilt of Alagna further down."

## Notes

1-15. ASCENT TO THE EMPYREAN. Heretofore the glories
of the heavens have shone like stars in glorious night. In the
Empyrean, God (the Sun) shines forever in the fullness of His
glorious day, obscuring all other heavenly bodies except as they

reflect His light. The ascent into the Empyrean, therefore, is a dawning, and Dante's figure for it is based on an earthly dawn.

When the sun is at its noon height over India (about 6000 miles away) dawn is just beginning in Italy and the Earth's shadow is almost a level line (level bed) out into space (i.e., nearly perpendicular to a line dropped from the zenith). Then the stars directly overhead begin to fade, the dimmest first, then the brighter. Then as dawn (Aurora, the serving maid of Apollo, the Sun) draws nearer, all the stars go out, even the loveliest and brightest.

Just so nine rings of the three trinities of Angelic beings fade as Dante and Beatrice ascend into the first dawning of the direct vision of God. Obviously the dimmer outer rings would fade first, then the others in order.

12. *embraced by what Itself embraces:* The Angel Rings seem to contain God within their rounds, whereas it is God who contains them and all else.

22-33. THE BEAUTY OF BEATRICE. As Dante ascended each new heaven and became more able to perceive, Beatrice grew more beautiful (was able to reveal more of herself to his senses). Now fully disclosed in the direct light of the Empyrean she surpasses conception: only God can realize her full beauty.

On another level it is only natural that Dante stand inarticulate before the full beauty of Divine Revelation. What religious man could think himself equal to describing the entire beauty of Revelation? (Such inarticulateness is all the more effective when it overtakes a man who boasted of his powers in *Inferno,* IV, 100-102, XXV, 91-99, XXXII, 7-9, and in *Paradiso,* II, 1-18.)

35-36. *to a clarion of greater note than mine*: Does Dante mean that a greater poet will follow to sing the full beauty of Beatrice? He has just said that only God can fully realize her beauty.

I think it is no accident that Dante says "clarion" rather than "lyre." The Day of Judgment will be announced by a clarion call, and on that day the souls of all mortals may look upon Beatrice in her full beauty. Dante's "clarion" must occupy itself with drawing its long and arduous theme to a conclusion.

39. *the greatest sphere*: The Primum Mobile. *heaven of pure light*: The Empyrean.

43. *both hosts of Paradise*: The Angels and the Blessed.

44. *one of them*: The Blessed. Those who once wore mortal bodies which shall be returned to them on Judgment Day. Within the Mystic Rose Dante does see the radiances of the

Blessed with their lineaments etched upon them. He is offered this sight as a special dispensation in a climactic act of *caritas*.

47. *visual spirits*: See XXVI, 70-72.

52. *The Love*: God. *that keeps this Heaven ever the same*: All the other heavens rotate in constant change. The Empyrean, reflecting God's unchanging and unchangeable perfection, is always the same.

54. *and thus prepares the candle for His flame*: Dante has several times been blinded by the light that prepared him for better vision. Here the candle of his soul is put out by the splendor of the Empyrean to be relit by the light of God Himself.

60-66. As Dante makes clear in line 95 below, the sparks are Angels and the flowers, the Blessed. The river may be taken as the endless flowing of God's grace. Some religious commentators suggest that the two banks represent the Church. As verified by lines 76-78 below, the rubies of line 66 should be taken to be Angels and the bands of gold as the Blessed.

77. *jewels*: Dante says "topazes" and the topaz was believed to have the power of reflecting things without distortion, certainly a relevant suggestion in context, though "topazes" here does not accord with "rubies" in line 66.

82 ff. *no babe in arms*: "Except ye be converted and become as little children, ye shall not enter into the kingdom of heaven" (*Matthew*, XVIII, 3).

87. *better mirrors*: The better to reflect God.

88-89. *my eyes' eaves*: His eyelashes. Dante has, of course, plunged his face into the river. It may seem odd to say that he drank with his eyes, but note that this is a river of light, and that it is to wash the last mortal weakness from his eyes that Dante is drinking. See also the common idiom: "My eyes drank in the sight of it."

95-97-99. *I saw*: Now and then in the *Paradiso* Dante says "I saw." More often he uses some such phrase as "there appeared to me" or "it manifested itself." Such phrasing is deliberate. "I saw" implies an action of the speaker's own powers. Heaven, however, is a gift of grace: Dante does not see it through his own powers; rather it manifests itself to him as an act of love, and does so not in its true essence but in manifestations graspable by Dante's mortal mind.

Here, however, Dante uses "I saw" as one of his rare triple rhymings on the same word. In Dante an unusual device always indicates unusual stress. It occurs, moreover, at one of the great climaxes of the poem.

For Dante has just experienced the first direct revelation of God. Until he drank from the stream he could not see things with the spontaneous intuition of heavenly souls, who partake directly of the mind of God. Now he, too, has achieved the beginnings of Paradisal power. This is the true rebirth, the spiritual enlargement to which the entire journey has been directed. And soon now, as Virgil left him below, Beatrice will leave him to take her throne among the hosts of the Blessed, though in a larger sense she will be with him forever, both her soul and Dante's being contained in God.

108. *power*: Virtue. The ability to influence what lies below it. *motion*: Its own rapid revolution.

112 ff. THE MYSTIC ROSE. As ever in Paradise, the heavenly beings manifest themselves to Dante at the highest level he is capable of grasping at each point of his development. At every stage they have sent their manifestations down to him as an act of love. They themselves remain forever in the direct presence of God.

Now, his vision at last approaching perfection, Dante sees them in their supreme heavenly state, ranked tier on tier in a huge stadium that gives forth the appearance of an enormous white rose basking in the eternal springtime of the direct light of God. Note, however, that he sees the rose not directly (even at this point he is not yet ready) but as a vision reflected in the sea of God's light.

For purposes of placing Dante in relation to it, the Rose may be thought of as an immense, truncated, inverted, floating cone marked off in many tiers. The tier first reflected to Dante from that sea of light is the bottom one, the upper tiers being only partially visible at this point. The nimbus of the bottom tier (lines 115-116) is far greater than the circumference of the Sun (lines 104-105).

114. *those who had won return*: The loyal angels, having never left, would not have won return.

116-117. *what then must be its measure*: There are more than a thousand tiers. If the lowest is greater by far than the circumference of the Sun, what must be the dimensions of its upper ring, a thousand steps up from such magnitude?

118-123. On earth we see near things in detail and far things indistinctly. The laws of nature, however, are God's agencies and have no force where God rules without inter-mediaries. So, despite the galactic dimensions of the rose, Dante sees all in minute detail, not only each being in that multitude, but the quality of each one's ecstasy.

124 ff. *Into the gold of the rose:* The central corona of the rose, from which the petals grow, is always golden, or so it was in Dante's time, though some modern hybrids no longer have a golden center. *Beatrice drew me:* If the Mystic Rose is con-ceived as a vast circular stadium Dante and Beatrice are now in the center of the arena looking up at the tiers.

132. *few are wanted before all is done*: As with so many other revelationists, Dante believes God will not long endure the evils of mankind and that the trump of Judgment will soon sound.

136. *Henry*: Henry VII of Luxemburg, Emperor 1308-1313. He was not, strictly speaking, referred to as Henry the Great, but I have been forced to call him that for purposes of rhyme. See *Purgatorio*, VII, 96, note, and for the background of Henry's attempt at order in Italy see *Purgatorio*, VI, 100, note. In the *Purgatorio* Dante says Henry came too late. Here he says he came before the time was ripe. In either case the result was the same and Dante attributes Henry's failure to the evil designs of the bad popes Beatrice now goes on to denounce before the full court of Heaven. It is certainly relevant, here, to note that Dante placed his one hope of returning to Florence on the outcome of Henry's efforts to settle the hatreds of Italian politics.

138. *already annointed*: As Holy Roman Emperor.

140. *you*: You Italians.

142. *The prefect*: The pope. *The holy court*: Rome, the Vatican. Here Dante intends Clement V, who worked to defeat Henry's policy, though he professed to support it.

143-144. I have found it necessary to translate the intent rather than the phrasing of Dante's lines here. Literally rendered, they would read: "Who will not walk with him the same road openly and covertly," a strange figure that has Clement walking beside Henry on two separate roads at the same time.

145. *God will not long permit*: Clement died eight months after Henry, on April 20, 1314.

147. *where Simon Magnus, headfirst in the pit*: With the Simoniacs in the Third Bolgia of the Eighth Circle *(Inferno,* XIX). There the sinners are stuffed head-first into a tubelike baptismal font, their feet kicking the air, their soles aflame. As each replaces his successor in selling holy office, the earlier tenant is shoved down into some undescribed lower pit, sealed from the eyes of all.

149. *the guilt of Alagna*: Boniface VIII. He was born at Alagna (or, variantly, Anagna).

# CANTO XXXI

`The Mystic Rose
The Angel Host
Beatrice Leaves Dante
St. Bernard`

THE SECOND SOLDIERY of the Church Triumphant is the ANGEL HOST and Dante now receives
a vision of them as a SWARM OF BEES in eternal
transit between God and the Rose.

Dante turns from that rapturous vision to speak to
Beatrice and finds in her place a reverend elder. It is
ST. BERNARD, who will serve as Dante's guide to the
ultimate vision of God. Bernard shows Dante his
LAST VISION OF BEATRICE, who has resumed her
throne among the blessed. Across the vastness of
Paradise, Dante sends his soul's prayer of thanks to her.
BEATRICE SMILES down at Dante a last time, then
turns her eyes forever to the Eternal Fountain of God.

Bernard, the most faithful of the worshippers of the
Virgin, promises Dante the final vision of God through
the Virgin's intercession. Accordingly, he instructs Dante
to raise his eyes to her throne. Dante obeys and burns
with bliss at the vision of her splendor.

Then, in the form of a white rose, the host
　　of the sacred soldiery appeared to me,
　　all those whom Christ in his own blood espoused.　3

But the other host (who soar, singing and seeing
　　His glory, who to will them to his love
　　made them so many in such blissful being,　6

like a swarm of bees who in one motion dive
   into the flowers, and in the next return
   the sweetness of their labors to the hive)                    9

flew ceaselessly to the many-petaled rose
   and ceaselessly returned into that light
   in which their ceaseless love has its repose.                 12

Like living flame their faces seemed to glow.
   Their wings were gold. And all their bodies shone
   more dazzling white than any earthly snow.                   15

On entering the great flower they spread about them,
   from tier to tier, the ardor and the peace
   they had acquired in flying close to Him.                    18

Nor did so great a multitude in flight
   between the white rose and what lies above it
   block in the least the glory of that light;                  21

for throughout all the universe God's ray
   enters all things according to their merit,
   and nothing has the power to block its way.                  24

This realm of ancient bliss shone, soul on soul,
   with new and ancient beings, and every eye
   and every love was fixed upon one goal.                      27

O Threefold Light which, blazoned in one star,
   can so content their vision with your shining,
   look down upon us in the storm we are!                       30

If the barbarians (coming from that zone
   above which Helice travels every day
   wheeling in heaven with her beloved son)                     33

looking at Rome, were stupefied to see
   her works in those days when the Lateran
   outshone all else built by humanity;                         36

what did I feel on reaching such a goal
  from human to blest, from time to eternity,
  from Florence to a people just and whole—      39

by what amazement was I overcome?
  Between my stupor and my new-found joy
  my bliss was to hear nothing and be dumb.      42

And as a pilgrim at the shrine of his vow
  stares, feels himself reborn, and thinks already
  how he may later describe it—just so now      45

I stood and let my eyes go wandering out
  into that radiance from rank to rank,
  now up, now down, now sweeping round about.      48

I saw faces that compelled love's charity
  lit by Another's lamp and their own smiles,
  and gestures graced by every dignity.      51

Without having fixed on any part, my eyes
  already had taken in and understood
  the form and general plan of Paradise:      54

and—my desire rekindled—I wheeled about
  to question my sweet lady on certain matters
  concerning which my mind was still in doubt.      57

One thing I expected; another greeted me:
  I thought to find Beatrice there; I found instead
  an elder in the robes of those in glory.      60

His eyes and cheeks were bathed in the holy glow
  of loving bliss; his gestures, pious grace.
  He seemed a tender father standing so.      63

"She—where is she?" I cried in sudden dread.
  "To lead you to the goal of all your wish
  Beatrice called me from my place," he said;      66

"And if you raise your eyes you still may find her
in the third circle down from the highest rank
upon the throne her merit has assigned her."  69

Without reply I looked up to that height
and saw her draw an aureole round herself
as she reflected the Eternal Light.  72

No mortal eye, though plunged to the last bounds
of the deepest sea, has ever been so far
from the topmost heaven to which the thunder
sounds  75

as I was then from Beatrice; but there
the distance did not matter, for her image
reached me unblurred by any atmosphere.  78

"O lady in whom my hope shall ever soar
and who for my salvation suffered even
to set your feet upon Hell's broken floor;  81

through your power and your excellence alone
have I recognized the goodness and the grace
inherent in the things I have been shown.  84

You have led me from my bondage and set me free
by all those roads, by all those loving means
that lay within your power and charity.  87

Grant me your magnificence that my soul,
which you have healed, may please you when it slips
the bonds of flesh and rises to its goal."  90

Such was my prayer, and she—far up a mountain,
as it appeared to me—looked down and smiled.
Then she turned back to the Eternal Fountain.  93

And the holy Elder said: "I have been sent
  by prayer and sacred love to help you reach
  the perfect consummation of your ascent.      96

Look round this garden, therefore, that you may
  by gazing at its radiance, be prepared
  to lift your eyes up to the Trinal Ray.      99

The Queen of Heaven, for whom in whole devotion
  I burn with love, will grant us every grace
  because I am Bernard, her faithful one."      102

As a stranger from afar—a Croat, if you will—
  comes to see our Veronica, and awed
  by its ancient fame, can never look his fill,      105

but says to himself as long as it is displayed:
  "My Lord, Jesus Christ, true God, and is this then
  the likeness of thy living flesh portrayed?"—      108

just so did I gaze on the living love
  of him who in this world, through contemplation,
  tasted the peace which ever dwells above.      111

"Dear son of Grace," he said, "you cannot know
  this state of bliss while you yet keep your eyes
  fixed only on those things that lie below;      114

rather, let your eyes mount to the last round
  where you shall see the Queen to whom this realm
  is subject and devoted, throned and crowned."      117

I looked up: by as much as the horizon
  to eastward in the glory of full dawn
  outshines the point at which the sun went down;      120

by so much did one region on the height
  to which I raised my eyes out of the valley
  outshine the rays of every other light.      123

And as the sky is brightest in that region
   where we on earth expect to see the shaft
   of the chariot so badly steered by Phaeton,   126

while to one side and the other it grows dim—
   just so that peaceful oriflamme lit the center
   and faded equally along either rim.   129

And in the center, great wings spread apart,
   more than a thousand festive angels shone,
   each one distinct in radiance and in art.   132

I saw there, smiling at this song and sport,
   she whose beauty entered like a bliss
   into the eyes of all that sainted court.   135

And even could my speech match my conception,
   yet I would not dare make the least attempt
   to draw her delectation and perfection.   138

Bernard, seeing my eyes so fixed and burning
   with passion on his passion, turned his own
   up to that height with so much love and yearning  141

that the example of his ardor sent
new fire through me, making my gaze more ardent.

## Notes

1-12. In XXX, 43, Beatrice promised that Dante would see both
hosts of Paradise. The first host is of the sacred soldiery, those who
were once mortal and who were redeemed by Christ. They are
seated upon the thrones of the Mystic Rose in which are gathered
eternally the essences of all those heavenly souls that manifested
themselves to Dante in the various spheres below, moved by
*caritas* to reveal themselves to Dante at the various levels of his
developing understanding. How these souls could be eternally
within the Rose while yet manifesting themselves to Dante in the
various spheres is, of course, one of the mysteries to be grasped

only by revelation. The essential point is that Dante becomes better able to see; the vision of Heaven unfolds to him ever more clearly and ever more profoundly.

The second soldiery is of the angels who never left heaven. They soar above the Rose like Heavenly bees, in constant motion between the Rose and the radiance of God. Unlike earthly bees, however, it is from God, the mystical hive of grace, that they bring the sweetness to the flower, bearing back to God, of course, the bliss of the souls of Heaven. (See lines 16-18).

The first host is more emphatically centered on the aspect of God as the Son; the second, on the aspect of God as the Father.

13. See the vision of God and Heaven in *Ezekiel*, I, 14 ff.

14. See the similar vision in *Daniel*, X, 4 ff.

22-24. God illuminates all things in the exact degree that each is worthy of illumination (which is to say, able to receive it), and nothing may block from any other thing the light it is in condition to receive. No soul, that is to say, can receive less of God than it is able to contain at any given stage of its development.

27. *one goal*: God.

32. *Helice*: The nymph Helice (I am afraid the reader will have to Anglicize her name as HEL-ees) attracted Zeus and was turned into a bear by jealous Hera. Zeus translated his nymph to heaven as Ursa Major, the constellation of the Great Bear which contains the Big Dipper. Arcas, her son by Zeus, was translated to Ursa Minor, within which he forms the Little Dipper.

The two dippers, being near the pole, are always above the horizon in the northland, the zone from which the barbarian came.

35. *the Lateran*: The Lateran is today a section of old Rome. Here Dante uses it to signify Rome in general.

39. *from Florence to a people just and whole*: This is Dante's last mention of Florence. Note that Florence has not improved but that on the universal scale it has become too insignificant for the sort of denunciation he once heaped upon it.

42. *my bliss was to hear nothing and be dumb*: At such a moment of ecstasy Dante wants neither to speak nor to hear others speak, but only to stand rapt before the glory of such revelation.

Note that Dante believes he is standing next to Beatrice. "To hear nothing" must mean he does not even wish to hear her speak. On the personal level, such a feeling might seem an affront to his lady; yet there is no affront: even she, as she herself would insist, must be silent before the greater vision. The figure of Beatrice is a complex symbol. To simplify matters for the beginning reader of Dante, I have taken her allegorically in simplest terms as Divine Revelation. So taking her, Dante's seeming rejection of her blends harmoniously with the total of his vision, for if Beatrice is Divine Revelation (an agent of God), Dante is now near God Himself (that which Revelation is meant to reveal).

43. *shrine of his vow*: It was a custom of the pious, as thanks for an answered prayer, to win forgiveness of sins, or as a testimony of faith, to vow a journey to a stated shrine or temple. Such pilgrimages were often dangerous. Travel was rare in the Middle Ages, and the pilgrim returned from far shrines was much sought after for the hopefully miraculous, and in any case rare, news he brought back. How could Dante, having traveled to the Infinite Summit, fail to think ahead to the way he would speak his vision to mankind?

58. *One thing I expected; another greeted me*: Dante expected to see Beatrice. He sees instead St. Bernard. As Virgil, his service done, vanished at the top of Purgatory, so now Beatrice has left Dante, though not to vanish but to resume her throne among the blessed. In the next passage Dante will look up and see her there.

60. *an elder*: St. Bernard (1090-1153), the famous Abbot of Clairvaux, a contemplative mystic and author. Under him the Cistercian Order (a branch of the Benedictines with a stricter rule than the original order) flourished and spread. All Cistercian monasteries are especially dedicated to the Virgin, and St. Bernard is particularly identified with her worship.

66. *Beatrice called me from my place*: In succeeding Beatrice, Bernard clearly becomes the allegorical figure of Contemplation, and so a progress of the soul: From Human Reason or Aesthetic Wisdom the soul mounts to Revelation at which time the final bliss becomes Contemplation of God as He reveals Himself.

Bernard, himself one of the most famous contemplatives of the church, has a second function. The ultimate revelation must come as a special grace and grace can be granted in answer to the prayers of the worthy. The worthiest being in the Mystic Rose is the Virgin and Bernard as her special servitor will pray to her that she pray God to grant Dante's most ardent wish.

68. *the third circle down*: In the Mystic Rose (see diagram in XXXII) Mary sits in the topmost tier, Eve directly below her, Rachel (the Contemplative Life) below Eve. Beatrice sits to the right of Rachel. In Dante, of course, every mention of three must suggest trinity, but the reader is left to decide for himself the significance of the Mary-Eve-Rachel trinity.

73-75. To what altitude the sound of thunder reaches through the atmosphere and how far that would be from the bottom of the deepest sea are questions a scientist might perhaps determine. For Dante the upper height would be the top of the atmosphere and he would have understood that upper limit as being close to the moon. Whatever the specifications, the poetic force of the passage powerfully suggests vast dimensions.

81. *to set your feet upon Hell's broken floor*: As she did when she descended to Limbo (as, of course, a manifestation) to summon Virgil.

103. *a Croat*: Probably used here in a generic sense to signify the native of any far off Christian land, but Croatia, aside from lying at one of the outer limits of Christianity, was also known for the ardor of its religious belief.

104. *our Veronica*: From *vera icon*, the true image. Certainly the most famous relic in St. Peter's, the Veronica was the handkerchief of the faithful follower ever after known as St. Veronica. She gave it to Jesus to wipe the blood from his face on the road to Calvary, and what was believed to be the true likeness of Jesus was believed to have appeared on what was believed to be the cloth in what was believed to be His own blood.

110-111. According to legend, Bernard was rewarded for his holiness by being permitted a vision of Heaven's blessedness while he was yet on earth.

112-117. The way to perfect consummation is ever upward toward God. Dante has been staring at Bernard, awed by that vision of holiness. In modesty and as an act of loving guidance, Bernard tells him to prepare his eyes for the ultimate vision by looking up to Mary on her throne.

118-123. The comparison is not, as careless readers sometimes take it to be, between a dawn and a sunset (whose brightnesses would be approximately equal) but between the eastern and western horizons at dawn. Bright as Heaven is, Mary outshines it as the east outshines the west at daybreak.

124-129. The shaft of the chariot of the Sun would project ahead of the horses. It would, therefore, be the first point of light of the new dawn, that moment when light glows on the eastern rim while the horizon to north and south is still dark. Thus Mary not only outshines all heaven as the east at daybreak outshines the west, but even at the uppermost tier of the blessed, those radiances at either side of her are dim by comparison.

132. *art*: Motion. No two angel beings are exactly equal in their brightness, nor in the speed of their flight. These festive angels are, of course, another manifestation of the Angel Hierarchy. At this height of heaven and revelation, it should not seem contradictory for them to revolve forever around God while they forever circle Mary. The two circlings are clearly meant to be one. Heaven, moreover, reveals itself in one manifestation after another of the truth only God can entirely grasp.

The labels within the figure, reading the petals and tiers:

- Peter
- Beatrice
- John the Evang.
- Souls who believed in Christ descended (Christians)
- Christian Children (baptized)
- The of the
- Christian Saints
- Augustine
- Benedict
- Francis
- Lucy
- John Baptist

**THE MYSTIC ROSE** (after Gardner)
No specific number of petals or of tiers should be under-

Mary

Eve

Rachel

Sarah

Rebecca

Judith

Ruth

Hebrew Women

Adam

Moses

Pre-Christian Children

(Pre-Christians)

Souls who believed in Christ to come

Yellow
Rose

Anna

stood. The dotted lines indicate the parts of the rose
which Dante does not describe in detail.

# CANTO XXXII

*St. Bernard*
*The Virgin Mary*
*The Thrones of the Blessed*

*HIS EYES FIXED BLISSFULLY on the vision of the Virgin Mary, Bernard recites the orders of the Mystic Rose, identifying the thrones of the most blessed.*

*MARY'S THRONE is on the topmost tier of the Heavenly Stadium. Directly across from it rises the THRONE OF JOHN THE BAPTIST. From her throne to the central arena (The Yellow of the Rose) descends a LINE OF CHRISTIAN SAINTS. These two radii form a diameter that divides the stadium. On one side are throned THOSE WHO BELIEVE IN CHRIST TO COME; on the other, THOSE WHO BELIEVED IN CHRIST DESCENDED. The lower half of the Rose contains, on one side, the PRE-CHRISTIAN CHILDREN SAVED BY LOVE, and on the other, the CHRISTIAN CHILDREN SAVED BY BAPTISM.*

*Through all these explanations, Bernard has kept his eyes fixed in adoration upon the Virgin. Having finished his preliminary instruction of Dante, Bernard now calls on him to join in a PRAYER TO THE VIRGIN.*

Still rapt in contemplation, the sainted seer
    assumed the vacant office of instruction,
    beginning with these words I still can hear:    3

"The wound that Mary healed with balm so sweet
    was first dealt and then deepened by that being
    who sits in such great beauty at her feet.    6

Below her, in the circle sanctified
  by the third rank of loves, Rachel is throned
  with Beatrice, as you see, there at her side.                    9

Sarah and Rebecca and Judith and she
  who was the great-grandmother of the singer
  who for his sins cried, 'Lord, have mercy on me!'— 12

as I go down the great ranks tier by tier,
  naming them for you in descending order,
  petal by petal, you shall see them clear.                        15

And down from the seventh, continuing from those
  in the first six tiers, a line of Hebrew women
  forms a part in the tresses of the rose.                         18

Arranged to form a wall thus, they divide
  all ranks according to the view of Christ
  that marked the faith of those on either side.                   21

On this side, where the flower is in full bloom
  to its last petal, are arranged all those
  whose faith was founded upon Christ to Come;                     24

on that, where the half circles show the unblended
  gaps of empty seats, are seated those
  whose living faith was fixed on Christ Descended.                27

And as, on this side, the resplendent throne
  of Heaven's Lady, with the thrones below it,
  establishes the line of that division;                           30

so, facing hers, does the throned blessedness
  of the Great John who, ever holy, bore
  the desert, martyrdom, and Hell's distress;                      33

and under him, forming that line are found
  Francis, Benedict, Augustine, and others
  descending to this center round by round.                        36

Now marvel at all-foreseeing profundity:
  this garden shall be complete when the two aspects
  of the one faith have filled it equally.                    39

And know that below that tier that cuts the two
  dividing walls at their centerpoint, no being
  has won his seat of glory by his own virtue,               42

but by another's, under strict condition;
  for all of these were spirits loosed from flesh
  before they had matured to true volition.                  45

You can yourself make out their infant graces:
  you need no more than listen to their treble
  and look attentively into their faces.                     48

You do not speak now: many doubts confound you.
  Therefore, to set you free I shall untie
  the cords in which your subtle thoughts have
                                        bound you.           51

Infinite order rules in this domain.
  Mere accidence can no more enter in
  than hunger can, or thirst, or grief, or pain.             54

All you see here is fixed by the decree
  of the eternal law, and is so made
  that the ring goes on the finger perfectly.                57

These, it follows, who had so short a pause
  in the lower life are not ranked higher or lower
  among themselves without sufficient cause.                 60

The king in whom this realm abides unchanging
  in so much love and bliss that none dares will
  increase of joy, creating and arranging                    63

he minds of all in the glad Paradise
  of His own sight, grants them degrees of grace
  as He sees fit. Here let the effect suffice.                    66

Holy Scripture clearly and expressly
  notes this effect upon those twins who fought
  while still within their mother. So we see                      69

how the Supreme light fittingly makes fair
  its aureole by granting them their graces
  according to the color of their hair.                           72

Thus through no merit of their works and days
  they are assigned their varying degrees
  by variance only in original grace.                             75

In the first centuries of man's creation
  their innocence and the true faith of their parents
  was all they needed to achieve salvation.                       78

When the first age of man had run its course,
  then circumcision was required of males,
  to give their innocent wings sufficient force.                  81

But when the age of grace came to mankind
  then, unless perfectly baptized in Christ,
  such innocents went down among the blind.                       84

Look now on her who most resembles Christ,
  for only the great glory of her shining
  can purify your eyes to look on Christ."                        87

I saw such joy rain down upon that face—
  borne to it by those blest Intelligences
  created thus to span those heights of space—                   90

that through all else on the long road I trod
  nothing had held my soul so fixed in awe,
  nor shown me such resemblances to God.                          93

The self-same Love that to her first descended
   singing *"Ave Maria, gratia plena"*
   stood before her with its wings extended.      96

Thus rang the holy chant to Heaven's Queen
   and all the blessed court joined in the song,
   and singing, every face grew more serene.      99

"O holy Father, who endures for me
   the loss of being far from the sweet place
   where fate has raised your throne eternally,      102

who is that angel who with such desire
   gazes into the eyes of our sweet Queen,
   so rapt in love he seems to be afire?"      105

Thus did I seek instruction from that Great One
   who drew the beauty of his light from Mary
   as the morning star draws beauty from the sun.      108

And he: "As much as angel or soul can know
   of exultation, gallantry, and poise
   there is in him; and we would have it so,      111

for it was he who brought the victory
   to Mary when the Son of God had willed
   to bear the weight of human misery.      114

But let your eyes go where my words point out
   among this court, and note the mighty peers
   of the empire of the just and the devout.      117

Those two whose bliss it is to sit so close
   to the radiance of the Empress of All Joy
   are the two eternal roots of this our rose:      120

The one just to the left of her blessedness
   is the father whose unruly appetite
   left man the taste for so much bitterness;      123

and on her right, that ancient one you see
   is the father of Holy Church to whom Christ gave
   the twin keys to this flower of timeless beauty.   126

And that one who in his prophetic sight
   foretold the evil days of the Sweet Bride
   won by the spear and nails, sits on his right.   129

While by the other father and first man
   sits the great leader to whom manna fell
   to feed an ingrate and rebellious clan.   132

Across the circle from Peter, behold Anna.
   She feels such bliss in looking at her daughter
   she does not move her eyes to sing 'Hosanna!'   135

And opposite the father of us all
   sits Lucy, who first urged your lady to you
   when you were blindly bent toward your own fall.   138

But the time allowed for this dream vision flies.
   As a tailor must cut the gown from what cloth is
                       given,
   just so must we move on, turning our eyes   141

to the Primal Love, that as your powers advance
   with looking toward him, you may penetrate
   as deep as may be through His radiance.   144

But lest you should fall backward when you flare
   your mortal wings, intending to mount higher,
   remember grace must be acquired through prayer.   147

Therefore I will pray that blessed one
   who has the power to aid you in your need.
   See that you follow me with such devotion   150

your heart adheres to every word I say."
And with those words the saint began to pray.

## *Notes*

**1-3.** *Still rapt in contemplation*: Of the Virgin. His eyes have not left her. Nor do they turn again to Dante. Following his own preachment in XXXI, 112-117, he keeps his eyes on high. The text permits the assumption that Bernard turns his eyes from the Virgin to look at the various parts of the Mystic Rose as he identifies them, later, for Dante. Certainly, however, Bernard could identify every detail of the Rose without having to look at it, and every quality of Dante's mind and style would be better honored by thinking of Bernard as staring adoringly on the Virgin throughout. *the vacant office of instruction*: Formerly held by Beatrice. *I still can hear*: A rhyme-forced addition, not in Dante's text.

**4-6.** Mary, Mother of God, sits in the uppermost tier. At her feet in the second tier sits Eve, Mother of Man. *the wound*: Original sin. *balm so sweet*: Jesus. *opened*: The first fault, Eve's disobedience. *driven deeper*: Her seduction of Adam, thus spreading sin to all mankind. *in such great beauty*: Eve, having been created directly by God, was perfect in her beauty.

**8-9.** *Rachel . . . Beatrice at her side*: See *Inferno*, II, 102: "Where I was sitting with the ancient Rachel." Rachel, the younger wife of Jacob, symbolizes the contemplative life, as her sister Leah, also Jacob's wife, symbolizes the active life. In relation to Bernard she may be taken allegorically to be Contemplation and he to be the Contemplative Soul.

**10-12.** *Sarah*: Wife of Abraham. *Hebrews*, XI, 11-14, cites her as the mother (by miraculous fertility in her old age) of the Jews who foresaw Christ's coming and believed in him. *Rebecca*: Wife of Isaac. *Judith*: She killed Holofernes and freed the Jews. *and she*: Ruth, great-grandmother of David. *that singer*: David. *who for his sins*: His lust for Bathsheba, wife of Uriah. In order to marry Bathsheba, David sent Uriah to his death in the first line of battle. David's lament is in *Psalm L*.

Thus, the first descending rank, down tier by tier from Mary, is made up of Hebrew women, mothers of the children of God.

**18.** *part . . . tresses*: As if the rose were a head of hair and that vertical row of Hebrew women formed a part in it. In the next line the part becomes a wall.

**22.** *in full bloom*: That half of the rose-stadium that holds the pre-Christian believers would naturally be completely filled. On the other side there are thrones waiting for those who have yet to win salvation through Christ Descended. Dante, in fact, is laboring to earn one of them for himself. The Day of Judgment will be upon mankind when the last throne is filled, for Heaven will then be complete.

32-33. *the Great John*: The Baptist. He denounced Herod Antipos and was beheaded two years before the Crucifixion. He had to wait in Limbo for two years, therefore, till Christ came for him at the Resurrection. For the Harrowing of Hell, see *Inferno*, V, 53, note.

40 ff. *below that tier*: The lower half of the rose-stadium contains the blessed infants, the souls of those who died before they had achieved the true volition of reason and faith. They could not, therefore, win salvation by their own merit. *but by another's, under strict condition*: The necessary qualification for election is belief in Christ. These souls were too young at death to have formed their faith. Salvation is granted them not directly through belief in Christ but through the faith and prayers of their parents, relatives, and others of the faithful who interceded for them.

49. *many doubts*: The infants are ranked in tiers that indicate degrees of heavenly merit. But if they were saved through no merit of their own, how can one be more worthy than the other? Such is Dante's doubt, which Bernard goes on to set at rest by telling him, in essence, that God knows what He is doing.

58-59. *These . . . who had so short a pause*: The infants paused only briefly in the mortal life.

62. *dares*: I have no explanation of Dante's word choice here. "Not to dare" cannot fail to suggest intimidation. But in Paradise there can be no daring: every soul is in bliss exactly to the degree it is capable of bliss, and its capacity keeps increasing as it looks upon God. To dare (*ausare,* or in modern Italian, *osare*) must be taken as an impurity from the mortal vocabulary (in the sense of "even to think of") and not strictly of the heavenly tongue.

66. *the effect*: The cause is buried in God's mind. The effect must speak for itself.

67-72. The reference here is to Jacob and Esau. According to Genesis, XXV, 21 ff., they were at odds while still in their mother's womb. (Cf. the legend of Polyneices and Eteocles, twin sons of Oedipus and Jocasta.) Dante follows St. Paul *(Romans,* IX, 11-13) in interpreting the division between Jacob and Esau as a working of God's unfathomable will. "Even as it is written, Jacob I loved, but Esau I hated." Man can note the will of God in such matters ("the effect") but cannot plumb its causes. *according to the color of their hair*: For what may seem to be superficial reasons. Esau (*Genesis,* XXV, 25) was red-headed.

81. *sufficient force*: To mount to Heaven.

84. *among the blind*: Among the souls of Hell. Such infants were assigned to Limbo.

85. *on her who most resembles Christ*: The Virgin Mary.

88-99. THE GLORY OF THE VIRGIN. As Bernard directs, Dante fixes his attention on Mary and beholds her blazing in a splendor that rains down upon her in a host of angel beings. These fly from God to the Rose and back again like bees between the hive and the flower, with the difference that these bees bring the rain of light to the flower and are themselves the glorious rain.

88. *that face*: Mary's.

94. *the same Love*: The archangel Gabriel, the Angel of the Annunciation. Dante seems to conceive of Gabriel suspended in air before her, repeating the blissful chant of the Annunciation as he had first hymned it in Nazareth.

112. *the victory:* (Dante says "the palm.") Of God's election. Some commentators gloss it as Mary's triumph over all other Jewish women, all of whom would have been eager to bear the promised Messiah; and possibly so, but to be chosen by God would be triumph enough itself, and any thought of outshining the ladies of the neighborhood would be trivial by comparison.

118-126. *Those two*: Adam and St. Peter. Adam as Father of Mankind, Peter as Father of the Church. Note that Peter has the place of honor on the right.

127. *that one*: St. John the Evangelist. His *Apocalypse* was received as the prophetic book in which the entire history of the Church is foretold. He sits on Peter's right.

131. *that leader*: Moses. As the second great figure of the Old Testament he sits to the left of Adam.

133-135. *Anna*: Ste. Anna, Ste. Anne, mother of the Virgin. Her position directly across the circle from Peter's puts her to the right of John the Baptist. *does not move her eyes to sing 'Hosanna'*: Like all the other heavenly beings, she constantly sings the praise of God. All others, naturally enough, look up as they sing. She, however, is so filled with bliss by the sight of Mary that she does not turn her eyes from her blessed daughter. She praises God while looking at Mary. This detail can be interpreted in many ways, but all of them, of course, must center on the special position of Mary in Catholic doctrine and feeling.

136-138. *Lucy*: See *Inferno*, II, 97-100. It was she who first sent Beatrice to rescue Dante from the Dark Wood of Error. She sits opposite Adam. She would, accordingly, be to the left of John the Baptist.

139-141. The time granted for Dante's vision is limited. As a tailor must cut the gown from what cloth he is given, so Dante must get on with it, making what he can of his experience in the time allotted him.

142-144. In the act of looking at God man is given the power to see Him. Such is the gift of grace, and to the extent that grace is given, a man may see more or less deeply into God's glory.

148. *that blessed one*: Mary.

# CANTO XXXIII

---

*St. Bernard*
*Prayer to the Virgin*
*The Vision of God*

ST. BERNARD *offers a lofty* PRAYER TO THE
VIRGIN, *asking her to intercede in Dante's behalf, and
in answer Dante feels his soul swell with new power
and grow calm in rapture as his eyes are permitted
the* DIRECT VISION OF GOD.

*There can be no measure of how long the vision
endures. It passes, and Dante is once more mortal and
fallible. Raised by God's presence, he had looked into
the Mystery and had begun to understand its power
and majesty. Returned to himself, there is no power in
him capable of speaking the truth of what he saw. Yet
the impress of the truth is stamped upon his soul,
which he now knows will return to be one with God's
Love.*

"Virgin Mother, daughter of thy son;
   humble beyond all creatures and more exalted;
   predestined turning point of God's intention;     3

thy merit so ennobled human nature
   that its divine Creator did not scorn
   to make Himself the creature of His creature.     6

The Love that was rekindled in Thy womb
   sends forth the warmth of the eternal peace
   within whose ray this flower has come to bloom.     9

Here, to us, thou art the noon and scope
   of Love revealed; and among mortal men,
   the living fountain of eternal hope.   12

Lady, thou art so near God's reckonings
   that who seeks grace and does not first seek thee
   would have his wish fly upward without wings.   15

Not only does thy sweet benignity
   flow out to all who beg, but oftentimes
   thy charity arrives before the plea.   18

In thee is pity, in thee munificence,
   in thee the tenderest heart, in thee unites
   all that creation knows of excellence!   21

Now comes this man who from the final pit
   of the universe up to this height has seen,
   one by one, the three lives of the spirit.   24

He prays to thee in fervent supplication
   for grace and strength, that he may raise his eyes
   to the all-healing final revelation.   27

And I, who never more desired to see
   the vision myself than I do that he may see It,
   add my own prayer, and pray that it may be   30

enough to move you to dispel the trace
   of every mortal shadow by thy prayers
   and let him see revealed the Sum of Grace.   33

I pray thee further, all-persuading Queen,
   keep whole the natural bent of his affections
   and of his powers after his eyes have seen.   36

Protect him from the stirrings of man's clay;
   see how Beatrice and the blessed host
   clasp reverent hands to join me as I pray."   39

The eyes that God reveres and loves the best
   glowed on the speaker, making clear the joy
   with which true prayer is heard by the most blest.  42

Those eyes turned then to the Eternal Ray,
   through which, we must indeed believe, the eyes
   of others do not find such ready way.  45

And I, who neared the goal of all my nature,
   felt my soul, at the climax of its yearning,
   suddenly, as it ought, grow calm with rapture.  48

Bernard then, smiling sweetly, gestured to me
   to look up, but I had already become
   within myself all he would have me be.  51

Little by little as my vision grew
   it penetrated further through the aura
   of the high lamp which in Itself is true.  54

What then I saw is more than tongue can say.
   Our human speech is dark before the vision.
   The ravished memory swoons and falls away.  57

As one who sees in dreams and wakes to find
   the emotional impression of his vision
   still powerful while its parts fade from his mind—  60

just such am I, having lost nearly all
   the vision itself, while in my heart I feel
   the sweetness of it yet distill and fall.  63

So, in the sun, the footprints fade from snow.
   On the wild wind that bore the tumbling leaves
   the Sybil's oracles were scattered so.  66

O Light Supreme who doth Thyself withdraw
   so far above man's mortal understanding,
   lend me again some glimpse of what I saw;  69

make Thou my tongue so eloquent it may
    of all Thy glory speak a single clue
    to those who follow me in the world's day;    72

for by returning to my memory
    somewhat, and somewhat sounding in these verses,
    Thou shalt show man more of Thy victory.    75

So dazzling was the splendor of that Ray,
    that I must certainly have lost my senses
    had I, but for an instant, turned away.    78

And so it was, as I recall, I could
    the better bear to look, until at last
    my vision made one with the Eternal Good.    81

Oh grace abounding that had made me fit
    to fix my eyes on the eternal light
    until my vision was consumed in it!    84

I saw within Its depth how It conceives
    all things in a single volume bound by Love,
    of which the universe is the scattered leaves;    87

substance, accident, and their relation
    so fused that all I say could do no more
    than yield a glimpse of that bright revelation.    90

I think I saw the universal form
    that binds these things, for as I speak these words
    I feel my joy swell and my spirits warm.    93

Twenty-five centuries since Neptune saw
    the Argo's keel have not moved all mankind,
    recalling that adventure, to such awe    96

as I felt in an instant. My tranced being
    stared fixed and motionless upon that vision,
    ever more fervent to see in the act of seeing.    99

Experiencing that Radiance, the spirit
  is so indrawn it is impossible
  even to think of ever turning from It.                    102

For the good which is the will's ultimate object
  is all subsumed in It; and, being removed,
  all is defective which in It is perfect.                   105

Now in my recollection of the rest
  I have less power to speak than any infant
  wetting its tongue yet at its mother's breast;            108

and not because that Living Radiance bore
  more than one semblance, for It is unchanging
  and is forever as it was before;                          111

rather, as I grew worthier to see,
  the more I looked, the more unchanging semblance
  appeared to change with every change in me.               114

Within the depthless deep and clear existence
  of that abyss of light three circles shown—
  three in color, one in circumference:                     117

the second from the first, rainbow from rainbow;
  the third, an exhalation of pure fire
  equally breathed forth by the other two.                  120

But oh how much my words miss my conception,
  which is itself so far from what I saw
  that to call it feeble would be rank deception!            123

O Light Eternal fixed in Itself alone,
  by Itself alone understood, which from Itself
  loves and glows, self-knowing and self-known;             126

that second aureole which shone forth in Thee,
  conceived as a reflection of the first—
  or which appeared so to my scrutiny—                      129

eemed in Itself of Its own coloration
  to be painted with man's image. I fixed my eyes
  on that alone in rapturous contemplation.   132

Like a geometer wholly dedicated
  to squaring the circle, but who cannot find,
  think as he may, the principle indicated—   135

so did I study the supernal face.
  I yearned to know just how our image merges
  into that circle, and how it there finds place;   138

but mine were not the wings for such a flight.
  Yet, as I wished, the truth I wished for came
  cleaving my mind in a great flash of light.   141

Here my powers rest from their high fantasy,
  but already I could feel my being turned—
  instinct and intellect balanced equally   144

as in a wheel whose motion nothing jars—
by the Love that moves the Sun and the other stars.

## Notes

1-39. ST. BERNARD'S PRAYER TO THE VIRGIN MARY.
No reader who has come this far will need a lengthy gloss of
Bernard's prayer. It can certainly be taken as a summarizing statement of the special place of Mary in Catholic faith. For the rest
only a few turns of phrase need underlining. 3. *predestined turning
point of God's intention*: All-foreseeing God built his whole scheme
for mankind with Mary as its pivot, for through her He would become man. 7. *The Love that was rekindled in thy womb*: God.
In a sense he withdrew from man when Adam and Eve sinned. In
Mary He returned and Himself became man. 35. *keep whole the
natural bent of his affections*: Bernard is asking Mary to protect
Dante lest the intensity of the vision overpower his faculties. 37.
*Protect him from the stirrings of man's clay*: Protect him from the
stirrings of base human impulse, especially from pride, for Dante is
about to receive a grace never before granted to any man and the

thought of such glory might well move a mere mortal to an hybris that would turn glory to sinfullness.

40. *the eyes*: Of Mary.

50. *but I had already become*: i.e., "But I had already fixed my entire attention upon the vision of God." But if so, how could Dante have seen Bernard's smile and gesture? Eager students like to believe they catch Dante in a contradiction here. Let them bear in mind that Dante is looking directly at God, as do the souls of Heaven, who thereby acquire—insofar as they are able to contain it—God's own knowledge. As a first stirring of that heavenly power, therefore, Dante is sharing God's knowledge of St. Bernard.

54. *which in Itself is true*: The light of God is the one light whose source is Itself. All others are a reflection of this.

65-66. *tumbling leaves . . . oracles*: The Cumean Sybil (Virgil describes her in *Aeneid*, III, 441 ff.) wrote her oracles on leaves, one letter to a leaf, then sent her message scattering on the wind. Presumably, the truth was all contained in that strew, could one only gather all the leaves and put the letters in the right order.

76-81. How can a light be so dazzling that the beholder would swoon if he looked away for an instant? Would it not be, rather in looking at, not away from, the overpowering vision that the viewer's senses would be overcome? So it would be on earth. But now Dante, with the help of all heaven's prayers, is in the presence of God and strengthened by all he sees. It is by being so strengthened that he can see yet more. So the passage becomes a parable of grace. Stylistically it once more illustrates Dante's genius: even at this height of concept, the poet can still summon and invent new perceptions, subtlety exfoliating from subtlety.

The simultaneous metaphoric statement, of course, is that no man can lose his good in the vision of God, but only in looking away from it.

85-87. The idea here is Platonic: the essence of all things (form) exists in the mind of God. All other things exist as exempla.

88. *substance*: Matter, all that exists in itself. *accident*: All that exists as a phase of matter.

92. *these things*: Substance and accident.

109-114. In the presence of God the soul grows ever more capable of perceiving God. Thus, the worthy soul's experience of God is a constant expansion of awareness. God appears to change as He is better seen. Being perfect, He is changeless within himself, for any change would be away from perfection.

130-144. The central metaphor of the entire *Comedy* is the image of God and the final triumphant inGodding of the elected soul returning to its Maker. On the mystery of that image, the metaphoric symphony of the *Comedy* comes to rest.

In the second aspect of Trinal-unity, in the circle reflected from the first, Dante thinks he sees the image of mankind woven into the very substance and coloration of God. He turns the entire attention of his soul to that mystery, as a geometer might seek to shut out every other thought and dedicate himself to squaring the circle. In *Il Convivio*, II, 14, Dante asserted that the circle could not be squared, but that impossibility had not yet been firmly demonstrated in Dante's time and mathematicians still worked at the problem. Note, however, that Dante assumes the impossibility of squaring the circle as a weak mortal example of mortal impossibility. How much more impossible, he implies, to resolve the mystery of God, study as man will.

The mystery remains beyond Dante's mortal power. Yet, there in Heaven, in a moment of grace, God revealed the truth to him in a flash of light—revealed it, that is, to the God-enlarged power of Dante's emparadised soul. On Dante's return to the mortal life, the details of that revelation vanished from his mind but the force of the revelation survives in its power on Dante's feelings.

So ends the vision of the *Comedy*, and yet the vision endures, for ever since that revelation, Dante tells us, he feels his soul turning ever as one with the perfect motion of God's love.

## MENTOR Classics

☐ **THE ILIAD OF HOMER translated by W. H. D. Rouse.**
A brilliant prose translation of Homer's great epic about
the Trojan War by a noted English scholar.
(#MT650—75¢)

☐ **THE ODYSSEY OF HOMER translated by W. H. D.
Rouse.** A modern prose translation of the world's great-
est adventure story, the travels of Ulysses.
(#MT677—75¢)

☐ **EIGHT GREAT COMEDIES edited by Sylvan Barnet,
Morton Berman and William Burto.** Complete texts of
the great comic plays from Aristophanes to Shaw, and
essays on the comic view. (#MY787—$1.25)

☐ **EIGHT GREAT TRAGEDIES edited by Sylvan Barnet,
Morton Berman and William Burto.** The great dramatic
literature of the ages, eight memorable tragedies by
Aeschylus, Euripides, Sophocles, Shakespeare, Ibsen,
Strindberg, Yeats and O'Neill. With essays on tragedy
by Aristotle, Emerson and others. (#MY740—$1.25)

☐ **THE SATYRICON by Petronius, translated by William
Arrowsmith.** A classic recreation of Nero's pleasure-
loving Rome by the cultured cynic, Petronius. In a
brilliant new translation. (#MQ1027—95¢)

☐ **LIFE STORIES OF MEN WHO SHAPED HISTORY from
PLUTARCH'S LIVES (abridged), edited by E. C. Linde-
man.** A distinguished selection taken from the John and
William Langhorne translation. (#MT983—75¢)

---